GW00468042

Understanding Entrepreneurship

Definition, Function and Policy

MAGNUS HENREKSON

MIKAEL STENKULA

Studentlitteratur

Copying prohibited

All rights reserved. No part of this publication may be reproduced or transmitted in any form or by any means, electronic or mechanical, including photocopying, recording, or any information storage and retrieval system, without permission in writing from the publisher.

The paper and ink used in this product are eco-friendly.

Art. No 39196
ISBN 978-91-44-11196-4
First edition
1:1

© The authors and Studentlitteratur 2016
www.studentlitteratur.se
Studentlitteratur AB, Lund

Cover design: Francisco Ortega
Cover illustration: alphaspirit/shutterstock.com

Printed by Mediapool Print Syd AB, Estonia 2016

CONTENTS

© THE AUTHORS AND STUDENTLITTERATUR

© THE AUTHORS AND STUDENTLITTERATUR

© THE AUTHORS AND STUDENTLITTERATUR

© THE AUTHORS AND STUDENTLITTERATUR

FOREWORD

Phenomena such as private property rights, contractual freedom, well-functioning price formation and the free movement of goods, people and capital are important prerequisites for creating prosperity and avoiding the arbitrary use of power.

The Industrial Revolution and the establishment of liberal market systems made a rapid increase in average life expectancy and standard of living possible. The political influence of the vast majority of the people was minor at first, but it eventually picked up steam. Political democratization was gradual; it took until the beginning of the post-war period for men and women in all Western countries to enjoy full political rights.

It is almost impossible for us to appreciate the conditions under which people lived before the advent of broad-based economic development and the establishment of the rule of law. However, a 1651 quote from English philosopher Thomas Hobbes conveys a vivid picture:

> In such condition there is no place for industry, because the fruit thereof is uncertain, and consequently, not culture of the earth, no navigation, nor the use of commodities that may be imported by sea, no commodious building, no instruments of moving and removing such things as require much force, no knowledge of the face of the earth, no account of time, no arts, no letters, no society, and which is worst of all, continual fear and danger of violent death, and the life of man, solitary, poor, nasty, brutish, and short.[1]

---

1 Thomas Hobbes, *Leviathan*, XIII.9.

The modern human has existed for more than 50,000 years, while the ideas and institutions necessary for economic development have only existed for a couple of hundred years. Moreover, rapid economic development would not have arisen without innovative entrepreneurs, who managed to simultaneously create a customer base for their innovative products and, by investing and employing labor, generate purchasing power for workers and savers.

However, during the inter-war period, the view of the entrepreneur's role in the development process changed radically. Large corporations— not entrepreneurs—came to be seen not only as more efficient producers of existing goods and services but also as the engines of innovation and technological change. Even Joseph Schumpeter, until then known as the foremost advocate of the crucial role of entrepreneurship and the individual entrepreneur, argued that the individual entrepreneur would not be important for economic development in the future. On the contrary, he claimed that "even the renewal function itself is being reduced to routine."

The individual entrepreneur was increasingly considered an anachronism. However, a reversal would occur. With the oil crises and stagflation of the 1970s, people started to doubt large corporations' innovativeness and ability to create wealth. The first signs that bigger was not necessarily better emerged. Large corporations were increasingly considered inflexible and unable to adapt to new market conditions and increasingly quality-conscious consumers. Meanwhile, the founders of high-tech firms were regarded as the heroes of our times and the most important business leaders of the new generation.

Commentators, politicians and scholars began to commonly assert that the world had entered into "the age of the entrepreneur." This trend was particularly evident in the latter half of the 1990s, when visionary entrepreneurs both embodied the spirit of the times and were able to attract considerable capital from external investors.

Today, most leading observers have a more nuanced view. The need for *both* individual entrepreneurship and large, efficient firms is the only reasonable conclusion. The economist William Baumol speaks aptly about "the David-Goliath symbiosis."

Both in Sweden and abroad, much has been said and written about the importance of entrepreneurship, but few research-based textbooks more

© THE AUTHORS AND STUDENTLITTERATUR

extensively explain the nature of entrepreneurship, the ways in which it affects society and the role of politics. We hope that this book can fill this gap.

For many contemporary readers, using the traditional "he" may come off as sexist, while using "he or she" may seem overly cumbersome. Therefore, in this book, we have decided to use "she" in odd-numbered chapters and "he" in even-numbered chapters.

We thank Fredrik Andersson, Henrik Berglund, Niklas Elert, Dan Johansson, Eric Rehn and Tino Sanandaji for their constructive comments on earlier drafts of this manuscript. All the remaining errors and shortcomings in this book are ours alone.

Stockholm, February 2, 2016

Magnus Henrekson   *Mikael Stenkula*

© THE AUTHORS AND STUDENTLITTERATUR

CHAPTER 1

Introduction

Giving a fair account of a country's economic history is impossible without discussing the companies that have played a central role in its development. Inevitably, behind these company names stands a founder and a strong driving force—the entrepreneur. When the Industrial Revolution—the first phase in the process of modern economic growth—began in Great Britain, entrepreneurs such as James Watt, Henry Bessemer, Robert Owen and Samuel Greg were the front men. When the United States surpassed Great Britain and became the technologically leading economy around 1900, its ascension was largely the result of the efforts of entrepreneurs such as John D. Rockefeller, Dale Carnegie and Henry Ford, innovators such as Thomas Alva Edison and Alexander Graham Bell and creative financial capitalists such as J. P. Morgan.

Likewise, Swedish industrialization, which took off in the 1860s, has been associated with specific entrepreneurs such as Lars Magnus Ericsson, Göran Fredrik Göransson, Alfred Nobel, André Oscar Wallenberg, Sven Wingquist and Johan Petter Åhlén.[1] A single person with a strong vision and business idea is often behind each of the more recently founded companies that have grown considerably in the post-war period. Ingvar Kamprad's IKEA, Ruben Rausing's Tetra Pak and Erling Persson's H&M are probably the best-known examples, but an individual founder and a successful entrepreneur is also behind most of the companies that have entered the Swedish stock market since the deep crisis in the early 1990s.

---

1 See Johnson (2006) for a presentation of many successful entrepreneurs in Sweden from the 17th century until the present.

Given these entrepreneurial successes, does entrepreneurship or the work of individual entrepreneurs explain why some countries, such as Sweden and the United States, are rich, while other countries, such as Sierra Leone and Burma/Myanmar, are extremely poor? A country's business sector development seems to be closely related to its entrepreneurs. However, to what extent is claiming that a country is rich because of its entrepreneurs possible? What would Sweden's growth trajectory have looked like if we momentarily pretended that the great entrepreneurs associated with the Swedish industrial breakthrough had never been born or had chosen to emigrate to the United States? Perhaps the Swedish economy would still have undergone a process similar to the one that actually took place, even if it may have seemed a bit different. In any event, without a scientifically based understanding of the function of entrepreneurship, determining its importance with regard to a country's historical, contemporary and future development is impossible.

In this book, we intend to analyze and explain what entrepreneurship is and why entrepreneurship plays a crucial role with regard to creating prosperity, growth and employment in a country. Our analysis is based on an extensive body of theoretical and empirical literature. Both Swedish and international conditions will be discussed.

No entrepreneurs in the standard neoclassical models are used and referred to in economic analyses, which complicates any attempt to interpret and explain the received view in economics regarding the role of entrepreneurship. This neglect of entrepreneurs is not as odd as it may seem at first glance. During the inter-war period, economics became increasingly formalized and mathematically oriented. The role of the entrepreneur does not readily lend itself to mathematical formalization, which partly explains why entrepreneurship was once excluded from the mainstream framework.

Reducing specific aspects of the entrepreneurial function to make it mathematically tractable has been possible, but several important aspects cannot be expressed mathematically in the same way as many other economic mechanisms are. The neoclassical toolbox is insufficient in capturing all the facets of the entrepreneurial function.[2] Therefore, the role of the entrepreneur in economic theory has largely been restricted to aspects that can be integrated into formal mathematical models.

---

2 Barreto (1989) and Bianchi and Henrekson (2005).

 © THE AUTHORS AND STUDENTLITTERATUR

Before the breakthrough of modern microeconomic theory in the inter-war period, the entrepreneur and the entrepreneurial function were often discussed and analyzed among contemporary scholars. Leading economists throughout history, including Richard Cantillon (18th century), Jean-Baptiste Say (19th century) and Irving Fisher (early 20th century), all analyzed the role of the entrepreneur in the economy. Today, many consider Joseph Schumpeter, who was active during the first half of the 20th century, to be the father of modern entrepreneurship theory.

The entrepreneurial element in both micro- and macroeconomics is sparse at best and is sometimes even completely absent from the teaching material that today's economics students encounter.[3] The simplest microeconomic models do not include businesses or businesspeople and entrepreneurs. Business activity is reduced to a so-called production function that mechanically maps the maximum production that can be obtained with a certain amount and combination of inputs. In the basic macroeconomic models, growth results from investment, technical change and increased inputs of labor. These models also neglect entrepreneurs.

These models say nothing about who, subject to uncertainty, assumes the role of combining resources in the form of capital (financial and physical), labor (with different education and intrinsic abilities) and knowledge to produce the goods and services demanded and who does so in the form of a firm that pursues economic profit. Instead, this complex task has been implicitly assumed to work; therefore, it has been excluded from the formal analysis.

As a result, a sizable share of the early research on entrepreneurship has fallen outside mainstream economics or has landed in other academic disciplines, such as business studies, sociology and economic psychology.[4] However, by the end of the 1960s, influential economist William J. Baumol highlighted this shortcoming in the traditional economic analysis in his now classic observation that "the theoretical firm is entrepreneurless—the Prince

---

3 Johansson (2004) and Phipps, Strom and Baumol (2012).
4 Two important sources for readers who seek more in-depth overviews of the extensive field of entrepreneurship research are the collections published by Edward Elgar in the *International Library of Entrepreneurship Series* (30 volumes to date) and the journal *Foundations and Trends in Entrepreneurship*.

of Denmark has been expunged from the discussion of Hamlet."[5] Research on entrepreneurship is now well established in management, and research on entrepreneurship and the importance of individual entrepreneurs began thriving within the so-called Austrian tradition in economics. The Austrian school focuses less on formal modelling.

However, research on entrepreneurship has exploded since the early 1990s, and many attempts have been made to find scientific evidence for the crucial importance of entrepreneurship in economic development and wealth creation. Even within mainstream economics, scholars have recently once again become interested in the role of the entrepreneurial function in the economy. The importance of entrepreneurship for growth and employment is now also a natural element in policy discussions, in both Sweden and other countries as well as in international organizations such as the European Union, the Organisation for Economic Co-operation and Development (OECD) and the World Bank.

The book is organized as follows. In chapter 2, we provide a brief background by discussing what a firm is and why it exists. In chapters 3–6, we thoroughly examine what entrepreneurship really is, how it should be defined and how it can be measured. In chapters 7 and 8, we discuss why entrepreneurship is of crucial importance and examine the role of entrepreneurship in economic growth and employment creation. In chapters 9–11, we address the determinants of entrepreneurship and discuss how these may be analyzed based on economic theory. In chapters 12–14, we discuss economic policy and entrepreneurship based on the discussion in the previous chapters. In chapter 15, we conclude with a brief summary and some important conclusions.

5 Baumol (1968, p. 66).

© THE AUTHORS AND STUDENTLITTERATUR

What Do We Mean by Entrepreneurship?

In this first part, we systematically discuss what entrepreneurship really is, how it should be defined, and which measurements are typically used to empirically quantify the degree of entrepreneurial activity in an economy. We also position the entrepreneur in a larger context. The entrepreneur does not operate in a vacuum and depends on a range of actors with complementary competencies to realize his ideas. The entrepreneur plays a central role in what we refer to as the competence structure.

In chapter 2, we discuss what firms really are and why they exist. In chapters 3 and 4, we discuss what the term "entrepreneurship" means. This discussion shows that entrepreneurship is a multidimensional concept that has been defined in several different ways over the years. In chapter 5, we adopt an empirical perspective and examine the various ways in which the extent of entrepreneurial activity has been measured in the empirical literature.

Entrepreneurship cannot be measured in a distinct and unambiguous manner. Instead, we present a number of both "narrow" and "wide" measures that researchers use. Chapter 6 addresses the entrepreneur from a wider perspective. Here, we discuss the importance of various complementary actors and the role of risk capital in helping firms be capable of developing and prospering. In this chapter, we also analyze the differing roles of small, new and large firms in the economy.

Once we have determined what entrepreneurship is and how we reckon that it should be defined, we will discuss why entrepreneurship is important in Part II.

CHAPTER 2

What is a Firm, and How is it Organized?

Entrepreneurship is closely linked to firms and the operation of firms. Social, political and institutional entrepreneurship, which are not necessarily associated with running a firm, also exist. Social entrepreneurship involves pursuing social objectives or solving a social problem without seeking economic profit. Political and institutional entrepreneurship concern influencing a country's institutions/rules by acting entrepreneurially within the framework of the political system.

This book deals exclusively with the kind of entrepreneurship that is conducted within profit-seeking firms. Therefore, before we proceed to more directly analyze entrepreneurship, we will discuss what a firm is, why it exists and how it can organize its activities. In this chapter, we will explain how the ways that research scholars have viewed firms have evolved over time. In a more forward-looking section, we will also attempt to explain how globalization changes the conditions for running a firm and, in turn, entrepreneurship.

2.1 Why Do Firms Exist?

What is a firm and what is its function? Economic transactions can be organized in two fundamentally different ways: (i) independent actors who interact with each other in the market, and (ii) transactions that occur internally within a firm. Nobel Laureate Ronald Coase argued in the 1930s that, in many cases, firms exist because transaction costs may be lower when interactions are performed within an organization rather than in the market.

More than anyone else, 2009 Nobel Laureate Oliver Williamson has furthered Coase's analysis by studying the factors that influence transaction costs. According to Williamson, three important changes occur when transactions are moved from the market into the firm:

- a relationship based on authority arises (hierarchy replaces market);
- individual incentives are weakened; and
- new costs arise.

If an authority-based relationship is formed, many coordination problems and conflicts of interest can be solved. This relationship requires the creation of an internal bureaucracy, which, in turn, leads to new costs. Since the early 1970s, a comprehensive body of literature has emerged that has attempted to expand the debate on the effect of transaction costs—i.e., why they may vary within and outside the firm and what determines the firm's boundaries.[1]

Economic agents and firms must continually decide whether producing a certain good or service themselves or buying the good or service in question from somebody else is more profitable. This is usually referred to in the literature as the *make-or-buy decision*.[2] On the one hand, problems and costs associated with coordination and incentives will arise if a firm primarily uses internal transactions to carry out its economic activities. On the other hand, in this case, the firm may take advantage of economies of scale and use the firm as protection to avoid having its high-value transactions identified and mimicked by its competitors. If the firm instead decides to buy goods and services in the market, it faces the opposite problem of high transaction costs.

Transaction costs: Costs associated with carrying out a transaction or an economic exchange. These costs include the time and effort required to find a counterpart, to negotiate a mutually acceptable agreement and to ensure that the transaction is carried out. Economists usually refer to three different types of costs: costs for contact, contract and control.

---

1 See, for instance, the articles in Williamson and Masten (1999).
2 See, e.g., Besanko, Dranove and Shanley (1996).

© THE AUTHORS AND STUDENTLITTERATUR

In a theoretical world without contract costs and costs associated with asymmetric information or uncertainty, imagining a firm that only operates through contract-based agreements between independent individuals is possible. A firm may be considered a nexus (or a bundle) of contracts, which are necessary for managing uncertainty, coordination problems, opportunism and other complications in the economy.

Hence, we may envision two ideal types of firms that reflect the two solutions to this problem: the integrated firm and the network firm (see *Figure 2.1* and *Figure 2.2*). In the integrated firm, the bulk of the economic activity that is required to produce the final product occurs within the firm. In the network firm, only the absolute core activities take place within the firm

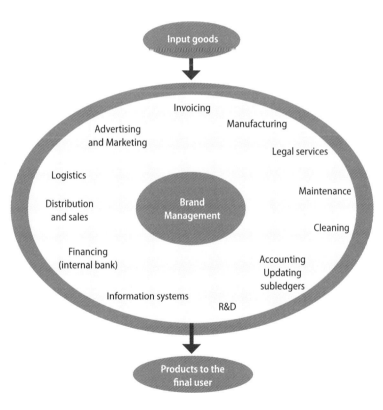

Figure 2.1 The integrated firm.

Note: In the integrated large corporation, the bulk of the economic activity that is required to obtain the final product occurs within the corporation.

Figure 2.2 The network firm.

Note: In the network firm, only the absolute core activities occur within the firm, while everything else, including manufacturing, research and development, distribution and marketing, is outsourced to third parties.

(management, strategic brand and design management, and coordination of research and development [R&D]). Everything else, including manufacturing, distribution and the execution of R&D, is outsourced, i.e., purchased from third-party producers. On the one hand, compared with the integrated firm, the network firm is very small in terms of employees. On the other hand, the network firm will have far higher sales per employee. With few exceptions, firms are positioned somewhere in between these two ideal types.

2.2 The View of Firms from a Historical Perspective

For a long time, many economists and politicians—on both the right and the left and on both sides of the "Iron Curtain"—believed that the best route to industrialization and economic development was through mass production

© THE AUTHORS AND STUDENTLITTERATUR

Incentive: Something that motivates an individual to perform an action. For example, economic incentives may be material rewards in the form of salaries, bonuses or profit-sharing plans that an employer may distribute to encourage a specific behavior or effort.

Incentive problems: Problems that occur in designing a reward structure in such a way that a desired behavior is encouraged and achieved.

Coordination problems: Problems that occur when the behavior or expectations of different actors are hard to coordinate, which make achieving a desired behavior or choice more difficult.

Economies of scale: The cost advantage that enterprises obtain due to size, output, or scale of operation, with the cost per unit of output generally decreasing with increasing scale as fixed costs are distributed over more units of output.

Contract costs: The costs of obtaining a (legally binding) contract. These costs may include the negotiation of the agreement's content, the drafting of the explicit agreement (the text of the agreement) and the cost of legal expertise and assessments.

Information costs: The costs of information gathering and the evaluation of this information.

of relatively standardized products via specialized capital equipment and technology. The obtainable benefits through increased economies of scale, increased specialization and standardized mass production were generally considered greater than the increased costs that resulted from weakened individual incentives, growing information problems and the bureaucratization of large organizations. Bigger might have been more boring, but it was considered more efficient. In the 1950s and 1960s, large production units organized within the framework of the vertically integrated corporation were considered one of the most important elements in the model for economic and social development that came to be known as Fordism. The principal tradeoff was between the inherent inefficiency of small firms and the risk that the large vertically integrated corporations would abuse their market power and evolve into inefficient monopolists.

The future was believed to belong to the giant corporations. The importance of individual effort and individual incentives was thought to be decreasing. Canadian-born Harvard professor John Kenneth Galbraith was one of the most emphatic proponents of a policy favoring large corporations. A famous quotation from 1956 aptly illustrates his view:

> There is no more pleasant fiction than that technological change is the product of the matchless ingenuity of the small man forced by competition to employ his wits to better his neighbor. Unhappily, it is a fiction.[3]

However, for an extended period, the large corporations were seen not only as more efficient producers but also as the leading engines of innovation and technological change. In 1942, Joseph Schumpeter, who had been known as the most adamant believer in the importance of the individual entrepreneur, concluded that "What we have got to accept is that [the large-scale enterprise] has come to be the most powerful engine of progress."[4]

In light of these predominant views, economic policy unsurprisingly focused on favoring the large, bureaucratically organized organizations, which included both large corporations and public monopoly producers. Many countries came to use state-owned firms and regulations as a counterweight to large corporations. Although the latter were considered necessary for growth, the increasing concentration of resources and power, along with the reduced pluralism that ensued, also raised serious concerns.

The perception of large corporations as the unrivalled engines of innovation and growth began to be challenged in the late 1970s. The changing nature of technological development, the growing importance of the service sector, and the reduced need for standardized mass production all contributed to reduce the advantages of large corporations. In 1979, Massachusetts Institute of Technology (MIT) researcher David Birch published the much-discussed study entitled *The Job Generation Process*. Birch showed that small firms were far more important than previously thought in terms of creating new jobs.[5] In another important breakthrough in the early 1980s, entrepreneurship scholar Zoltan Acs found that smaller American steelworks, the so-called "mini mills," successfully competed with the super-sized steel companies—in an industry that epitomized the Fordist

---

3 Galbraith (1956, p. 86).
4 Schumpeter (1942, p. 106).
5 Birch (1979).

  © THE AUTHORS AND STUDENTLITTERATUR

way of organizing economic activities.[6] These mini mills not only created jobs but also contributed to groundbreaking innovations in the steel sector.[7] Both Birch's and Acs' studies contributed to a modified view of the importance of small firms.

In 1984, economist Michael Piore and political scientist Charles Sabel, both at MIT, published an influential book entitled *The Second Industrial Divide*. They argued that the era of large-scale mass production and the concomitant institutional setup had ended. What had begun in the United States at the beginning of the 20th century had spread to Europe and Japan, but these economies' production system were facing "a second divide" based on "flexible specialization" and smaller firms, which worked in networks and relied on strong local and regional ties to a greater degree than large corporations.

2.3 Firms in the 21st Century

Ronald Coase has already noted that the boundary between market and inter-firm transactions varies over time and across activities.[8] Today the technological development and the increasingly sophisticated use of information and communications technologies (ICTs) to control production and distribution (the so-called ICT revolution) contribute to a shift in the boundary between market and inter-firm activities. Many factors explain this shift. First, the extent to which technological change gives rise to economies of scale in production has seemingly decreased. In many cases, small-scale operations and factors such as proximity to customers make the small units superior. Second, major changes in technologies and markets create new business opportunities and entirely new products. Totally new products are often produced more efficiently in newly established firms, which have been founded to produce these very products. Third, the new technologies help make the market more efficient, which reduces transaction costs in the market and reduces the need for large firm units.[9]

---

6 Acs (1984).
7 Christensen and Raynor (2003). They use the term "disruptive innovations."
8 Coase (1937).
9 See, for instance, Carlsson (1999), Baldwin and Johnson (1999) and Loveman and Sengenberger (1991).

However, this is not the entire picture. Developments in ICT have also made it possible for large organizations to remain flexible and efficient. Firms that have experienced strong growth have been able to remain productive and avoid soaring transaction costs. ICT has allowed firms to change their governance models, even if the flat, non-hierarchical organizational model has not become as prevalent or delivered the results that many observers expect.[10] The ICT revolution has also provided a basis for many new business models and innovations that are network products, which provides large firms with extensive customer bases with an advantage and makes small firms' entry and survival more difficult.

Network product: A good or service whose value depends on how many people use it.

Today's technologies often make cooperating and combining resources in the market rather than within the firm more advantageous. When information can be disseminated instantly and at a low cost to many people in diverse geographic locations, the value of centralized and bureaucratic decision making declines. Individual specialists can be their own managers and can coordinate and enhance their work by cooperating with different partners. Through the emergence of global information networks, such micro-firms are also able to access and benefit from the global cache of information, expertise and funding that was previously only available to large multinational corporations. Small firms may thus benefit from many of large firms' advantages without having to give up the flexibility and creativity that is more easily achieved in small firms. However, large multinational corporations are not waning in importance. Many very large—and successful—firms have utilized ICT to develop well-functioning markets within the framework of existing firms. ICT contributes to both organizational and product innovation. Apple and Google are two prominent cases in point.

Therefore, many firms have reorganized their activities according to the setup that characterizes the network firm. When firms expose a growing share of their activities to market forces, opportunities are also created for

---

10 Wulf (2012).

   © THE AUTHORS AND STUDENTLITTERATUR

new firms to take over a large share of the activities that are sold in the market (outsourcing). On an international scale, large corporations have gone through a painful process of corporate downsizing since the 1980s. This trend has been reversed in recent years. Some firms have backsourced activities that are considered especially valuable to the firm. For example, some firms reclaim large parts of their R&D activities and locate them close to their production plants to be able to take advantage of synergies between the two.

GLOBALIZATION

The flow of goods, services, capital and workers between countries and continents has increased in pace and volume in recent decades. The global market offers many opportunities for progress and firm development, but it also presents some challenges. When the value chain within firms is broken up and fragmented, each individual part will be allocated where it is the most beneficial from the firm's perspective. The improved means of transportation and communication, important drivers of globalization, have changed the conditions for industrial organization and logistics. National borders play an increasingly smaller role in locational decisions. However, whether outsourcing (the transfer of portions of work to external domestic or foreign suppliers) and offshoring (the relocation of a business process to another country either within the firm or to another supplier) will continue to grow increasingly important is unclear.

Part of the restructuring that is taking place—and that will take place— can be viewed in the form of international outsourcing and offshoring as a successful adaptation in the wake of globalization, whereby domestic production "climbs up the value chain," enabling continued growth and real wage increases for the domestic labor force. Meanwhile, unprofitable activities may be outsourced and developed in an environment in which they are competitive. However, a certain part of the relocation may result in potentially profitable and employment-generating activities being located outside a country's borders and thus not becoming a part of that country's economy.

Forces are also concurrently working in opposite directions, as is apparent in the ongoing wave of mergers and acquisitions of large firms. This trend is largely driven by the economies of scale in distribution and marketing focused on the end-users, which are gradually becoming more global. In many areas, increasingly larger firms are required to manage and further develop global brands and to manage the development of new product generations. In other words, the advantages of economies of scale seem to remain, perhaps becoming even more important, within certain business activities.[11] Developments in ICT may help large and growing businesses to remain effective without "drowning" in information and coordination problems.

However, this trend and the trend toward more and increasingly specialized firms are not contradictory. In many cases, large firms will continue to act as buyers of sophisticated products for which smaller firms handle part of the production. For example, large pharmaceutical companies might outsource research and clinical trials to small firms, or independent engineers and designers outside the large companies play an important role in developing new car models.

2.4 Chapter Summary

In this chapter, we have learned the following:

- Firms exist because transaction costs would be too high if each actor had to independently interact with every other actor in a market.
- The optimal firm size depends on the incentive and coordination problems that are associated with the building of hierarchies within a firm as well as the extent of a firm's economies of scale.
- Until the late 1970s, large corporations were considered crucial for economic development, whereas small and new firms were considered to be of increasingly lesser importance. This view was practically reversed in the early 1990s, but it has since become more balanced; small and young firms as well as large, mature firms are playing important roles in innovation and economic growth.
- Globalization and ICT developments have affected both large and small firms' opportunities to interact in the market. At this stage, which type of firm that benefits the most from these developments is unclear.

---

11 Andersson, Braunerhjelm and Jakobsson (2006, chapter 5) and Ekholm and Hakkala (2006).

  © THE AUTHORS AND STUDENTLITTERATUR

CHAPTER 3

What is Entrepreneurship?

The term "entrepreneur" originates from the French verb *entreprendre,* which means to supply or create a "space" to be able to do something. In the public debate, entrepreneurship often refers to new firms and/or self-employment. The term is used somewhat differently in the economic literature, which often focuses on the entrepreneur's unique role in the economy, not on the firm's organizational form. According to Robert Hébert and Albert Link, who have written several works on perceptions of the entrepreneur throughout history, there are at least twelve different definitions for what an entrepreneur does.[1] The entrepreneur has been defined as a risk taker, a capital owner, an innovator, a decision maker, an industrial leader, a business leader/superintendent, an organizer and coordinator of economic resources, a business owner, an employer of factors of production, a contractor of goods and services, an arbitrageur and an allocator of resources among alternative uses. Hence, no consensus exists regarding how the concept should be defined.

The first person to emphasize the entrepreneur's key role in the economy was French economist Richard Cantillon (ca. 1680–1734).[2] This role was recognized in his book *Essai sur la Nature du Commerce en Général,* which was published posthumously in 1755 but was circulated privately starting in 1730. In this book, Cantillon describes an emerging market economy based on private property, with three types of economic agents:

---

1 Hébert and Link (1989, 2006).

2 Cantillon's *Essai* soon sank into oblivion, and it was not rediscovered until the late 19th century. Today, many people consider the book the first systematic analysis of the workings of a market economy, preceding Adam Smith's *The Wealth of Nations* by more than 40 years. Cantillon has even been called "the father of enterprise economics" (Nevin 2013).

© THE AUTHORS AND STUDENTLITTERATUR

- landowners, who are financially independent;
- entrepreneurs, who are acting in the market with the goal of making a profit; and
- employees.

Cantillon depicts the entrepreneur as the crucial agent in the economic process. In Cantillon's view, entrepreneurs make all decisions and conduct all activities pertaining to production, distribution and trade, while landowners, who generally determine aggregate demand, play a passive role.

The entrepreneurial function has thus been discussed on many occasions. Even if the function of the entrepreneur has been described in several ways, distinguishing some distinctive features that recur in many writings is possible. In this chapter, we will systematically examine what entrepreneurship really is.

3.1 The Four Classical Entrepreneurial Functions

Distinguishing four classical entrepreneurial functions is possible. *Figure 3.1* summarizes these four functions and links them to the social scientists who are considered the first to identify and emphasize particular functions. In this section, these four social scientists and their contributions are discussed in detail. Several more recent contributions are generally either refined variations of one of these four function or combinations of them.

JOSEPH A. SCHUMPETER

Few people dispute that Joseph A. Schumpeter (1883–1950) is the most important scholar within entrepreneurship research. In his book *The Theory of Economic Development*, originally published in German in 1911, Schumpeter singled out the individual entrepreneur as the *primus motor* for economic growth and the development process. According to Schumpeter, the entrepreneur is primarily an innovator who identifies and introduces new and innovative "combinations" of available factors of production—a creative process for which he coined the felicitous term "creative destruction." According to Schumpeter, innovations do not need to be new goods or services, but they may also consist of the following:

© THE AUTHORS AND STUDENTLITTERATUR

Figure 3.1 The four classical entrepreneurial functions and their intellectual originators.

- new production methods,
- new markets,
- new resources, or
- new organizations/organizational forms.

In Boxes 3.1 and 3.2, we present two Schumpeterian entrepreneurs. They were involved in two completely different activities on completely different scales, but they were both innovators because they organized activities in new and different ways.

Box 3.1

Sam Walton (1918–1992)—the entrepreneur who created the world's largest company and raised the standard of living for low-income earners

Sam Walton was a former employee of JC Penney and ran a retail franchise. When Walton's employer dismissed his idea to open up low-price stores in small towns in the United States, he went on to found Wal-Mart in 1962. More than twenty years later, in 1985, Sam Walton had become the richest man in the United States according to *Forbes Magazine*. Wal-Mart grew to be the largest employer in the world, and, in recent years, it is estimated to have contributed a considerable share of the productivity growth in the American economy.[14]

In 2014, Wal-Mart owned more than 11,000 department stores in 27 countries (sometimes under different names). It is the world's largest company in terms of both turnover and the number of employees (2.2 million). Wal-Mart's customers are mostly low-income earners, and

---

3 Hausman and Leibtag (2009).

© THE AUTHORS AND STUDENTLITTERATUR

studies show that the company has contributed significantly to reducing the prices of the products that weigh heavily in the consumer baskets of low-income earners.

However, the company has been criticized for contributing to reduced diversity and the weakening of social capital, as part of the existing retail sector may be outcompeted when Wal-Mart is established in small-town communities.

SOURCE: BASKER (2007), HAUSMAN AND LEIBTAG (2009) AND THE COMPANY WEBSITE: WWW.WALMART.COM.

Box 3.2

Christina Wahlström—the midwife who challenged the public monopoly

In the early 19th century, midwife training was organized throughout Sweden, and midwifery was starting to require formal certification. In the 19th century, midwifery was an area where there were many female entrepreneurs. However, during the 20th century, private providers were increasingly pushed back, and the 1970 healthcare reform gave county councils a *de facto* monopoly on all kinds of obstetric care.

Christina Wahlström had been employed as a midwife within the Stockholm County Council for more than ten years when she founded the maternity care company Mama Mia in 1988. She founded Mama Mia because she did not think that the persons needing care were receiving the services to which they were entitled. The company was initially completely privately funded and experienced major losses until 1992, when a new political leadership took over the County Council. The new leadership introduced a so-called "maternity allowance," and pregnant women were allowed to use any caregiver without incurring any additional costs.

Christina Wahlström has managed to broaden the activities of private caregivers. For example, midwives in private health care have been given the right to prescribe birth control pills.

In 2012, the company had grown to become one of Scandinavia's largest private companies within the maternity care sector, with over 6,000 admitted mothers and approximately 100 employees.

SOURCE: DU RIETZ (2013) AND THE COMPANY WEB SITE: HTTP://WWW.MAMAMIA.SE.

© THE AUTHORS AND STUDENTLITTERATUR

ISRAEL M. KIRZNER

Israel M. Kirzner (born in 1930) belongs to what is frequently referred to as the Austrian tradition. Unlike Schumpeter, he sees the entrepreneur as an arbitrageur who discovers and acts on unexploited profit opportunities in the economy. These opportunities may exist because of imbalances in the market or an inefficient use of existing resources. They do not need to originate from anything genuinely new or innovative, as claimed by Schumpeter. However, a particular form of attention or alertness—an ability to identify and recognize opportunities that others have not yet discovered—is required. According to this approach, the individuals who are best able to discover unexploited opportunities are the true entrepreneurs.

Kirzner's entrepreneur can be characterized as a "creator of equilibrium." Through her actions, the Kirznerian entrepreneur pushes the economy toward equilibrium—a state in which no unexploited opportunities exist and in which all the existing production capacity is being used in the best way possible. In equilibrium, exploitable entrepreneurial opportunities no longer exist.

Nevertheless, the above description is too simplistic. Kirzner uses actually two distinct approaches to entrepreneurship that are directed at different readers, which further complicate his perspective. The aforementioned perspective (called Mark I) is the one most associated with Kirzner, and it is directed at mainstream economists for whom the equilibrium concept plays a central role. For economists who are trained in the Austrian tradition, to which Kirzner himself belongs, he developed an alternative perspective regarding the entrepreneur (Mark II). This perspective cannot be integrated into mainstream neoclassical theory. In his Mark II theory, Kirzner emphasizes uncertainty over time and entrepreneurship as a creative process. According to this theory, no discoverable objective opportunities push the economy toward equilibrium. Here, Kirzner is linked more closely with both Schumpeter, Knight, and other scholars within the Austrian tradition.[4]

---

4 Korsgaard et al. (2015)

FRANK KNIGHT

Frank Knight (1885–1972) is often regarded as the third of the "big three" within modern entrepreneurship research. Knight focuses on the entrepreneur's role as a decision maker under so-called *genuine uncertainty*.[5] In contrast to risk, genuine uncertainty refers to a situation in which no calculable probability distribution of possible outcomes exists, not even in principle. In many cases, none of the possible outcomes is known. This uncertainty is a common and particularly weighty problem that entrepreneurs face. Someone needs to make decisions subject to uncertainty, and, according to Knight, the entrepreneur assumes this role. The entrepreneur is thus a bearer of uncertainty.

To illustrate the difference between risk and genuine uncertainty, the reader could ponder the difference between investments in public firms and investments in an innovation start-up. When investing in public firms, historical records and data can often be used to calculate an expected outcome distribution reasonably well. However, when investing in an innovation start-up, forming an equally clear notion regarding the outcome—or even its probability distribution—is impossible before the product is fully developed and introduced in the market. Before attempting to implement an idea in practice, predicting the technical problems that may arise or the actual existence of a market for the product is impossible.

JEAN-BAPTISTE SAY

A fourth function that has been assigned to the entrepreneur is the role of coordinator. Jean-Baptiste Say (1767–1832) is widely considered the first scholar to analyze this function of the entrepreneur. Say clearly distinguishes the entrepreneur's role and her compensation from that of the capitalist, the owner of natural resources (the landowner) and the worker (the wage earner). To produce a good, one needs capital (both physical and financial), natural resources, labor and entrepreneurship. According to Say, someone has to monitor and decide how knowledge, labor and capital should be

---

5 However, later research argues that Knight's theory of entrepreneurship is not as elaborate as the theories of Schumpeter and Kirzner. Knight mainly discusses the differences between risk and uncertainty and between profit and interest, while his discussion of entrepreneurship is sketchy and more fragmented (Brooke 2010).

  © THE AUTHORS AND STUDENTLITTERATUR

organized and used.[6] Without this coordinating function, no firm activities would occur, which is precisely why such a role is a crucial function of the entrepreneur. Say also claims that supply and demand not only exist with regard to labor and capital but also with regard to entrepreneurship.

3.2 Newer Research on the Entrepreneurial Function

Over time, different traditions have developed that have emphasized the four functions described in *Figure 3.1* differently. To show how entrepreneurship research has evolved, we will in this section discuss recent research contributions and highlight a few new important scholars in the field of entrepreneurship research.

THE INDIVIDUAL, THE ORGANIZATION AND THE TYPE OF EMPLOYMENT

During the infancy of modern entrepreneurship research in the 1960s, scholars tended to focus on social and psychological factors: Who is the entrepreneur, and which personal characteristics does she possess compared with those of the average citizen? Is the entrepreneur rich or poor, immigrant or native, young or old, male or female? Does she have a low or high level of education? Is she less risk averse, and does she generally manage stress better than other people do? Does the entrepreneur have more self-confidence and a greater need for personal autonomy? And so on. Even the possible existence of specific "entrepreneurship genes" was discussed, and many analyses explored the characteristics that influence a person's likelihood of becoming an entrepreneur. These kinds of studies still exist, even though they do not generate as much interest as they used to.

At the same time, another research field emerged. Instead of asking who will become an entrepreneur, researchers in this field believed that examining what an entrepreneur does, regardless of any common characteristics among entrepreneurs, would be useful.[7] They argued that the difference between entrepreneurs and non-entrepreneurs is that the former create new organizations or new structures. These researchers focused on analyzing

---

6 Say (1845). Posthumously published.
7 Gartner (1988).

© THE AUTHORS AND STUDENTLITTERATUR

the existence of start-ups. By necessity, the analysis of small firms and self-employed individuals provided an important foundation for this research tradition. After all, most new firms are small in the beginning, and most start-ups are founded by self-employed individuals. Labor market economists' entrepreneurship research mainly focused on the form of employment: Is a person employed in a firm or self-employed? For these entrepreneurship scholars, entrepreneurship often became synonymous with self-employment.

Focusing on a particular type of firm or business owner can help provide a clearly defined quantitative measurement of the entrepreneurial activity in the economy, which is a clear advantage of this approach. Empirical research in economics requires a well-defined metric (which is comparable over time, across individuals and preferably across geographical units) of the phenomenon that one seeks to analyze. Instead of asking exactly what characterizes an entrepreneur, researchers can analyze whether entrepreneurship—measured, for example, by the number of start-ups in a certain area during a certain period—is positively related to factors such as improvements in productivity, economic growth or increased employment. However, the disadvantage is that researchers ultimately produce clear-cut metrics that fail to fully capture the multi-faceted phenomenon of entrepreneurship. However, this dilemma is not unique to entrepreneurship research.

Many scholars have analyzed the importance of different types of firms or business owners, arguing that they are examining the effects of entrepreneurship in the economy. The results from this type of research have often been ambiguous. A similar approach has been used to examine the impact of various institutions on entrepreneurship. These results are often ambiguous as well. The question is whether the measures that researchers use are sufficiently accurate indicators of the extent of entrepreneurial activity. We will address this essential question in some detail in chapters 4 and 5.

ENTREPRENEURIAL OPPORTUNITIES AND EXPLOITATION

Since the early 1990s, a new research program has emerged; the entre-preneurial opportunity is center stage, which primarily relates to the definitions of the entrepreneurial function that both Schumpeter and Kirzner presented. Entrepreneurship is about discovering, evaluating and exploiting

© THE AUTHORS AND STUDENTLITTERATUR

opportunities by creating something new. Not all start-ups are innovative. Likewise, not all innovations are created in start-ups. In fact, a large share of all entrepreneurial activities takes place in already established firms. The scholars in this field are trying to identify and study the few organizations that create something that is genuinely novel—an innovation—which they introduce in the economy as more valuable goods and services. These organizations may be large or small, new or old.

In other words, entrepreneurship research has shifted from primarily studying the forms of entrepreneurship to trying to understand how, when and why an entrepreneurial opportunity is exploited—regardless of form. This exploitation does not have to occur within an organization, nor does the entrepreneur have to be a business owner. Scott Shane at Case Western Reserve University and Sankaran Venkataraman at the University of Virginia are two management scholars who have made significant contributions in this tradition, often named "the individual-opportunity nexus." They define entrepreneurship as a scholarly field that "seeks to understand how opportunities to bring into existence 'future' goods and services are discovered, created, and exploited, by whom, and with what consequences." Their definition of the field is thus closely aligned with the views of Schumpeter and Kirzner (Mark I).[8]

Economists Harvey Leibenstein and William Baumol have also made important conceptual contributions.[9] Leibenstein distinguishes between "routine" entrepreneurship and "Schumpeterian" entrepreneurship, the former referring to ordinary leadership in a well-known environment and the latter referring to non-routine leadership in an unknown environment that is rife with uncertainty. Baumol makes a similar distinction when he distinguishes between "innovative" and "imitative" entrepreneurship.

British entrepreneurship scholar Mark Casson's perspective closely relates to those of Knight and Say. He defines an entrepreneur as "someone who specializes in taking judgmental decisions about the coordination of scarce resources."[10] The essence of Casson's definition is captured by the expression "judgmental decisions," which refers to decisions that must be

---

8 Venkataraman (1997) and Shane and Venkataraman (2000). The quote is from Venkataraman (1997, p. 120).

9 Leibenstein (1968) and Baumol (1993, 2010).

10 Casson (2003, p. 20).

© THE AUTHORS AND STUDENTLITTERATUR

made under uncertainty when the decisive factor is the individual's ability to perceive and correctly interpret all relevant circumstances. This definition implies that different individuals, with exactly the same objectives and interests and subjected to exactly the same circumstances, may still make *different* decisions because individuals do not have the same information or they interpret the same information differently. According to Casson, entrepreneurs specialize in making decisions under such conditions. Non-entrepreneurs may be seemingly rational and maximize their expected utility, but they may be stuck in old routines, lack relevant information or be unable to grasp that they lack relevant information and are thus bound to make erroneous decisions. The "judgmental decision making" that characterizes entrepreneurs is based more on creative thinking than what is implicitly assumed in established neoclassical decision theory. The latter theory is valid only for non-entrepreneurial decision making.

SARAS SARASVATHY

Casson's and especially Knight's lines of thinking are closely linked to what American entrepreneurship scholar Saras Sarasvathy calls *effectuation*.[11] By effectuation, Sarasvathy refers to the specific problem-solving method that she believes must characterize entrepreneurial decisions. Entrepreneurs must make decisions under uncertainty, when no perfectly predictable future exists and when the final result is far from foreseeable. The entrepreneurial process itself largely explains why the future is uncertain. The entrepreneur's future preferences are not fixed; instead, they are continuously influenced and updated based on how the entrepreneurial process plays out. Instead of working toward achieving a predetermined objective, the entrepreneur focuses and bases her efforts on the available resources. In this way, the entrepreneur—to the greatest degree possible—tries to control the future without trying to predict it.

To illustrate her approach, Sarasvathy compares the case of a chef who is about to prepare a meal with a more traditional "causal" decision-making process. According to the traditional method, the chef decides to prepare a specific meal and comes up with a recipe for this meal. The chef buys the

---

11 Sarasvathy (2001, 2009).

   © THE AUTHORS AND STUDENTLITTERATUR

ingredients and then goes through the recipe point by point until the meal is prepared. According to the "effectual" method, the chef bases her meal on the ingredients that she has at home and uses her creativity to compose a possible meal. Unforeseen events—for instance, when a sauce begins to separate when new ingredients are mixed in—are a part of the process and lead to new experiences and insights from which the chef can learn. The chef may end up with no dish or with a repulsive dish. However, because the chef has not followed any predetermined and known recipe, she may also succeed in creating something new, tasty and unique. Sarasvathy believes that the most successful "expert entrepreneurs" work in this fashion when making decisions and that this method can be taught. If she is right, almost anyone can become more entrepreneurial.

THE AUSTRIAN TRADITION

Many of the arguments presented in this chapter, particularly Casson's views, closely relate to the view of the Austrian School of Economics regarding individuals' actions and choices. Ludwig von Mises, Friedrich von Hayek and the previously mentioned Israel Kirzner are key figures in this tradition.[12] According to the economists of the Austrian School, people usually do not behave as calculating robots who choose *one* strategy among a number of identifiable options, where the outcome is (probabilistically) known. Sometimes we are unsure of what we really want to achieve; wishes and objectives manifest themselves over time as we accumulate new experiences. The future is not only unknown but also sometimes "unknowable." We do not always know the possible future outcomes, which is not simply because it is costly to extract useable knowledge from the available information. Characteristics such as ambition, boldness and creativity thus come into play; traditional decision-making theory, which almost by definition excludes entrepreneurial decision making, allows little room for such characteristics.

However, the Austrian theories are not homogeneous, and other Austrian scholars have developed alternate views on entrepreneurship that differ from those of Kirzner (Mark I). For example, Ludwig Lachmann rejects the idea that an entrepreneurial opportunity is something that an

12 See Kirzner (1997), Hayek (1945) and von Mises (1949).

alert person discovers based on a sudden revelation. Opportunities arise and develop when ideas are explored in practice. By constantly considering new information that originates in the market and your own practical experiences, one may get entrepreneurial insights into how the company's resources may be restructured and improved. Lachmann refutes the notion that entrepreneurial activities have an inherent tendency to move the economy toward equilibrium. The thoughts that Kirzner later developed on entrepreneurship (Mark II) often responded to criticism against his earlier work (Mark I) that other economists within the Austrian tradition raised.

George S.L. Shackle is another economist in the Austrian tradition who analyzes entrepreneurship. Like Lachmann, he rejects Kirzner's (Mark I) notion of the entrepreneur as someone who creates equilibrium. Shackle completely rejects equilibrium as a concept, regardless of whether the entrepreneur pushes the economy toward or away from this imagined equilibrium. Instead, he stresses the entrepreneur as a creative actor who uses her imagination to visualize entrepreneurial opportunities. In reality, only subjective opportunities based on the imagination of various individuals exist. In fact, every individual exercises entrepreneurship when she faces decisions that cannot be resolved based solely on objective facts and that instead require subjective interpretations of what may happen in the future.[13]

Other critics, such as Nicolai Foss and Peter Klein, assert that "judgmental decision making" captures the essence of entrepreneurship far better than Kirzner's "alertness." They argue that alertness neither assumes uncertainty nor has any opportunity cost; in other words, the entrepreneur does not have to expend any effort to notice an entrepreneurial opportunity. It just requires the right (innate) talent. However, entrepreneurship requires action under uncertainty, which presupposes an ability to exercise judgmental decision making.[14]

THE NEOCLASSICAL TRADITION

Nobel Laureate Theodore W. Schultz has been the most eager economist to attempt to integrate the entrepreneurial function into neoclassical mainstream

---

13 Shackle (1979). See Ricketts (2002, p. 69–71).
14 Foss and Klein (2010a, 2010b).

  © THE AUTHORS AND STUDENTLITTERATUR

theory.[15] In recent years, other scholars have followed in Schultz's footsteps by attempting to integrate entrepreneurship into neoclassical growth models. However, in those models, the entrepreneurial role is invariably narrowly defined, not capturing the extensive and complex functions that scholars outside mainstream economics attribute to the entrepreneur.[16]

For a factor of production to be integrated into mainstream neoclassical theory, the calculation of its (expected) marginal productivity must be possible. Such calculations are reasonably straightforward for labor and capital, but they are more doubtful with regard to entrepreneurship. Still, Schultz simply postulates that calculating entrepreneurship's marginal productivity is possible, thus turning it into just another regular factor of production, which can be bought and sold in the market at a given price. However, if entrepreneurship, as Knight and Casson maintain, concerns making judgmental decisions regarding the coordination of scarce resources under uncertainty—for example, when starting a new firm or opening up a new market—then the entrepreneur's marginal productivity cannot be defined in advance. Therefore, a regular market in which supply and demand, including the markets that exist for other inputs such as raw materials and financial capital, determine the price of entrepreneurship cannot exist.

As entrepreneurship research has evolved and deepened, the analysis has gradually become more complex and multifaceted. Instead of discussing whom an entrepreneur is or what an entrepreneur does, scholars have increasingly focused on the entrepreneurial process. Today, scholars not only distinguish between entrepreneurial and non-entrepreneurial activities but also between various forms of entrepreneurship. To establish an even deeper understanding of entrepreneurship as a concept, we will discuss some of these differences more thoroughly before we proceed to discuss how we believe entrepreneurship should be defined today. We will discuss the following differences:

- Discovered versus created opportunities (section 3.3)
- Equilibrium versus non-equilibrium (section 3.4)

---

15 Schultz (1980).

16 See, for instance, Segerstrom, Anant and Dinopoulos (1990), Helpman (1992), Aghion and Howitt (1992) and Acemoglu, Aghion and Zilibotti (2006). Bianchi and Henrekson (2005) provide an overview.

- Entrepreneurship versus non-entrepreneurial self-employment (section 4.1)
- Intrapreneurs versus entrepreneurs (section 4.2)
- Productive versus unproductive and destructive entrepreneurship (section 4.3)
- Institutional entrepreneurship (section 4.4)
- High-growth firms and high-impact entrepreneurship (section 4.5)

3.3 Discovered versus Created Opportunities

Many distinctions in descriptions of the entrepreneur may relate back to Schumpeter's and Kirzner's approaches to entrepreneurship, including the question of whether an entrepreneur creates or discovers the opportunities that she exploits.[17]

The notion of discovered entrepreneurship is based on the premise that *objective* opportunities in the real economy are simply waiting to be discovered. According to this approach, a person does not need to generate any new knowledge; instead, noticing—or discovering—the opportunities that have yet to be exploited is crucial. The affinity with Kirzner's alertness is self-evident.

The idea of creative entrepreneurship, which can be linked to Schumpeter, is not based on objective opportunities. In this view, opportunities depend on individuals' input. Individuals apply their creativity and skills to create new opportunities. The opportunities are considered *subjective* and are linked to the individual actor's ability to create and exploit something novel.

Therefore, entrepreneurship is not simply an attempt to respond to an expected demand among prospective customers that no one has acted on before. It may also involve creating something that customers have yet to imagine and have thus been unable to demand. If Gottlieb Daimler and Carl Benz had asked their potential customers what they demanded in the 1880s, these customers would have replied that they wanted a faster horse with more stamina that required fewer resources. They would not have responded that they wanted a metal-sheeted covered carriage that was propelled by a mixture of liquid hydrocarbons rather than pulled by a horse.

---

17 See Alvarez (2005) for an in-depth discussion of this distinction.

© THE AUTHORS AND STUDENTLITTERATUR

On the one hand, discovered entrepreneurship implies a fixed number of opportunities to be discovered in the economy. As existing opportunities are exploited, fewer remain to be discovered. In a supposed final state—an equilibrium—all the entrepreneurial opportunities will be exhausted. On the other hand, creative entrepreneurship implies essentially infinite potential—only human creativity sets the limits.

However, this interpretation of discovered entrepreneurship is far too simplistic. A more realistic view of the entrepreneurial process posits that the discovery of an opportunity gives rise to additional exploitable opportunities. The number of opportunities will not gradually fall because of entrepreneurial activity; instead, self-reinforcing processes emerge, whereby the discovery and exploitation of opportunities generate new opportunities. When new methods, techniques or products are introduced, new questions and ideas emerge, which lead to new opportunities. When the computer mouse was introduced in the market, it paved the way for the development of other pointing devices and wireless mice. Bill Gates would not have been able to develop Microsoft if Steve Jobs, Ed Roberts and others had not created the personal computer. Steve Jobs and Steve Wozniak would not have been able to develop their personal computer if Gordon Moore and Intel had not developed the microprocessor. Intel would not have been able to develop the microprocessor if John Bardeen, Walter Brattain and William Shockley had not invented the transistor in 1947. And so on.

New opportunities may also be created or discovered as the economy grows and pertinent conditions evolve. For example, changes in consumer preferences continually give rise to new opportunities that entrepreneurs can exploit.[18] A telling example of this phenomenon is the emergence of the Internet and social media and the significant impact both have had on how people spend their leisure time on different activities. The demand for physical capital goods that require a considerable commitment of one's time is clearly declining and is being replaced by a demand for experiences and different kinds of online services.

The existence of one type of opportunity does not preclude the existence of the other type. Furthermore, the difference between creating and discovering does not have to be so clear-cut. For instance, the pharmaceutical company

18 Holcombe (2003).

Pfizer once tried to develop a new cardiac medication. The drug did not have the positive features that were demanded. However, the company found that the drug had side effects that it had not originally considered. This drug is now sold as Viagra, which has contributed in excess of 1.5 billion dollars in annual revenue to Pfizer in recent years.

Critics, particularly entrepreneurship scholars who stress the uncertainty of entrepreneurial activities, argue that the discussion surrounding created or discovered opportunities is misguided. They assert that opportunities are neither discovered nor created. Discovered opportunities presuppose the existence of objective opportunities based on a given and probabilistically predictable future, which is impossible if one assumes uncertainty. Created opportunities presuppose that the entrepreneur, perhaps based on her subjective interpretation, has created an (objective) opportunity that should be saleable. However, what has been created is a new technology, an economic activity, a business model or a firm. According to these critics, judgmental decision making under uncertainty is not an objective product or opportunity that can be bought and sold.

One way of interpreting opportunities involves sidestepping the theoretical distinction between created and discovered opportunities and seeing opportunities as a bundle of more or less clearly envisioned subjective views on the potential opportunities that are relevant to different people in various situations and for very different reasons.[19] Therefore, an alternative approach that is linked to uncertainty and "judgmental decisions" views opportunities as "imagined" instead of discovered or created. Individuals may interpret reality in various ways and imagine different opportunities that are difficult to transmit to others and that are subsequently exploitable or not.[20]

In a conceptual study, Per Davidsson and his colleague Marco Tonelli argue that the concept of entrepreneurial opportunities currently hampers the possibility of gaining more knowledge about the entrepreneurial process. They instead propose the concept of *New Venture Ideas* (NVIs), which they

19 Berglund (2007).
20 Klein (2008).

© THE AUTHORS AND STUDENTLITTERATUR

define as "imagined future ventures."[21] These ideas change and adapt to additional circumstances during the process, when the entrepreneur—guided by her partially implicit and incomplete idea of the imagined business project—works toward realizing the project's goals.

3.4 Equilibrium versus Non-Equilibrium

A further distinction, which may also be linked to the different views that Kirzner and Schumpeter expressed regarding the role of the entrepreneur, concerns whether entrepreneurship pushes the economy toward or away from equilibrium.

From an economic perspective, Schumpeter's view of entrepreneurship as a creative process—aptly dubbed "creative destruction"—can be interpreted as though the entrepreneur disequilibrates the economy, i.e., pushes it away from equilibrium. When entrepreneurs contribute new knowledge, new production opportunities are created, while existing products and activities become obsolete. The economy will hence move *away* from equilibrium. New opportunities set the economy in motion. Without entrepreneurship, the economy would be in a state of permanent equilibrium, what Schumpeter calls "a circular flow"—a state devoid of innovations—while entrepreneurs' efforts would upset the equilibrium.

Kirzner's notion of entrepreneurship as a discovery process can be interpreted in the exact opposite way; that is, the entrepreneur helps move the economy toward equilibrium. In this equilibrium, no unexploited opportunities exist, and all existing production capacity is used in the most value-creating way possible. In equilibrium, no new entrepreneurial opportunities exist to exploit. According to Kirzner, this imagined equilibrium is never attained, as the economy is constantly changing, moving toward new equilibria. Therefore, the potential equilibrium is an ever-changing, elusive target. In the basic neoclassical analysis, this movement toward equilibrium is assumed to occur automatically in frictionless markets.

---

21 Davidsson and Tonelli (2013). They write, "New Venture Ideas (NVIs) are 'imagined future ventures' or, more precisely, the evolving, changing and usually implicit and incomplete outlines of a future venture that give direction to action in processes of attempted creation of new economic activities."

In reality, entrepreneurship is one of the main mechanisms for bringing the economy to the point at which supply equals demand.

Kirzner's entrepreneurs are needed to push the economy toward equilibrium because the potential, though never attained, equilibrium (i.e., when supply equals demand in all markets) is constantly changing. Many factors may explain this constant change, including changes in the composition of the population, changes in preferences (tastes), changes in world market prices for inputs, and new competitors.[22] However, the equilibrium in the economy may change for another reason: innovations are introduced in the economic system. These innovations may be new technologies, new production methods or new business models. They can be anything that adds value to society and alters what is optimal for consumers and producers in the economy (the equilibrium). Schumpeterian entrepreneurs play a crucial role in producing such innovations.

The two approaches complement each other. The entrepreneur contributes to an economy that is moving away from equilibrium by introducing innovations in the market. The disequilibrium that emerges in the market will result in new opportunities for other entrepreneurs to exploit, which will once again move the economy closer to a new equilibrium.[23] *Figure 3.2* shows how equilibrating and disequilibrating entrepreneurship interact. We initially assume that every market in the economy is in equilibrium. New knowledge, which may take the form of new combinations of existing knowledge, makes it possible for Schumpeterian entrepreneurs to introduce innovations. These innovations pull the economy away from equilibrium, thus creating opportunities for Kirznerian entrepreneurs to push the markets toward a new equilibrium. As the figure shows, different shocks that do not originate from Schumpeterian entrepreneurs may also push markets away from equilibrium and introduce opportunities for Kirznerian entrepreneurs.

22 See, for instance, Drucker (1998) for a discussion on changes within the company/industry and outside the company/industry and the ways in which these changes affect innovation opportunities.

23 See Baumol (2010) and Holcombe (2007). However, some scholars maintain that these two notions cannot be combined in this manner. For instance, Glancey and McQuaid (2000) claim that the process that pushes the economy back toward equilibrium originates from imitation and that it should thus not be defined as entrepreneurship. See also Kirzner (1999) for a discussion of how his theory relates to Schumpeter's analysis.

  © THE AUTHORS AND STUDENTLITTERATUR

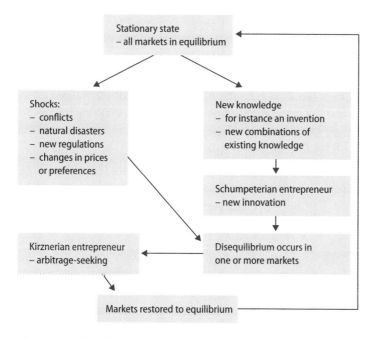

Figure 3.2 Different forms of entrepreneurship. Source: Based on Gunter (2012).

The figure also shows how the role and function of the entrepreneur complement the neoclassical model, which mainly focuses on identifying and analyzing equilibria.

The distinction between equilibrating and disequilibrating entrepreneurship can be graphically illustrated in yet another way. *Figure 3.3* depicts a production possibility frontier *PP*. The curve indicates the maximum combinations of two goods that can be produced with a certain amount of input. A discovering and equilibrating entrepreneur can be said to push the economy from point *A* inside the production possibility frontier, where the use of available resources is inefficient, toward an efficient use of existing resources on the curve at point *B*.

A creative and disequilibrating entrepreneur instead shifts the entire production possibility frontier outward to *P'P'* by introducing innovations. Equilibrating entrepreneurs will then gradually move the economy in the direction of the new production possibility frontier *P'P'*. Initially, reaping the full potential of the innovation may not be possible. For example, the economy may end up at point *C*. Eventually, the economy may reach a point on *P'P'*, but innovations will likely have already pushed the production possibility frontier further outwards.[24]

Figure 3.3 illustrates a case in which the resources (inputs) that can be used are given and the entrepreneur finds new ways of using existing inputs to a greater extent (*A → B*) or in a more value-creating way (*B → C*). The use of modern ICTs to streamline logistics and distribution in the retail sector illustrates this mechanism at work. If we assume two types of retailers, those that sell perishable goods and those that sell consumer durables, the use of modern ICT in both of these sectors can produce more with given inputs; however, making the necessary investments in hardware and

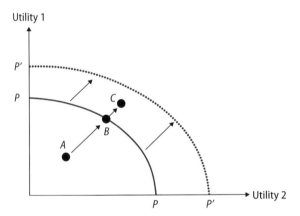

Figure 3.3 Equilibrating and disequilibrating entrepreneurship.

Note: Distinguishing between moving the economy to a point that is closer to the production possibility frontier and pulling the entire production possibility frontier outward is one way of distinguishing between equilibrating and disequilibrating entrepreneurship. The available factors of production are assumed fixed when such an analysis is undertaken. The entrepreneur who helps move the economy closer to the production possibility frontier does so by finding more valuable ways of using the existing factors of production, while the entrepreneur who helps push the production possibility frontier outwards does so by combining the existing factors of production in a more value-creating way. Source: Based on Boettke and Coyne (2003).

---

24 Boettke and Coyne (2003) conduct a similar analysis.

  © THE AUTHORS AND STUDENTLITTERATUR

software, training the staff to use the new systems and implementing all of the organizational changes that are required to benefit from the full potential of the new technology takes a long time.[25]

Let us conclude this chapter with a portrait of someone who, to an unusually high degree, embodied most of the functions assigned to the entrepreneur in this chapter: the Swedish florist and entrepreneur Bengt Nygren (see Box 3.3).

Box 3.3

Bengt Nygren—the man who revolutionized the floral industry

Bengt Nygren (born in 1931) was once as well known in Sweden as IKEA's founder Ingvar Kamprad and H&M's founder Erling Persson. Nygren grew up in a working-class family in Sundsvall, an industrial town some 600 km north of Stockholm. He began working as an errand boy and gardener at age 14. He started his first company, a flower plantation, as a teenager. Within a year, he had also opened his first store.

In the early 1950s, the distribution and sale of flowers was conducted using obsolete and inefficient methods. The value chain from production to consumption was handled by different actors, and the last stage, the sale to consumers, was extremely labor intensive. The staff dealt with one customer at a time, and bouquets and flower arrangements were created in the store "flower by flower."

Nygren systematically changed this process. He founded his own whole-sale business in 1956 and imported flowers from Italy, which secured access to inexpensive flowers all year round. Before orders were placed with Italian suppliers, Nygren had taken orders from the floral shops, implying that the flowers were already sold when they arrived in Sweden. Previously, much waste had characterized this phase of the process, when the wholesalers ordered flowers themselves and then tried to sell them to retailers. The logistics of the wholesale business also became increasingly efficient.

---

25 See Litan and Rivlin (2002) and Brynjolfsson and McAfee (2014), who reach similar conclusions in analyses of the long-term effects of ICT on production methods and productivity growth.

© THE AUTHORS AND STUDENTLITTERATUR

The wholesale price could thereby be drastically reduced, but the retailers did not lower their prices commensurately. Instead, they preserved the previous retail price and just increased their profit margins. As the consumer price did not decrease, the sales volume remained unchanged. Nygren reacted by starting a chain of flower shops of a completely new kind. The first store was opened in 1960 under the name Buketten ("The Bouquet"). Supply was standardized; the bouquets were pre-packaged; and the shops were designed to maximize efficiency. In Nygren's words, he had "worked out practically every step that the staff takes in the store. The customers do the job."[26]

Meanwhile, Nygren expanded his flower plantations and quickly became one of the most prominent gardeners in Sweden. At the same time, imports from Italy increased.

By 1967, Buketten had grown to become Europe's largest floral retail chain and Europe's largest horticultural company, and it continued to expand at a rapid pace. The first blow came with the oil crisis in 1973–74, which led to a sharp rise in costs, particularly for greenhouse cultivation. However, Nygren managed to survive the crisis, and, as long as industry demand did not collapse, the company's outlook was good thanks to Nygren's superior concept based on low prices, high turnover and efficient logistics.

The company had already expanded by establishing itself in Norway. In 1978, Nygren was invited to collaborate with an American company to establish 1,000 flower shops in France and Germany. However, the Riksbank (the central bank of Sweden) did not authorize Nygren to transfer the required cash to finalize the investment, thus barring the transaction. He then sold Buketten and left Sweden. Five years later, Buketten filed for bankruptcy.

Instead of continuing to develop his entrepreneurial ventures, Nygren, who was just a little over 45 years old, moved to the United Kingdom, where he increased wealth through some successful real estate transactions. A few years later, he moved to the Caribbean, where he still lives.

In the late 1960s, Swedish society was radicalized, and entrepreneurs, particularly those who had managed to become wealthy by founding and building successful companies, were unpopular. Nygren was severely

---

26 Olivecrona (1970, p. 132).

   © THE AUTHORS AND STUDENTLITTERATUR

attacked by the chairman of the Social Democratic youth movement (SSU), Bosse Ringholm, who would later become Minister of Finance between 1999 and 2004. Ringholm stigmatized Nygren as "antisocial and subversive," even though Nygren had made cut flowers affordable for working-class families. In Nygren's words, "The money I have made and make each year in this way is a pittance compared to the money that consumers make from my ideas, which I have developed to make money."[27]

Nygren's innovative entrepreneurship shows that, even though successful entrepreneurs often become very wealthy when building their companies, the bulk of the value created is passed on to consumers in two ways: (i) imitating competitors establish themselves in the market, which increases supply and lowers prices, or (ii) the entrepreneur lowers the price and reduces her margins to discourage potential competitors from entering the market.

Why did Nygren's entrepreneurial venture end in bankruptcy, while Ingvar Kamprad and Erling Persson continued to expand and conquer new markets outside Sweden? Exceedingly high tax rates on inheritance, wealth, dividends and income, combined with restrictive foreign exchange controls (not abolished until 1989) made it virtually impossible for Nygren to obtain the resources necessary to expand his business outside Sweden.[28]

In the decades following World War II, the foundation was laid for IKEA and H&M, which are now large global retail chains, and the principal owners remain unthreatened as number one and number two, respectively, on the list of Sweden's wealthiest individuals. Neither Ingvar Kamprad nor Erling Persson would probably have been able to expand internationally if they had not left Sweden at a critical stage in the development of their companies, thereby avoiding harsh taxation and currency restrictions. If Nygren had emigrated in 1973 as Ingvar Kamprad did, today's market might have included a major international floral retail chain with its roots in Sweden. If Nygren had continued to own and build the company, he too would likely have been one of the richest individuals in the world.

SOURCE: NYGREN AND ERICSON (2005), OLIVECRONA (1970) AND JÖRNMARK (2007).

---

27 Olivecrona (1970, p. 138).
28 Henrekson (2015).

3.5 Chapter Summary

In this chapter, we have learned the following:

- According to the four classic entrepreneurial functions, the entrepreneur can be considered an innovator, an arbitrageur, an uncertainty bearer and a coordinator.
- Each function is typically associated with a particular leading scholar: Joseph A. Schumpeter, Israel M. Kirzner, Frank Knight and Jean-Baptiste Say.
- A number of traditions have developed concurrently, and they emphasize different aspects of entrepreneurship. Recent research tends to further elaborate or combine the four classic functions.
- Several contemporary researchers have emphasized that the entrepreneur makes judgmental decisions regarding the coordination of scarce resources or that she is someone who specializes in judgmental decision making under uncertainty.
- The entrepreneur may be regarded as someone who creates or discovers an entrepreneurial opportunity. According to a more subjective interpretation, the entrepreneur should be viewed as someone who imagines an entrepreneurial opportunity that no one else can see or is willing to finance.
- The entrepreneur may also be regarded as someone who moves the economy toward or away from equilibrium. These two approaches complement each other.

© THE AUTHORS AND STUDENTLITTERATUR

CHAPTER 4

Entrepreneurship— Some Further Distinctions

As we have seen in the previous chapter, entrepreneurship is a multi-dimensional concept that numerous economists and management scholars have scrutinized and analyzed. However, discussing the somewhat elusive nature of entrepreneurship may be fruitful before we move on to the next chapter and discuss entrepreneurship from an empirical perspective. In this chapter, we will thus make a few further distinctions regarding what entrepreneurship is and what it is not. The chapter ends with a discussion regarding how we reckon that entrepreneurship should be defined.

4.1 Entrepreneurship versus Non-Entrepreneurial Self-Employment

The motive behind or reason for becoming a business owner likely differs across individuals, and a classification of entrepreneurship may be based on such differences. An individual may become an entrepreneur because he has discovered or created a business opportunity that he would like to pursue. However, an individual may also start a firm because he lacks some other means of income. To distinguish between these two different types of self-employment, scholars usually talk about opportunity entrepreneurship in the former case and about necessity entrepreneurship in the latter.[1] Some authors instead distinguish between pull and push factors. An individual may be "pulled" into running a firm to exploit a business idea, or he may be "pushed" into starting a firm because he has no other acceptable way to make a living.[2]

---

1 Reynolds et al. (2002)
2 Storey (1994).

© THE AUTHORS AND STUDENTLITTERATUR

To be defined as entrepreneurial, a firm should be innovative, and it should normally have an explicit ambition to grow. Therefore, necessity entrepreneurship should not be regarded as entrepreneurship. An unemployed person should not be defined as an entrepreneur if he is forced to start an ordinary taxi service in an already crowded market and does not contribute anything innovative or find an unexplored opportunity. Many companies "only" help the owner(s) make a living and only act locally, having neither the desire nor the ability to expand their activities. Therefore, a more accurate term for this category would be *necessity self-employment*.[3] This group represents a large share of the self-employed, especially in developing countries (artisans, farmers, street vendors), and they often play an important role in the economy. Non-entrepreneurial self-employment sometimes transforms into opportunity entrepreneurship. After starting a business, the now self-employed person may discover an untapped niche or create an innovation that contributes to the development of the industry.

Based on the underlying motive for becoming an entrepreneur, scholars have recently started discussing *ambitious entrepreneurship*, which refers to entrepreneurs who enter the entrepreneurial process to create as much value as possible. The entrepreneur has not been forced to start an entrepreneurial activity, and to be defined as an "ambitious entrepreneur" it is not sufficient to discover an exploitable entrepreneurial opportunity. He must have far-reaching ambitions to fully exploit the opportunity that he has discovered. In other words, ambitious entrepreneurship is a subset of opportunity entrepreneurship. Many scholars believe that ambitious entrepreneurship drives economic development. Still, just because an entrepreneur asserts that he wants and expects to expand does not mean that these plans will be realized. High ambitions alone are insufficient. Instead of classifying entrepreneurship based on underlying motives, entrepreneurs can be classified based on what they actually achieve. We will return to this important distinction.[4]

In *Table 4.1*, we summarize the various motives behind self-employment. It can be a way of getting a better life or the best way to realize the full entrepreneurial potential of an idea. However, it is frequently a way to circumvent regulations and obstacles that are set up within a firm or the

---

3 Necessity self-employment is thus one type of non-entrepreneurial self-employment
4 See Stam et al. (2012).

 © THE AUTHORS AND STUDENTLITTERATUR

labor market's overregulation of employees. Self-employment may also be an alternative path into the labor market for minority groups that face discrimination. In addition, self-employment may increase opportunities for rent seeking and tax avoidance or tax evasion.

Rent seeking refers to individual efforts that aim to create private gains that lead to social losses rather than social gains. However, the individual entrepreneur who is focused on maximizing his own utility sees no difference (in principle) between rent seeking and profit maximization through market transactions.[5]

Table 4.1 Motives behind self-employment.

	Entrepreneurial	Non-entrepreneurial
First best	Pursue a business opportunity most suitably pursued in a new firm.	Seek independence, a certain life style, etc.
		Local service production, working in networks in temporary projects.
Second best	Inferior management by current employer bars efficient intrapreneurship. Mechanism to escape effects of discrimination or lack of social capital for marginal groups.	Safety valve to circumvent excessive labor market regulations. Means to achieve flexibility hindered by other regulations. Mechanism to escape effects of discrimination or lack of social capital for marginal groups. Necessity self-employment.
Unproductive/ predatory	Set up a business to exploit subsidies and tax breaks rather than creating value for customers. Fraud. Looting, warfare, etc.	Transform consumption expenditure into tax-deductible business costs. Fraudulence, where revenue is partly unreported, etc.

Note: The table lists the major motives behind self-employment. Intermediate cases also exist. For instance, entrepreneurial self-employment may be partially pursued in search of independence. "First best" means that the choices are both privately and socially optimal. "Second best" implies that the optimal choice is blocked by regulations or some other institutional barrier, but self-employment may still more or less offset the negative effects that arise.

Source: Developed further from Henrekson (2007).

5 Buchanan (1980).

© THE AUTHORS AND STUDENTLITTERATUR

When the rules of the game do not leave much room for rent seeking and when productive entrepreneurship is always rewarded and executed in existing firms, the only reason to become self-employed is a desire for independence. However, in reality, some ideas will be best suited for development within the framework of a new firm with a single individual as the founder. Therefore, in a dynamic economy, entrepreneurial start-ups and self-employed individuals will always exist, even in optimally designed institutional settings.

Start-ups and self-employment are thus not synonymous with entrepreneurship; nevertheless, they are the two most important channels through which individuals can realize their entrepreneurial ambitions. However, assuming a direct correlation between entrepreneurship and all start-ups or self-employment does not consider the different types of existing start-ups and self-employment that may be more or less entrepreneurial.

Entrepreneurship and self-employment may even be negatively correlated. In fact, successful entrepreneurship is expected to reduce the share of small firms (including the share of self-employed individuals) in the employment statistics because every successful entrepreneurial activity will result in an increase in the number of large companies. Successful companies may offer better career opportunities, thereby raising the opportunity cost of self-employment, which leads more people to choose to be employed rather than running their own firm. The effect is even stronger if the entrepreneur's firm competes directly with the self-employed, thus reducing the latter's share of the product market.

Wal-Mart illustrates the effect of successful entrepreneurship on self-employment. The growth of Wal-Mart resulted in, and even depended on, the elimination of thousands of small, local retail businesses. While the United States' population increased by over 50 percent between 1963 and 2002, the number of independent shops in the retail sector dropped by half.[6] Companies such as IKEA, H&M and Amazon have similarly reduced the number of self-employed individuals in their respective sectors. This trend is

6 Basker (2007).

© THE AUTHORS AND STUDENTLITTERATUR

not unique to the retail sector. For example, Starbucks has replaced a variety of establishments that were previously owned and operated by self-employed individuals. Even the emergence of companies such as Intel, Microsoft and Google probably reduces self-employment by offering better career opportunities, thereby raising the opportunity cost of self-employment.

Entrepreneurship is a channel through which companies with valuable innovations or companies that are organized more efficiently than their competitors increase their share of the aggregate economy. As these firms expand, they replace and absorb the previously self-employed by providing better options, which simultaneously results in a more prosperous economy and a lower rate of self-employment.

This reverse relationship between entrepreneurship and self-employment only appears paradoxical if entrepreneurship is defined as merely a contractual form of working for oneself. If entrepreneurs are instead viewed as individuals engaged in innovation and the creation of new firms and self employment is viewed as a general ownership solution for a wide range of motivations, the process is quite natural. Examples of non-entrepreneurial impetuses for self-employment include a preference for being one's own boss, a desire to offer one's skills and services to solve agency problems, better monitoring of employees, and regulation and tax avoidance or evasion (see *Table 4.1* above).

Obviously, entrepreneurship should not necessarily be promoted by actively counteracting self-employment and small firms. Many successful entrepreneurs have started out as self-employed individuals, and their firms were once small. Nevertheless, it is important to avoid the wrong-headed idea that the economy can be made more entrepreneurial by stimulating self-employment (more will be said on this issue in chapter 12).

Despite all the studies showing a strong negative relationship between a country's level of income and the rate of self-employment, some scholars have argued that a break in the trend in terms of the relationship between self-employment and the level of income has recently occurred. Some scholars have claimed that the share of self-employment in some of the world's richest countries has increased anew. They have asserted that the share of self-employment declined during the transition from a mainly agrarian society to an industrial society, only to rise again in the post-industrial era fueled by ICT and a rapid expansion of the service sector. Some studies also claim to have identified a weak U-shaped pattern in the share of self-employment over time, which they have then extrapolated.[7]

The main reason for such a trend reversal is technological change. This development has reduced transaction costs in the market, which has enabled increased specialization and the focus on the core business, as discussed in chapter 2. The large companies, with many diverse in-house activities, have gradually been able to outsource some of their operations to numerous smaller, specialized companies that are interconnected through networks in the market. However, the recent development in the countries that have experienced the strongest economic growth has hardly supported this hypothesis—quite the opposite.[8] Here one should also note that the two areas in the United States that are generally considered the most entrepreneurial— Silicon Valley and Boston/Cambridge—have some of the lowest rates of self-employment in United States.[9]

4.2 Intrapreneurs versus Entrepreneurs

As noted above, equating start-ups and self-employment with entrepreneurship is misguided. Entrepreneurship does not necessarily take the form of a start-up or self-employment. An individual can be entrepreneurial as an employee, which is usually referred to as *intrapreneurship*. An excellent example is Sigfrid Edström, the legendary head of the General Swedish Electric Company (ASEA) (see Box 4.1). Even organizations can become entrepreneurial if they create good conditions that promote entrepreneurial behavior in their employees. *Table 4.2* shows a classification of business owners and employees in entrepreneurial and managerial roles.

Table 4.2 Entrepreneurs and intrapreneurs.

	Business owners	Employees
Entrepreneurial	Innovator, risk taker	Intrapreneur
Managing	Head of firm without ambition to grow and/or change	Salaried manager

7 Wennekers et al. (2005) and Minniti, Bygrave and Autio (2006).
8 Carree and Thurik (2010).
9 Henrekson and Sanandaji (2014a).

 © THE AUTHORS AND STUDENTLITTERATUR

A discovery by a (potential) business owner or an employee does not have to be exploited by the discoverer himself. The most clear-cut case of entrepreneurship and intrapreneurship occurs when the same economic agent both discovers and exploits an opportunity. An innovation may also be exploited in other ways, as illustrated in *Table 4.3*.

Table 4.3 Discovery and exploitation.

		Discovered by	
		Business owner/individual	Employee/organization
Exploited by	Business owner/individual	Start-up firm Entrepreneurship	Spin-off
	Employee/organization	Acquisition/licensing	Internal development Intrapreneurship

Source: Based on Shane (2003).

Box 4.1

J. Sigfrid Edström (1870–1964)—a Swedish super-intrapreneur

Together with the combustion engine, electricity was the foundation for the Second Industrial Revolution. Around 1880, Swedish innovator Jonas Wenström patented a direct current generator. This patent became the foundation of the company that was called ASEA (Allmänna Svenska Elektriska Aktiebolaget or the General Swedish Electric Company) starting in 1890.

During the 1890s, ASEA expanded quickly, but the competition was tough. The internal organization suffered from major shortcomings, and ownership and cooperation agreements restricted the company and drained its financial resources. ASEA thus experienced a deep financial crisis in 1902. The company was forced to turn to its largest creditor, Stockholms Enskilda Bank, for reconstruction. An important part of this reconstruction was the recruitment of a new CEO. Marcus Wallenberg, Sr. (1864–1943) headed this recruitment, and he was set on J. Sigfrid Edström (1870–1964).

Edström's background made him perfect for the job. He was an electrical engineer from Chalmers University of Technology, and he had continued his studies in electrical and mechanical engineering at the University of

Zurich. He then worked for four years at leading electrical companies in the United States, such as Westinghouse and General Electric, before returning to Zurich as head of the electrification of the city's trams. He then became the head of Göteborgs Spårvägar, the tram company of Gothenburg, which was also to be electrified.

ASEA's deep crisis made Edström hesitant to accept the job offer. To accept the job offer, he demanded a high salary, bonuses and stock options (in AB Diesels Motorer, not in ASEA), a personal guarantee from the Wallenberg brothers for a compensation of SEK 100,000 (approximately 130 annual salaries for an average industrial worker at the time) if ASEA defaulted on its payments over the next five years.

Once at his post, Edström went to work with great determination. In 1904, ASEA already showed a small profit, and the company became the undisputed leader in the Swedish electrical industry over the next few years. In the early 1930s, all Swedish competitors had been acquired, and their activities had either been closed down or integrated into ASEA. The company had also expanded internationally. When Edström arrived in Västerås as the new CEO, the company had 1,400 employees, and its exports were negligible. When he resigned as CEO almost 31 years later, the company had 10,200 employees, and it was represented in 50 countries. Edström then stayed on as chairman of the board until 1949, and ASEA continued to grow during this period.

Edström was at the absolute top of the company for 46 years, and the transformation of a small company on the brink of bankruptcy into a global leader in power generation and power transmission would not have been possible without Edström's unique intrapreneurship. ASEA lives on today as part of the world-leading Swiss-Swedish corporation ABB, with its headquarters in Zurich and 150,000 employees globally.

Edström was also a notable social entrepreneur. In his youth, he was a successful athlete (holding the Swedish record for 150 meters). This interest led to a lifelong commitment to organizing the sports movement, and Edström is undoubtedly Sweden's most internationally renowned sports leader and administrator of all time. He became the first president of the Swedish Sports Confederation in 1901, was the driving force behind the Stockholm Olympic Games in 1912, and was the founder and first president (1913–1946) of the International Association of Athletics Federations (IAAF). In 1920, he was elected as a member of the International Olympic

© THE AUTHORS AND STUDENTLITTERATUR

Committee (IOC), becoming its vice-president in 1931. Starting in 1942 (he was formally elected in 1946), he was the IOC president, presiding over the 1948 and 1952 Olympic Games. He was instrumental in maintaining the Olympic Movement during the Second World War and in ensuring that the Olympic Games were held in 1948. According to the IOC website, he is considered the second most important person in the history of the Olympic Movement after founder Pierre de Coubertin.

Edström's social entrepreneurship was also extensive in the business community. He served as chairman of the Swedish Engineering Association, the Federation of Swedish Industries (Industriförbundet) and the Swedish Employers' Confederation (SAF). He was one of the instigators of the model of collective agreements, which reduced labor conflicts within the engineering industry after 1905, and presided over the negotiations between employers and the trade unions that resulted in the Saltsjöbaden Agreement of 1938. Furthermore, Edström helped found the International Chamber of Commerce and served as its president from 1939–1946. He was also a founding member of the Institute for Industrial and Social Research (IUI; since 2006 the Research Institute of Industrial Economics, IFN) and served as its chairman from 1939–1944; he was an initiator of Arosmässan, where he served as president for 37 years; and he was one of the founding members of the Sweden-America Foundation.

SOURCE: CARLSON AND LUNDAHL (2014), JOHNSON (2006) AND LIF (2015).

A discovery within an organization can lead to a spin-off, i.e., a new firm that is formed to exploit the discovery. For example, a firm's management may not believe in the employees' discovery, which could lead these employees to leave the firm and attempt to develop the discovery independently in a new firm. Furthermore, the discovery may not fit within the existing firm but may still be sufficiently interesting for development within the framework of a different legal entity, often one with more suitable and dedicated owners. However, founding a spin-off does not have to be as dramatic as starting a new and independent firm. One can also start a new firm within the company group or create a new division within the existing organization.

In addition to the intrapreneur's discovery not being met with the management's sympathy, the intrapreneur might think that he will not be sufficiently rewarded if the innovation becomes a commercial success because the profits will have to be shared with shareholders as well as with many other people in the organization. By taking the innovation and starting a new firm, if legally possible, a larger share of the profit may accrue to the intrapreneur. However, the intrapreneur's personal risk increases, and he loses his job security. The important point here is that spin-offs should not necessarily be considered knowledge theft; instead, they constitute a strategy for creating a more efficient incentive structure for the intrapreneur.[10] A possible solution to this problem could be the use of stock options or shares, an issue that we will return to in chapter 6. A potential business owner may also decide to try to sell the right to exploit his business idea, for example, via licensing, to existing firms. An incumbent firm may likewise acquire the self-employed individual's firm, if such a firm exists and has started operations, to secure and further develop the idea. These strategies frequently occur when the potential self-employed business owner lacks (sufficient) capital or is unable to raise capital from external investors. According to a Swedish study, mainly high-tech spin-offs are sold to large, frequently multinational, firms during the early stages. High start-up costs, significant financing needs and the large firms' considerable market power contribute to this trend.[11] If the acquired firm's founders remain with the firm after it has been bought, they start as intrapreneurs, become entrepreneurs when a spin-off is launched and then once again become intrapreneurs in the acquiring firm.

TACIT VERSUS CODIFIED KNOWLEDGE

Not all ideas can be realized through licensed production or through their sale in the form of a patent. Economics and other sciences sometimes distinguish between *tacit* and *codified* knowledge.[12] Tacit knowledge refers to knowledge that is directly linked to a specific person and of which we may partially be unaware. Tacit knowledge cannot be expressed in words or in mathematical formulae. Therefore, this form of knowledge is difficult to transfer from person to person. A long and arduous journey lies between research results

---

10 Rumelt (2005).
11 Andersson and Xiao (2014).
12 Hungarian philosopher Michael Polanyi originally coined the term "tacit knowledge" (Polanyi 1967).

  © THE AUTHORS AND STUDENTLITTERATUR

and a commercial product, and a great deal of the knowledge used and required is often tacit and linked to specific individuals. For example, the importance of tacit knowledge is clearly illustrated in a study that found that over 70 percent of all commercializable research results in the United States required the inventor's involvement to ensure the commercialization's success.[13]

The distinction between tacit and codified knowledge closely relates to Friedrich von Hayek's distinction between "scientific knowledge" and "knowledge of the particular circumstances of time and place."[14] The former is technical and formalizable expertise, while the latter is a practical form of knowledge that is linked to individuals' unique situations and experiences.

The problem does not merely concern tacit knowledge. Entrepreneurship is largely about developing and commercializing subjectively perceived opportunities. However, what one entrepreneur considers an opportunity worth exploring may seem completely irrelevant, unrealistic or even crazy to others. Under uncertain conditions, subjective judgments about the nature of reality cannot be sold. If no one else can recognize or understand the genius of an idea that an entrepreneur wants to develop, selling the idea in question will be impossible (whether or not it is protected by a patent). This challenge also explains why entrepreneurs often must start and/or lead a firm and obtain and organize any necessary additional resources.[15]

THE ORIGIN OF INNOVATIONS

Ove Granstrand and Sverker Alänge, scholars at Chalmers University of Technology, have identified the 100 greatest Swedish innovations in the post-war period (1945–1980) and identify the environments from which they originated.[16] According to the study, most innovations came from existing firms. Only 20 percent of the innovations were launched in start-ups (of which ten were spin-offs). However, one noticeable result in the study is that the share of new firms seemingly rises and thus gains importance.

---

13 Jensen and Thursby (2001).
14 Hayek (1945)
15 Foss and Klein (2012).
16 Granstrand and Alänge (1995).

Christian Sandström, another scholar at Chalmers University of Technology, has made a bold attempt to identify the top 100 Swedish innovations in the country's history.[17] He finds that innovators/inventors who were employed in firms created 47 percent of these innovations. Single individuals developed 33 percent of the innovations, and the remainder originated in universities. The importance of independent innovators has risen markedly since 1980—increasing to 45 percent of the innovations compared with 25 percent during the previous 25 years. Note that these two studies are based on relatively few observations and that this development over time should be interpreted with some caution.

Johan P. Larsson analyzes a new database of Swedish innovations developed at Lund University, which identifies 4,853 innovations developed between 1970 and 2007.[18] A definite majority of the innovations resulted from entrepreneurs who worked with customers and interacted with non-academic bodies to produce something better and cheaper or a new market niche. Of the innovations that showed an explicit collaboration—approximately 20 percent—only about one-seventh resulted from university collaborations. The desire to improve one's position in the market and to compete more efficiently is thus the main source of innovation. Firms whose innovations are driven by scientific findings and new technologies employ far fewer people during the innovation stage. In addition, they do not grow as quickly as firms that are engaged in market-driven, entrepreneurial innovations. If a discernable pattern exists, it reveals the opposite. Half of all innovations were developed by firms with more than 50 employees, and a quarter were developed by individuals or firms with no more than four employees.

In this context, distinguishing between inventions and innovations is also important. New knowledge or new inventions are only the first step in the innovation process. Inventions and scientific/technological discoveries do not necessarily have a market value; normally, an entrepreneur must identify a market opportunity. For an invention to become economically valuable and benefit the larger economy, someone must exploit the new knowledge by introducing new products, new intermediate goods, or creating new markets

17 Sandström (2014).
18 Larsson (2015). The database is documented in Sjöö et al. (2014).

                    © THE AUTHORS AND STUDENTLITTERATUR

or by introducing new production methods. In other words, an innovation is required. Innovations are defined from a market perspective, but they may traverse most industries and economic activities.

The entrepreneur, who does not need to be the same person or belong to the same organization as the inventor, plays a crucial role in this process. For example, many of the innovations that were introduced in the market by Apple and Microsoft were not invented by these companies; they were instead invented by other companies that were unable to exploit their own inventions. Someone must discover or create a business opportunity from an invention to develop an innovation that may benefit society. Before it experienced its breakthrough and grew into a large multinational company, McDonald's was nothing but a small restaurant in San Bernardino, California. Ray Kroc recognized the potential of this restaurant business and bought it from the McDonald brothers. The rest, as they say, is history.

4.3 Productive versus Unproductive and Destructive Entrepreneurship

A high degree of entrepreneurship is not necessarily something positive or something that affects society in a beneficial way. Normally, one imagines that an entrepreneur is focused on discovering and creating innovations and new markets that will benefit income growth and productivity. However, not all entrepreneurship is productive in terms of benefitting both the individual entrepreneur and society; entrepreneurship can also be unproductive or destructive.

As already noted, an entrepreneur may engage in rent seeking and use his entrepreneurial talents to pursue benefits or to evade taxes. These kinds of activities are easier to carry out, and they most commonly occur in places where the legal protection of private property is weak or where individuals in the political system primarily exercise power over large commercial entities. In these cases, entrepreneurial effort tends to be oriented toward the redistribution of wealth rather than the creation of wealth. Although this orientation benefits the individual entrepreneur, it harms society, i.e., it destroys social value. Entrepreneurial activity is normally directed toward the activities with the highest payoff. By no means do these activities necessarily also generate the most social value.

If an entrepreneurial action benefits the entrepreneur but harms society, it should be termed destructive. Unproductive or destructive activities that harm the economy and reduce social welfare include parts of the entrepreneurship in the informal sector, political corruption and lobbying to provide a certain special interest with political benefits and criminal activities, such as looting, smuggling and racketeering.

According to entrepreneurship scholar William Baumol, the development of a country's prosperity is primarily determined by the extent to which entrepreneurship is channeled into productive activities. The capitalist market economy has partly been successful because it makes creating private wealth through the production of goods and services that others are willing to purchase possible. Hence, talented people and efforts are directed toward value creation rather than unproductive wealth-redistributing activities.[19]

Throughout history, society's formal and informal institutions have clearly influenced the allocation of entrepreneurial effort between productive and unproductive/destructive activities. During extended periods of weak economic development, tremendous entrepreneurial effort has been exerted on warfare and looting (e.g., the Roman Empire, the Hundred Years' War between England and France, and the Belgian looting of Congo before the First World War). Alternatively, the scope for entrepreneurship has been heavily constrained because of totalitarian central governments (e.g., China during the Ming Dynasty, the Soviet Union, Castro's Cuba, and present-day North Korea). From a Swedish perspective, plenty of potential entrepreneurs existed even before the Industrial Revolution, but the relative payoff of activities implied that entrepreneurial talent was used for purposes other than innovation and company building—not least attempts at victory on the battlefield or the search for political favors and various monopoly privileges.

Today, unproductive entrepreneurship is more likely to appear in the form of costly litigation and questionable takeovers as well as with advanced tax evasion and other resource-intensive arrangements to avoid regulations and taxes. A study on entrepreneurship in Romania around 2000 by Christopher Coyne and Peter Leeson serves as a powerful illustration of the importance of this distinction:[20]

---

19 Baumol (1990).
20 Coyne and Leeson (2004, p. 23).

 © THE AUTHORS AND STUDENTLITTERATUR

There are two ways to interpret the situation in Romania. The standard interpretation, reflected in reports by development agencies, is that there are high barriers to entrepreneurs and, hence, a shortage of entrepreneurship. Another interpretation is that entrepreneurship in Romania is flourishing. The key is the distinction we made between productive, unproductive, and evasive entrepreneurship. Productive entrepreneurship is currently stagnant in Romania. Unproductive and evasive entrepreneurship, on the other hand, are alive and well.

Therefore, thinking of entrepreneurship exclusively in quantitative terms overlooks an important point. The rate of entrepreneurship in a society matters, but how entrepreneurial activities are channeled are equally important. The institutional framework and society's reward systems need to be designed to stimulate productive entrepreneurship. The aggregate level of entrepreneurial activity may differ across countries, but the allocation of that activity may be just as important. The problem marring a poorly performing economy is not necessarily the lack of entrepreneurial talent. Instead, entrepreneurial effort may be used in ways that are socially unproductive or destructive.

4.4 Institutional Entrepreneurship

By now, it should be evident that profit-seeking entrepreneurial activities are influenced by the institutional framework and the social reward system created through decisions in the political system. However, causality may also run in the opposite direction; that is, entrepreneurs may influence the institutional framework in a direction that is favorable to them. In fact, if an entrepreneur can obtain a return by trying to influence (or circumvent) regulatory frameworks, he is clearly strongly incentivized to do exactly that. Activities that aim to directly or indirectly influence the societal rules of the game are usually referred to as institutional entrepreneurship, and they have only recently attracted the attention of entrepreneurship scholars.[21]

In this context, we should also mention political entrepreneurship, whereby entrepreneurial politicians and activists attempt to change societal

---

21 Key research contributions in this area are collected in Henrekson and Sanandaji (2012).

PART I WHAT DO WE MEAN BY ENTREPRENEURSHIP?

rules in exchange for recognition, power and personal satisfaction. Successful political entrepreneurship, i.e., the political entrepreneur who succeeds in changing formal societal institutions in the direction that he desires, can have enormous effects on a country's continued development. Prominent examples of political entrepreneurs include Vladimir Lenin, Mao Zedong, Deng Xiaoping, Margaret Thatcher and the architects of the United States Constitution. Gustav Vasa (1496–1560), Axel Oxenstierna (1583–1654) and Johan August Gripenstedt (1813–1874) are among the political entrepreneurs who have greatly influenced the subsequent development of Sweden. Despite its importance, further analysis of political entrepreneurship is beyond the scope of this book.

Entrepreneurs may devote a great deal of effort in hopes of changing pertinent rules and laws to their own advantage. This form of entrepreneurship can be both productive and destructive. The current regulatory framework may very well prevent or unnecessarily increase the costs of different forms of productive entrepreneurial activities. By influencing the regulatory framework, the entrepreneur may ensure that entrepreneurial activities are facilitated or made possible. If this activity not only benefits the entrepreneur himself but also society, this form of institutional entrepreneurship can be productive for society. Of course, the opposite may also hold true if an entrepreneur lobbies for benefits that favor himself but harm society as a whole and reduce social welfare.

Table 4.4 shows how an entrepreneur may respond to the existing regulatory framework and provides examples of how the entrepreneur may act. The entrepreneur may try to abide by, alter or evade the regulatory framework. When an entrepreneur "evades the regulatory framework," he is not necessarily breaking the law. For example, within the legal framework, an entrepreneur may make a series of arrangements to reduce his tax liabilities, or he might develop business models that compete with existing actors in a way that falls outside the purview of the existing regulatory framework. The entrepreneur will behave according to his entrepreneurial capacity for implementation and will choose whatever produces the best return. Whether this behavior is productive or destructive is a separate issue. From the beginning, politicians should consider the existence of institutional entrepreneurship when planning for reforms related to the regulatory framework.

© THE AUTHORS AND STUDENTLITTERATUR

Table 4.4 The entrepreneur's approach to the regulatory frameworks of society.

	Abide	Alter	Evade
Productive	Pursue a socially valuable business opportunity within prevailing institutions.	Achieve regulatory changes that are economically advantageous for society.	Sidestep stifling labor market regulations through a new contractual form.
Destructive (or unproductive)	1. Sue competitors for a share of their profit. 2. Rogue states; rivalry between warlords.	Lobby for new regulations to protect an industry.	1. Illegal syndicates. 2. Smuggling. 3. Illegal activities that harm health and the environment.

Source: Based on Henrekson and Sanandaji (2011) and Elert and Henrekson (2015).

If an entrepreneur tries to alter the regulatory framework and succeeds, the induced change is likely to benefit the entrepreneur. However, if the evasive entrepreneurship is overwhelming, a change in the existing regulatory framework may also result, which may be socially beneficial or detrimental. In times of rapid change, circumventing the existing regulatory framework may be necessary, at least in the short run, to prevent the economy from slowing down before the regulatory framework has been reformed to better adjust to the new circumstances. Even a revolutionary breakthrough that is not at odds with existing legislation can make that legislation obsolete and necessitate changes. Much of today's legislation that is linked to ICTs did not exist 50 years ago because the technology, the business practices, and the goods and services did not yet exist. As entrepreneurs contributed to the evolution of the economy, the institutional framework needed to be adapted to new realities—not the other way around. A great deal of entrepreneurial activity has thus preceded the regulatory framework, and this activity has precipitated institutional reform and regulatory change by pushing at the framework's boundaries. In many cases, institutional reform and regulatory changes thus retroactively codify practices that have evolved in markets for new products that are based on new technologies.

The importance of institutional entrepreneurship has also been noticed in the risk capital sector. A new trend among risk capital firms involves employing people who act as "policy experts" or policy activists; these employees not only monitor sensitive policy areas but also promote regulatory changes that will benefit business areas in which they have economic interests. This trend is particularly prevalent in private equity firms that own firms in heavily regulated sectors.[22]

THE SHARING ECONOMY

More examples of circumventing entrepreneurship are emerging within the new sharing, or peer-to-peer, economy that the emergence of the Internet made possible. The worldwide company Airbnb is probably the most spectacular example of this trend. Airbnb is an online marketplace that matches people who want to rent and let private homes around the world. For travelers, finding housing through Airbnb may be a much cheaper alternative than staying in a hotel, while the renter is given the opportunity to increase his income.

Airbnb is able to operate in a grey area with regard to the regulatory framework—somewhere in-between the generally very liberal right to sublet one's home and the heavily regulated hotel market. However, in many countries, such activities are illegal. Some cities in the United States do not allow short-term subletting of private homes unless the owner obtains a special license and undergoes an inspection. Avoiding taxes and the extensive safety and security regulations that apply to licensed hotels is also possible. In cities with rent control, such as New York City, homeowners/landlords and even tenants can use Airbnb to circumvent rent control. Although the number of overnight stays that were arranged through Airbnb in 2015 was still small relative to the total number of overnight stays in the world, the company is already represented in 192 countries. The debate rages on about whether regulators will tighten the rules and make Airbnb and similar companies' operations in the new sharing economy more difficult or even completely prevent them from operating at all or whether pertinent regulatory frameworks will be adapted retroactively to accommodate new practices.

A second example is Uber, a new taxi service provider. Uber defines itself as an IT company that offers an internet-based service to order and pay for taxi rides. Uber allows the user to see the location of the driver, and vice

22 Watson (2013) and Lawler (2015).

 © THE AUTHORS AND STUDENTLITTERATUR

versa. When ordering a car, the customer can follow the car on a map in a smartphone application and see its expected arrival time. Payments are made through the application; Uber takes a percentage of the payment, and the rest goes to the driver. At the end of 2015, Uber was established in 68 countries, including Sweden. Uber can compete with taxis because it has managed to avoid being classified as a taxi company. Consequently, it has succeeded in bypassing a number of regulations and licensing requirements that apply to taxi companies and that create high entry barriers in most cities.

4.5 High-Growth Firms and High-Impact Entrepreneurship

Entrepreneurship scholars have increasingly emphasized that not all entrepreneurial activities are equally important for aggregate outcome variables, such as national economic growth and net job creation. The exploitation of an entrepreneurial discovery or the discovery itself may be of greater or lesser importance and of higher or lower quality.

Of all entrepreneurial activities, a mere fraction will leave a significant and lasting footprint on the economy. In 1995, David Birch coined the term "gazelles" to designate the most rapidly growing firms. Birch defined gazelles as firms that at least doubled their turnover every four years. He found that approximately four percent of American firms were gazelles, and they created 70 percent of all new jobs.[23] The rapidly growing gazelles were compared with "elephants," companies that tended to leave employment unchanged or reduce their number of employees, and to "mice," which started out small and stayed small. Sometimes, the term high-growth firms (HGFs) is used to refer to entrepreneurial firms that are characterized by high growth in employment and turnover. Today, "gazelle" is an accepted term for a high-performing, rapidly growing firm. In fact, the Swedish business daily *Dagens Industri* has an annual competition for "The Swedish Gazelle of the Year."[24]

To further substantiate that only certain firms contribute significantly to growth and development, scholars have started using the term high-

---

23 The gazelle hypothesis is published in Birch, Haggerty and Parsons (1995).
24 The term had its Swedish breakthrough when it was highlighted in the Centre for Business and Policy Studies' Economic Council's report *Företagaren i välfärdssamhället [The Entrepreneur in the Welfare State]* in 1998; see Henrekson (1998).

impact entrepreneurship (HIE). High-impact entrepreneurial activities commercialize key innovations or create disruptive breakthroughs in the marketplace. This type of entrepreneurship is often associated with high profits, massive growth and extensive employment expansion.[25] While "ambitious entrepreneurship" refers to the desire and motivation behind entrepreneurship, HIE (and HGF) is a label based on the actual outcome of the entrepreneurial activity. If policymakers want to benefit as much as possible from the positive effects of entrepreneurship, they should focus their policymaking on this type of entrepreneurship.

This type of entrepreneurship can be distinguished from what we have previously referred to as necessity self-employment. Entrepreneurship and self-employment can have entirely opposing natures and completely different functions or effects. Lumping together certain types of firms (new firms, small firms, and closely held firms) or business owners (self-employed individuals who run sole proprietorships, small business owners, and owners of closely held firms) and referring to this category as "entrepreneurship" overlooks an important point. Nothing suggests that only certain firms with a certain type of owner are or will be future gazelles or high-growth firms. Furthermore, nothing suggests that all gazelles can be found in a particular firm or ownership category. Considering the distinction between high-growth firms, on the one hand, and firms without any ambition or potential to grow, on the other hand, is very important when determining how to design economic policies. We will return to this important issue in the last part of this book.

However, using rapid growth as the sole criterion for the success of individual firms is overly simplistic. Many innovative, entrepreneurial firms may be acquired by established firms at an early stage in their development, and the actual growth occurs in the established firm. Many new entrepreneurs have an explicit strategy to seek to be acquired by someone else to commercialize their ideas.[26] If these companies are not growing, it is not a sign of failure. The full potential of the company's ideas might be best realized in large, established firms.

---

25 Acs (2008).
26 Gans and Stern (2003).

© THE AUTHORS AND STUDENTLITTERATUR

4.6 Our Definition of Entrepreneurship

The discussion of entrepreneurship as a concept in the current and previous chapters has shown that this concept is multi-faceted and that no consensus exists regarding how it should be defined. Some people have argued that entrepreneurship is associated with a particular form of market structure, for example, many small or new firms or many self-employed individuals compared with the number of employed individuals. However, as the major entrepreneurship theorists have shown (Schumpeter, Kirzner, Knight and Say), entrepreneurship should primarily refer to an economic function, activity or process—not to a specific form of employment or business structure. This economic function is supported and pursued by single individuals—entrepreneurs. In a strict sense, entrepreneurship is something that characterizes a person and something that a person pursues. This definition is in line with recent entrepreneurship research, but it disagrees with previous research and large parts of the empirical literature, which have used a more easily accessible quantitative metric, even though it has proven directly misleading in many cases.[27]

In the light of the previous analysis, we propose the following definition of entrepreneurship. Entrepreneurship is the ability and willingness of individuals, both independently and within organizations,[28]

- to discover and create new economic opportunities;
- to introduce their ideas in the market under uncertainty, making decisions regarding the localization, product design, use of resources and reward systems; and
- to create value, which often, though not always, means that the entrepreneur aims to expand the firm to its full potential.

In the definition of productive entrepreneurship, the willingness and ability to expand the venture to its full potential can be added. However, this trait is not necessarily obvious, as the closing and dismantling of firms can be an important entrepreneurial task. Similarly, the creation of value can be maximized by selling the firm to an external party. If the entrepreneurial

---

27 Henrekson and Sanandaji (2014a).
28 This definition closely relates to that of Wennekers and Thurik (1999).

activity is productive, the value created benefits both society and the entrepreneur. The entrepreneur may also fail and destroy value.

For the sake of clarity, we should reiterate that entrepreneurship is not a profession or a position and entrepreneurs do not constitute a distinct group in the same way that employees and capital owners do. An entrepreneur may also be—and often is—a capital owner or an employee. Being an entrepreneur is not synonymous with being a manager or with leading one's own firm. Instead, entrepreneurship involves discovering and introducing something new under uncertainty through judgmental decision making, while "normal" leadership or management may consist of more routine decisions that do not necessarily require the kind of skills that entrepreneurs must have. A regular manager is someone who is employed to carry out a well-defined set of tasks for a contracted compensation (compare *Table 4.2*), although at least some degree of entrepreneurship exists in all kinds of management. Without any form of entrepreneurship, existing firms would find it difficult to survive, as continual development and adaptation to changing conditions are usually required to cope with existing and potential rivals.

The development of Ford Motor Company is a clear-cut case that shows that making an entrepreneurial discovery is not enough to survive and thrive in the long run. With the help of the assembly line, Henry Ford's mass production resulted in huge profit and growth potential for the company. To maintain its position as a world leader, Ford had to continue developing and renewing its automotive products, which the founder failed to do. He did not realize quickly enough that demand had become more differentiated and that the lowest possible price on a standardized product was no longer the most important competitive element. Instead, Ford lost its previous advantage to General Motors (GM), where the intrapreneur Alfred P. Sloan introduced annual model changes and marketed multiple brands, which targeted different customer segments and thus did not compete with one another. These innovations, along with Henry Ford's reluctance to change, meant that GM became the unrivalled leader in the automotive industry in the early 1930s. During Sloan's entrepreneurial leadership, GM became the largest and most profitable company in history.[29]

29 Sloan and McDonald (1964).

© THE AUTHORS AND STUDENTLITTERATUR

In this light, entrepreneurship becomes a factor of production in its own right—one that is at least as important as (human and physical) capital and labor. As a factor of production, it differs in crucial ways from other forms of labor, as it cannot be purchased in an external market for the reasons explained above: a subjectively perceived opportunity that others do not recognize or value cannot have an economic value in the market that matches the entrepreneur's own valuation. However, entrepreneurship is also similar to other factors of production because economic activity increases the more it is employed and because its supply (or its allocation between productive and non-productive entrepreneurship) is sensitive to the relative return on productive entrepreneurship. The ability to discover and create new economic opportunities does not seem to be merely a form of acquired human capital. Still, this ability, in the broadest sense of the term, can seemingly be found in most people at least to some degree, given suitable social conditions and economic incentive structures. We will return to this issue later, particularly in the chapters on entrepreneurship and economic policy.

Entrepreneurship should not be regarded as a static phenomenon. A person might exercise entrepreneurship during a certain period and later become a more conventional manager or employee. Considering entrepreneurship a *continuum* is more realistic than regarding it as a phenomenon that can be delimited by sharply defined boundaries, whereby a certain activity is classified as entrepreneurial and another as non-entrepreneurial. An activity may be more or less entrepreneurial or may include a more or less entrepreneurial element. Finally, the entrepreneurial streak may change over time.

4.7 Chapter Summary

In this chapter, we have learned the following:

- Equating self-employment or start-ups and entrepreneurship is not possible.
- Employees may practice entrepreneurship, and they are then referred to as intrapreneurs.
- Entrepreneurship is not necessarily socially productive. Entrepreneurship can also be unproductive and destructive.

- Entrepreneurs may attempt to influence the politically determined institutional framework. This behavior is referred to as institutional entrepreneurship.
- Gazelles/high-growth firms and so-called high-impact entrepreneurship are particularly important for the development of the economy.
- A reasonable definition of entrepreneurship is the ability and willingness
    - to discover and create new economic opportunities,
    - to introduce ideas in the market under uncertainty, and
    - to create value.

© THE AUTHORS AND STUDENTLITTERATUR

Entrepreneurship—
The Empirical Picture

As we have stressed in the previous chapters, no obvious or undisputed definition of entrepreneurship exists, nor have researchers reached a consensus regarding how to measure it. Entrepreneurship is a complex and multidimensional concept that does not lend itself to simple and unambiguous quantification. In this chapter, we will review the empirical literature on entrepreneurship and assess whether our definition is consistent with the most frequently used measures of entrepreneurship. Using our definition as a starting point, we will present and discuss the advantages and disadvantages of the different measures of entrepreneurship. We will also use these measures to see how the degree of entrepreneurial activities varies between countries and regions. The level of entrepreneurship in Sweden will be discussed in detail.

5.1 The Rate of Self-Employment and Related Measures

Within empirical and econometric research, a functional and quantifiable measure must be defined, and economists have often used the number or rate of self-employed individuals, business owners, new firms or new business owners as an approximation of aggregate entrepreneurial activity. At best, these measures are rough approximations of the true rate of entrepreneurial activity. Entrepreneurship is much more than the registration of a new firm or a firm consisting of one self-employed person. Other measures of entrepreneurship include the growth or survival rate of start-ups. However, a high level of survival may be an indication of high entry barriers, which means that only firms with a high estimated probability of survival are founded and that the requirements for innovative entrepreneurship will be lower in existing firms. Still, high entry barriers are not good indicators of a favorable entrepreneurial environment. Recently, new and more encompassing measures of entrepreneurship have been developed.

If we use self-employment as a measure to approximate entrepreneurship, we can conclude that significant differences exist between countries. The same is true when we restrict the comparison to the richest countries—see *Figure 5.1*. In South Korea, the self-employment rate is more than 25 percent, while the rate in Norway and the United States is less than 7 percent. Sometimes major differences exist between countries that are usually considered relatively similar in many other respects; in Italy, the self-employed constitute approximately 25 percent of the workforce, while

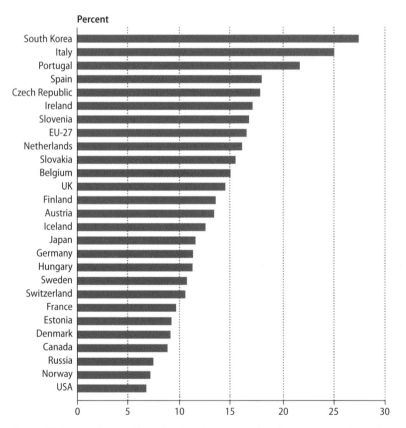

Figure 5.1 The number of self-employed, including unpaid family workers, as a share of the workforce, 2013. Source: OECD.

© THE AUTHORS AND STUDENTLITTERATUR

the share in France is less than 10 percent. According to data from the OECD, Sweden stands out with a relatively low self-employment rate. The low rate in the United States, a country that is generally considered one of the most entrepreneurial, suggests that the self-employment rate is not a good measure of the level of entrepreneurial activity in a country. Moreover, the statistics on self-employment in OECD countries are not fully comparable across countries. Therefore, one must use caution when comparing different countries. In a project called *Compendia* and based on OECD data, the Dutch research institute EIM has attempted to produce more comparable cross-country data.[1]

Overall, 30 percent of the working-age population in OECD countries state that they would like to participate in some kind of start-up activity. About ten percent also engage in some form of start-up activity, but only 1–2 percent realize their business ambitions each year. Of all the newly founded firms, 25 percent exit within a year, and 70 percent do not grow at all.[2] Based on these data, we can conclude that one should be skeptical of any attempt to equate what people report to be their entrepreneurial goals and what they actually achieve. Second, the weak survival rate and the total lack of growth for the overwhelming majority of new firms illustrate how misleading using start-up activity as an indicator of the level of entrepreneurial activity can be.

THE TEA INDEX

The Global Entrepreneurship Monitor (GEM), a large international comparative project, has developed an entrepreneurship index: the *Total Entrepreneurial Activity* (TEA) index. This index is defined as the proportion of working-age adults (18–64) in the population who either are involved in the process of founding a firm or are active as owner-managers of firms that are less than 42 months (3.5 years) old. The scope of the study and the number of countries participating in the GEM has increased significantly over time, and the study included 73 countries in 2014. In addition to attempting to measure entrepreneurial activity, this project has begun developing measures of attitudes toward entrepreneurship and of entrepreneurs' ambitions (for

1 See van Stel (2005).
2 OECD (2005).

example, making it possible to measure what we previously referred to as ambitious entrepreneurship).

Even if the TEA index is used as a measure of entrepreneurship, we can see major differences between countries, as shown in *Figure 5.2*. According to the GEM, developing countries such as Bolivia and Cameroon have a high share of entrepreneurs, whereas a low proportion of the population in Japan and Italy is attempting to start, or has recently started, a firm. The GEM has also attempted to distinguish between what they call necessity and opportunity-based entrepreneurship. Necessity self-employment is a better term for what the GEM refers to as necessity entrepreneurship. In *Figure 5.2.*, each bar has a dark and a light portion that indicates the share of each type. As *Figure 5.2* shows, one reason for the high share of entrepreneurs in developing countries is the high share of necessity self-employment, which largely reflects the adverse economic and institutional conditions in these countries. Developed countries, with their extensive safety nets and numerous alternative routes into the labor market, have lower shares of necessity self-employment.

Many new firms and/or high self-employment rates in developing countries do not necessarily indicate economic strength. A high self-employment rate more likely indicates that a large informal sector exists and that the country has not undergone industrialization and still operates as an agricultural society. Most likely, few of these start-ups, particularly those that classify as necessity self-employment, will contribute to growth and employment. A start-up among hundreds or thousands of similar firms and a start-up based on a new technical or organizational innovation are quite different.[3]

The TEA index is designed to reflect intentions and/or attempts to start a firm instead of being limited to actual start-ups. The measure also seems to be unrealistically high for some countries if we compare it with other indicators, such as the opening of new bank accounts.[4] In the same spirit, critics have argued that the TEA index overestimates the share of entrepreneurs because many people who claim to be starting a firm have ultimately not done so.[5]

3 OECD (2014).
4 OECD (2005, p. 20).
5 Hoffman (2007).

© THE AUTHORS AND STUDENTLITTERATUR

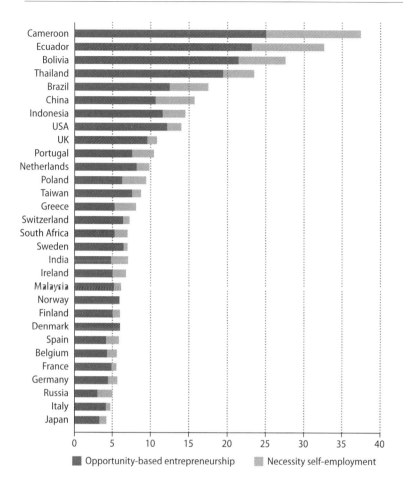

Figure 5.2 Opportunity-based entrepreneurship and necessity self-employment, 2014.

Note: *Total Entrepreneurial Activity* (TEA) is defined as the share of working-age adults (18–64) who either are involved in the process of starting a firm or are active as owner-managers of a firm that is less than 42 months (3.5 years) old. Only a selection of the 73 countries are included here. What we refer to as necessity self-employment is called necessity entrepreneurship in the study. Source: Singer, Amorós and Moska (2014).

© THE AUTHORS AND STUDENTLITTERATUR

Even if the share of business owners is lower in developed countries, their firms tend to be larger than those in developing countries. Hence, their contributions to employment may be equal to or even greater than those of firms in developing countries. Therefore, a larger share of the business owners in a developed country should be classified as entrepreneurial compared with those in a developing country.[6]

5.2 More Encompassing Measures of Entrepreneurship

The measures in section 5.1 are primarily problematic because they merely analyze different measures of the share of business owners in the economy and do not capture the qualitative aspect of entrepreneurship. To obtain a wider and more encompassing measure of entrepreneurship, the OECD launched what became the *Entrepreneurship Indicators Programme* (EIP) in 2006. The idea behind this program was to develop several different policy-relevant and internationally comparable measures of entrepreneurship, as no single measure can cover such a multifaceted concept. Instead, by creating several different measures, capturing different aspects of the entrepreneurship activity in an economy is possible. Since 2011, the OECD annually publishes the report *Entrepreneurship at a Glance*. Here, for multiple countries, data are presented on all the measures of entrepreneurship that have been developed. The report from 2014 includes some thirty countries and about twenty different measures. The measures cover many areas and include, among other things, the share of new and closed firms, venture capital investments (see Box 5.2 on p. 91), business growth, the size distribution of firms, productivity and job creation among surviving companies. Some measures are well established and based on official statistics. Other measures are being developed, and they currently cannot produce fully comparable cross-country data. Several of the new measures are only available for a few countries.[7]

Based on a variety of underlying factors, a new measure weighs these factors together to create an overall index of the entrepreneurship activity in the economy: the *Global Entrepreneurship and Development Index* (GEDI). Unlike the various measures presented in the EIP, this index

---

6 Ilmakunnas and Kanniainen (2001).
7 OECD (2014).

    © THE AUTHORS AND STUDENTLITTERATUR

facilitates easy and comprehensive comparisons between countries regarding entrepreneurship activity. The GEDI is based on measures in three areas: entrepreneurial attitudes, entrepreneurial abilities and entrepreneurial aspirations. The indicators in these three areas, which cover both individual and institutional measures, are weighed together to create a comprehensive index on entrepreneurship. The final weighing and the construction of the index will always be somewhat arbitrary. Many of the variables used in the index come from measures developed within the GEM.

Table 5.1 shows the ten countries with the highest rankings according to the GEDI. Eight of the ten countries are "Western countries." Taiwan and Singapore are the only non-Western countries in the top ten. Three Nordic countries and six countries from Western Europe are on the list.[8] At the bottom of the list of the 120 countries assessed, we find several African countries. Ranked third, Sweden seems to be a well-developed entrepreneurial country—in stark contrast to the picture presented by the TEA index and Sweden's share of self-employment.

Table 5.1 The ten most entrepreneurial countries according to the GEDI, 2014.

Country	GEDI	Country	GEDI
United States	82.5	Taiwan	69.5
Australia	77.8	Finland	69.3
Sweden	73.7	Netherlands	69.0
Denmark	72.5	United Kingdom	68.6
Switzerland	70.9	Singapore	67.9

Source: Acs, Szerb and Autio (2014).

FIRM GROWTH

Studying the growth of new firms is one way of further analyzing the level of entrepreneurship activity. Many firms must have—or relatively quickly reach—a certain size to be profitable. Entrepreneurship scholars sometimes discuss minimum efficient scale (MES), which refers to the level of production

---

8 The two other Nordic countries are ranked 11 (Iceland) and 14 (Norway).

at which the firm's average cost per produced unit is lowest. To survive in the long run, a new firm may need to reach this level. Therefore, many small and new firms must grow to survive in the long run.[9] However, growth takes time. For instance, it has taken almost 15–20 years for today's firms to reach a size of 50 employees or more. High-growth firms may be particularly important (see section 5.3). However, most firms do not grow at all, but this lack of growth is not necessarily problematic.[10] Many business owners do not aim to grow, but they can still play an important role in the economy, particularly as local producers of services. However, they should not be confused with entrepreneurial firms.

5.3 The Presence of High-Growth Firms

Prerequisites for rapid growth include the business owner's desire to grow rapidly and her expectation of being able to do so. The GEM also attempts to measure the share of the total entrepreneurial activity (those who state that they are in the process of starting or have started a firm in the past 3.5 years; TEA) that includes entrepreneurs who expect to be able to grow rapidly. In the GEM, this measure is known as high-growth expectation early-stage entrepreneurship. The term is defined as the proportion of TEA that expects to employ 20 or more people within five years.

This measure is available for 20 countries. *Figure 5.3* shows an average of this measure for the 2011–2013 period. Sweden is ranked in fifth place from the bottom. The share of new and young firms in Sweden that expect significant growth in employment is approximately six percent. Countries with particularly high growth ambitions include countries in Southeast Asia, the United States and a group of large countries in the European Union, including Germany and the United Kingdom. With its flexible labor market regulatory framework, Denmark is usually given a high position, but it did not participate in the 2013 survey. Finland and Norway also score relatively low, as do several of the countries in the European Union that have been the most affected by the financial crisis that started in 2008.

---

9 Audretsch (2002).
10 NUTEK (2005).

© THE AUTHORS AND STUDENTLITTERATUR

Some studies attempt to analyze the existence and the significance of rapidly growing firms. Unfortunately, no generally accepted definitions of gazelles or "high-growth" firms exist. Many issues must be considered when attempting to define high-growth firms. How much should a firm really grow to be defined as rapidly growing and for how long? Should one examine growth in turnover, in the number of employees, in value added or in some other variable? Should one examine absolute growth or relative growth?

The OECD uses a common definition, which requires that a firm has grown by more than 20 percent per year over a three-year period. The firm must also have at least ten employees at the beginning of the period in question. To be called a gazelle, the firm must also be no more than five years old (otherwise, it is simply referred to as a "high-growth enterprise"). A different option involves choosing a more arbitrary share of the fastest

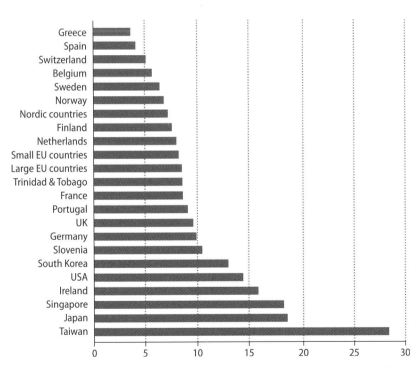

Figure 5.3 Share of TEA, according to the GEM, that expects to employ 20 or more people within five years, 2011–2013. Source: Braunerhjelm et al. (2014).

© THE AUTHORS AND STUDENTLITTERATUR

growing companies and then defining them as high-growth firms, for example, the 10 percent of all firms that grow most rapidly.

Based on current research about the importance of high-growth firms, one could conclude the following:[11]

- High-growth firms play a crucial role for employment growth and create a large proportion of all the new (net) jobs in the economy. This particularly holds true during recessions, when many high-growth firms continue to grow while other firms slow down.
- High-growth firms come in all sizes. Small firms are proportionally over-represented, but a small share of the high-growth large firms also create many new jobs.
- On average, high-growth firms are younger than other firms.
- Younger and small high-growth firms often grow organically (i.e., not through takeovers or mergers); therefore, they may contribute more to new employment than older and larger firms.
- High-growth firms are found in all industries, and high-tech industries are not over-represented.

A Swedish study shows that high-growth firms in Sweden accounted for 60 percent of the net generation of jobs between 2006 and 2009. Based on employment growth, the share of high-growth firms was eight percent in 2009.[12] However, few gazelles continue to grow rapidly for an extended period. In the Swedish study, so-called persistent high-growth firms—in other words, firms that continue to grow rapidly after the examined three-year period—are a mere seven percent of the high-growth firms in the first period. Even if gazelles are important for job creation, new gazelles must emerge on a continual basis to continue generating employment. One cannot rely on today's high-growth firms maintaining their rapid growth in the future.[13] Sven-Olov Daunfeldt and Daniel Halvarsson study the share of the

---

11 Henrekson and Johansson (2010), Haltiwanger, Jarmin and Miranda (2013) and Coad et al. (2014).

12 According to the OECD (2014), the share of high-growth firms, based on the OECD's own definition of high-growth firms, ranges from two to six percent. The share of gazelles is typically around one percent.

13 See Oreland (2012) for more information about this study.

   © THE AUTHORS AND STUDENTLITTERATUR

Table 5.2 Share of high-growth firms, percent.

Country	Share (%)	Country	Share (%)
United States	34	Italy	20
Hungary	33	Denmark	17
Poland	27	France	16
Czech Republic	26	Germany	14
Spain	26	Belgium	14
Ireland	24	Austria	14
Sweden	23	Netherlands	13
United Kingdom	22	Japan	8
Finland	20	*Average*	*20*

Note: High-growth firms are companies whose turnover has grown by more than 20 percent annually over a three-year period and that have between 50 and 1,000 employees at the end of the period. The study covers the 1999–2005 period, even if available data are missing for some countries for some years. Source: Teruel and de Wit (2011).

one-percent fastest growing companies over a three-year period that will also belong to the one-percent fastest growing companies in the upcoming three-year period. The probability of lasting rapid growth is not greater than one percent; less than one firm out of a hundred continues to be among the very top performers in the subsequent period.[14]

Finding international studies that compare the presence of high-growth firms and gazelles is difficult but not impossible. Two results are reported in *Table 5.2* and *Figure 5.4*. One result comes from the OECD, and the other comes from an academic study. The OECD's figures show both the share of high-growth firms and the share of gazelles, which are defined as high-growth firms no more than five years old. The OECD also shows the distribution between industries. The figure clearly shows that Sweden is not in a bad position, even though the United States and France have higher shares.[15] According to the second study, the United States is at the top, and Sweden is not far behind. Here, France does not have a prominent position. Japan has a

14 Daunfeldt and Halvarsson (2015).
15 The study only contains the Western European countries that are included in *Figure 5.4* (plus Luxembourg).

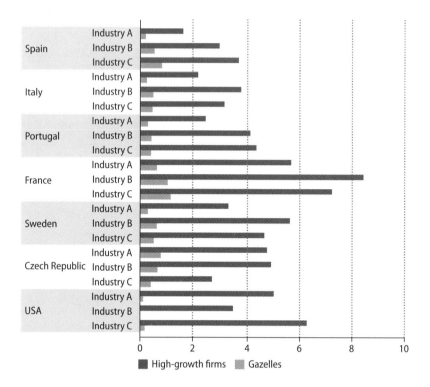

Figure 5.4 Share of high-growth firms and share of gazelles in different industries, 2008.

Note: Industry A = Manufacturing, Industry B = Services, Industry C = Construction. High-growth refers to the share of companies that initially had at least ten employees and whose employment growth has been higher than 20 percent per year for three years. High-growth firms that are no more than five years old are defined as gazelles. The United States has no data for the number of gazelles in industry B. Source: OECD (2014).

very low share of high-growth firms. The shares are also significantly higher in this study because different definitions for high-growth firms have been used. Hence, the exact definition of high-growth firms may significantly affect the results.[16]

A low share of high-growth firms may indicate that a country's entrepreneurial climate is unfavorable. However, if new firms in a particular country do not grow as much as in other countries, this relative lack of growth

---

16 See Daunfeldt, Elert and Johansson (2014) for an in-depth discussion regarding the definition of high-growth firms/gazelles and the ways in which the chosen definition affects the results.

© THE AUTHORS AND STUDENTLITTERATUR

cannot automatically be interpreted as a failure. Many firms may be acquired before they reach an expansion phase, and they are thus developed within the framework of established companies. In this case, one should consider why new firms are acquired and whether firms being acquired has a positive or negative effect on the economy. Such acquisitions are not necessarily bad from an entrepreneurial perspective.

5.4 Super-Entrepreneurship

A few entrepreneurs, such as Jeff Bezos (Amazon), Ingvar Kamprad (IKEA) and Steve Jobs (Apple), have been exceptionally successful. They did not merely build large, dominant companies; in many cases, they also created entirely new industries or completely reshaped an existing industry. One way of identifying these super-entrepreneurs involves scanning through *Forbes Magazine's* annual list of the world's dollar billionaires and identifying the people who built billion dollar fortunes by starting and growing their own companies. In one study, 996 super-entrepreneurs are identified in 53 countries for the 1996–2010 period.[17] Billionaire entrepreneurs are extremely rare. Nevertheless, they constitute a large share of the founders of the largest entrepreneurial companies. More than one-third (34 out of 100) of the largest companies in the United States, based on market value in 2010, were founded by entrepreneurs during the post-war period. Of these, half were founded by entrepreneur billionaires who appear on the *Forbes* list. Box 5.1 presents a historic Swedish super-entrepreneur, Christina Piper.

Box 5.1

Christina Piper—the merchant's daughter who became the super-entrepreneur of her time

Until 1921, Swedish women were not considered independent (granted majority) in the same way as adult men were. Widows enjoyed the largest degree of independence. Unsurprisingly, few prominent women appear in the early Swedish history of entrepreneurs.

---

17 Henrekson and Sanandaji (2014a).

© THE AUTHORS AND STUDENTLITTERATUR

Among Swedish women, the most successful entrepreneur is probably Christina Piper (1673–1752). She was the daughter of wealthy businessman Olof Törnflycht and was married at the age of 17 to 43-year-old count Carl Piper. Her husband was not wealthy, but he was closely allied to King Charles XII and thus held considerable sway in the Swedish government. He left Sweden in 1700 and spent the rest of his life in combat and as a prisoner of war. He died in Russian captivity in 1716, after his wife declined an offer to pay his ransom.

In her husband's absence and then as a widow, Piper could act at her own discretion and extend the family's properties, which she did with great skill. After the Danish province of Scania had been incorporated into Sweden, many estates were owned by economically needy or bankrupt heirs. Piper bought and gradually developed a large number of estates in Scania, including seven castles and their vast land holdings. She also bought large estates in the provinces of Östergötland and Västmanland.

She created six entailed estates, which are largely still in the family's possession. Today, her descendant Carl Piper at Högestad and Christinehof is the largest private landowner in Scania and Sweden's largest owner of productive agricultural land.

In 1725, she acquired the ailing alum works in Andrarum in Scania, and, as an entrepreneur, she was able to develop the business using her financial assets. Under her leadership, the alum works in Andrarum grew to be the largest of its kind in Northern Europe and the largest company in Scania, with 900 employees. Although her rule over the workers was quite regimented, she still built both a school and a hospital for them. She also introduced her own coinage system at the factory, which tied the employees even closer to the company.

Christina Piper was fully active until her death, and she continued to acquire land until she was 77. She was probably the richest private person in Sweden during the latter part of her life.

SOURCE: DU RIETZ (2013) AND JOHNSON (2006).

Figure 5.5 shows the number of super-entrepreneurs per million inhabitants. Hong Kong, Israel, the United States, Switzerland and Singapore are particularly successful with regard to creating super-entrepreneurs, while Europe (with some exceptions) and Japan have relatively few super-entrepreneurs per million inhabitants. The number of super-entrepreneurs

© THE AUTHORS AND STUDENTLITTERATUR

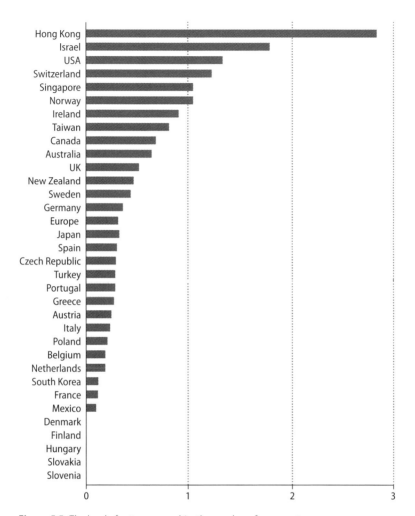

Figure 5.5 The level of entrepreneurship: the number of super-entrepreneurs per million inhabitants, 1996–2010. Source: Henrekson and Sanandaji (2014a).

per million inhabitants in Europe and Japan is almost exactly one-fourth of the number in the United States. As self-employment is often used as a measure of entrepreneurship, the relationship between the self-employment rate and the level of entrepreneurship (measured as the share of super-entrepreneurs) is quite striking. As shown in *Figure 5.6*, super-entrepreneurship and self-employment among the OECD countries is negatively correlated.

© THE AUTHORS AND STUDENTLITTERATUR

In the same study, two other measures of entrepreneurship are also examined to compare countries and regions. The first one is the share of today's 100 largest companies that were founded by entrepreneurs in the post-war period. The second measure is venture capital investments as a share of GDP. Because venture capital is almost invariably given to innovative and growth-oriented companies, this measure can be used to estimate the level of a country's entrepreneurial orientation. On the one hand, only 0.1 percent of all American companies receive venture capital at any time during their lifecycles. On the other hand, among the American companies that proved extremely successful and eventually went public, as many as two-thirds received venture capital financing at some point during their lifecycles. Therefore, most entrepreneurial firms with high potential received venture capital. Using venture capital to distinguish entrepreneurial firms with high potential from other firms thus seems reasonable. Total venture capital investment as a share of GDP is highly correlated with the number of entrepreneur billionaires per capita. See Box 5.2 for a discussion of venture capital.

Table 5.3 shows different measures of entrepreneurship in the United States, Europe and Asia. The United States has half as many self-employed individuals as Europe and Asia, but it has more than four times as many super-entrepreneurs per million inhabitants compared with Europe and about three times as many compared with Asia. Interestingly, the other two

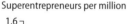

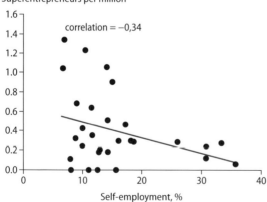

Figure 5.6
The number of super-entrepreneurs per million inhabitants, 1996–2010, and the self-employment rate in the OECD (2010). Source: Henrekson and Sanandaji (2014a).

© THE AUTHORS AND STUDENTLITTERATUR

measures of entrepreneurship show similar differences between the United States and Europe. Total venture capital investment as a share of GDP is more than five times as high in the United States. While 34 of the 100 largest American companies were founded by entrepreneurs during the post-war period, the corresponding figure for Europe is only seven of the 100 largest companies. Compared with Asia, Europe has clearly lower figures for two of the measures of entrepreneurship, although they are slightly higher when the degree of entrepreneurship is measured as venture capital investment as a share of GDP.

Table 5.3 Entrepreneurship in the United States, wealthy Asian countries and Western Europe according to three different measures.

	No. of super-entrepreneurs	Population in millions	Super-entrepreneurs per million inhabitants	Share of the 100 largest companies founded by an entrepreneur since 1945	Venture capital investment, % of GDP 2010	Self-employment
USA	411	307	1.34	34%	0.200	7.5%
Asia*	91	211	0.43	13%	0.024	16%
Europe‡	132	407	0.32	7%	0.036	15%

* Japan, South Korea, Taiwan, Singapore and Hong Kong. ‡ Germany, France, the United Kingdom, Italy, Spain, the Netherlands, Greece, Belgium, Portugal, Sweden, Austria, Denmark, Finland, Ireland, Luxembourg, Switzerland, Norway and Iceland. Source: Henrekson and Sanandaji (2015).

Box 5.2

Venture Capital

Of particular importance for the growth potential of smaller companies is the availability of a particular form of risk capital, known as venture capital (VC). Venture capital is characterized by its investment in unlisted companies and the venture capitalists' active participation in the target company's operations by providing, for instance, management skills, market knowledge and network contacts. The contributions of business angels and venture capital firms have been shown to be crucial for the success of mainly new and technology-based companies.

© THE AUTHORS AND STUDENTLITTERATUR

Analysts distinguish between two types of venture capitalists: business angels and venture capital firms. Business angels are private individuals who invest capital and knowledge during the early stages of newly founded and growing companies. Through the business angel, the business owner gains access to capital, skills and contacts through the former's network. A business angel often has experience as an entrepreneur and a business leader and has the time, dedication and personal wealth to invest in promising new business ideas.

Venture capital firms operate as financial intermediaries for potential entrepreneurs who seek potential investors and capital to finance their innovative high-risk projects. Within the framework of a limited partnership, institutional investors establish an agreement with a venture capital firm. The investors are owners with limited liability (limited partners) and the venture capital firm's representatives act as principal owners (general partners).

The lifespan of such a partnership is generally ten years. The usual arrangement is that the limited partners contribute 98–99 percent of the capital and the venture capital firm's general partners add 1–2 percent. When the return is allocated, 20 percent usually goes to the general partners, and 80 percent goes to the limited partners. This distribution applies to the return exceeding a certain hurdle rate, which historically has been around eight percent. General partners also receive an annual management fee of 1–2 percent.

The venture capital firm sifts out the best project proposals. The sorting is crucial, as a third party can hardly be—or become—as well informed regarding the investment project when the company's management is searching for financial support. In the companies that manage to obtain financing after the selection process, the venture capitalist usually assumes an active role in the ongoing decision-making process and in the planning and design of more long-term strategies. The venture capitalist sits on the board and plays a prominent role when key employees are recruited or when they are replaced because they—according to the venture capitalist's assessment—do not live up to expectations.

To exercise control, the venture capitalist doles out financial assistance in several installments. The results are evaluated at every stage, and support can be withdrawn if the company does not perform as expected. This arrangement is used to minimize the risk of opportunistic behavior and to strengthen the commitment of the company's management.

© THE AUTHORS AND STUDENTLITTERATUR

An interesting trend concerns private individuals' new online opportunities to be co-financiers of projects with established business angels. American AngelList, founded by serial entrepreneur Naval Ravikant, is a pioneer in this field. Another interesting trend is the emergence of accelerators, such as American companies Techstars and Y Company and the pan-European Seedcamp. The accelerator provides the innovator with an opportunity to quickly test whether an idea is exploitable. Some selected ideas and persons receive further assistance from individuals with start-up experience. They also often receive some start-up capital and a workspace in a creative environment.

Finally, venture capital firms are a subset of what is known as private equity (PE). In terms of volume, the PE sector is dominated by the buyout firms (more than 95 percent of the total volume), which buy mature companies that they then develop over a long period of time and resell, often by going public. Unfortunately, some confusion exists in this area. Buyout firms are often considered the same as PE, even though the term covers both venture capital firms and buyout firms.

Table 5.4 shows the correlation between the self-employment rate and the business ownership rate, the number of billionaire entrepreneurs per million inhabitants, venture capital investment as a share of GDP and the GEM's measure of entrepreneurship—the TEA index. In the table, we have also added the correlation between the self-employment rate and GDP per capita. The table shows that the number of billionaire entrepreneurs per million inhabitants and venture capital investment as a share of GDP is negatively correlated to the self-employment rate. GDP per capita is also negatively correlated with the self-employment rate. However, the GEM's TEA index is positively correlated with self-employment. If the share of venture capital investment and the number of billionaire entrepreneurs are better measures of entrepreneurship, self-employment and other measures that are closely related to self-employment (such as the TEA index and the business ownership rate) seem to be far too simplistic and even misleading.

Table 5.4 The correlation between self-employment and other entrepreneurship proxies (53 countries).

Entrepreneurship proxies	
Business ownership rate	0.69
Start-up rate (GEM TEA)	0.72
Billionaire entrepreneurs per million inhabitants	−0.33
Venture capital investment as a share of GDP	−0.21
GDP per capita	−0.63

Source: Henrekson and Sanandaji (2014a).

5.5 Entrepreneurship and Business Dynamics in Sweden

Thus far, we have discussed various quantitative measures of entrepreneurial activity. Analyzing business dynamics from different perspectives is another way of illustrating the entrepreneurial climate in, for example, Sweden. Therefore, we will study how the corporate structure, based on different size classes, has changed over time and analyze the creation and development of large Swedish corporations.

THE SWEDISH CORPORATE STRUCTURE

A country's corporate structure is not static; it changes over time as the economy evolves. The Swedish corporate structure at the end of the Second World War was dominated by large corporations and a strong concentration of private ownership, something that was strengthened in the 1950s and 1960s.[18] Some scholars have argued that a general pattern of structural changes in the West toward smaller production units became discernible in the early 1970s, but the differences between countries are significant with respect to the extent and the timing.[19] Concurrent with this trend, the development of Swedish firms with 10–199 employees was weak from the late 1960s to the early 1990s.[20]

---

18 Lindgren (1953) and Glete (1994).
19 Birch and Medoff (1994).
20 Henrekson and Johansson (1999).

  © THE AUTHORS AND STUDENTLITTERATUR

However, since the crisis of the early 1990s, the share of workers in firms with 10–199 employees has increased, while the share of workers employed in firms with more than 200 employees has decreased. The development is not as clear concerning companies with 1–9 employees. The size distribution is influenced by whether the statistics are corrected for company groups. Such correction implies that the parent company is merged with its subsidiaries to form a company group and that the new group is then assigned the correct size classification.

The employment share of firms with 1–9 employees after adjusting for the company group does not increase for the business sector as a whole. However, the employment share for firms with 1–9 employees in the manufacturing sector increases, whether or not it is adjusted for the fact that some firms are subsidiaries belonging to the same company group. In absolute numbers, approximately a quarter of a million more people were employed in firms with 10 199 employees in 2006 compared with the numbers in 1993. At the industry level, the construction, transport and communications industries can serve as industries in which firms with 10–199 employees have considerably increased their employment share. This share continued to increase between 2006 and 2009. Firms with 3–199 employees created approximately 300,000 new jobs in the economy during the 1990–2009 period. Most of these jobs were created in firms with 10–49 employees.[21]

Part of the increase probably resulted from changes related to the company group, but these changes do not fully explain this increase. Other explanatory factors are associated with the organization of firms (downsizing and outsourcing), private production of welfare-related services (such as health care, education, childcare and care of the elderly), and consolidation in some areas, including law firms and IT consultants.

The interpretation of changes in the share of people employed in different size classes must be clarified. Over time, firms may move from one employment size class to another because of increasing or decreasing employment levels. An increase in the share of people employed in medium-sized firms does not necessarily imply that medium-sized firms have contributed to this employment increase. For instance, the increase in the share may result from small firms increasing in size or large corporations

---

21 Heyman, Norbäck and Persson (2013).

© THE AUTHORS AND STUDENTLITTERATUR

shrinking, both of which are then reclassified as medium-sized firms. Hence, changes in the aggregate distribution between size classes may paint a biased picture of what is actually happening at the micro level or the firm level. How employment is distributed between size classes does not necessarily indicate where jobs are created or destroyed, and this distribution alone should not be used as a basis for policy conclusions regarding, for instance, suitable measures for increasing employment.

LARGE SWEDISH CORPORATIONS

Examining a country's large corporations can also be used as an indicator of the entrepreneurial environment. Truly successful entrepreneurs have managed to create and expand their activities and to develop large corporations. How many firms have grown and become quite large in Sweden over the past few decades? A detailed study has analyzed when today's largest entrepreneurial firms in Sweden were founded.[22] Unfortunately, no completely comparable study for other countries exists; thus, this presentation can be regarded as an illustration of the Swedish case.

Of the 100 largest Swedish companies in terms of employment in 2004, 34 of them started from scratch as a genuine start-up and have grown large over time. Therefore, they can be described as truly entrepreneurial.[23] None of these 34 companies was founded after 1970 (*Figure 5.7*). Examining the 100 largest companies in terms of turnover, the result is almost as dismal. Only two of the 38 truly entrepreneurial companies were founded after 1970: Tele2 and MTG (*Figure 5.8*). These two companies were the only new large corporations that were founded and grew large during the 35-year period from 1970–2004.[24]

However, many circumstances potentially influence founding dates. If a country has a larger share of older large corporations, the country was probably industrialized early. In Sweden, the period between 1880 and the First World War was highly favorable for starting new firms, which have since been able to grow and become very large. Successful entrepreneurial firms may also be acquired by other established actors before they have had

22 Axelsson (2006).

23 The other 66 large corporations are cooperatives, government-owned companies, foreign companies or companies that have been created through mergers and acquisitions or spin-offs.

24 See also NUTEK (2005).

          © THE AUTHORS AND STUDENTLITTERATUR

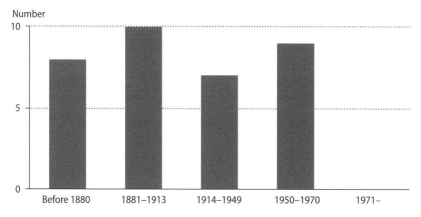

Figure 5.7 Founding years of Sweden's 34 largest genuinely entrepreneurial companies in terms of employment, 2004.

Note: The figure is based on 34 of the 100 largest companies in terms of employment. The other 66 companies are not genuinely entrepreneurial. Genuinely entrepreneurial companies are companies that were started from scratch as start-ups and have grown large over time. Source: Axelsson (2006).

the time to grow and become large. A well-functioning market for mergers and acquisitions may actually be a requirement for successful industrial development. Technological developments and globalization also influence the ways that firms are organized and the ways that they operate, and the entrepreneur's role has also changed. Two observable trends point in different directions. On the one hand, entrepreneurs increasingly start firms based on an idea with a global potential in an effort to sell the firm to a global actor. On the other hand, some firms have the global market in sight from the outset, so-called "born-global firms."[25]

Many people still believe that Sweden is doing well because of its large multinational companies and that these companies will continue to constitute the foundation of the national economy and to create new jobs. Large corporations are very important, but their significance has decreased sharply in the 2000s. *Table 5.5* lists the 20 largest Swedish public companies in terms of employment in 2000. The table shows that their share of employees in the Swedish private sector has decreased from almost ten percent of all employees in 2000 to just over six percent in 2012.

25 Halldin (2012).

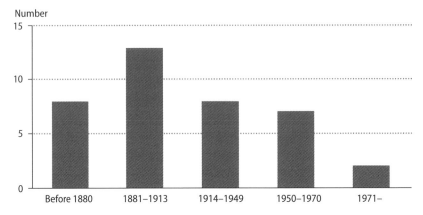

Figure 5.8 Founding years of Sweden's 38 largest genuinely entrepreneurial companies in terms of turnover, 2004.

Note: The figure is based on 38 of the 100 largest companies in terms of turnover. The other 62 companies are not genuinely entrepreneurial. Genuinely entrepreneurial companies are companies that were started from scratch as start-ups and have grown large over time. Source: Axelsson (2006).

Table 5.6 shows that just over one-third of all private sector employees in 2011 were working in firms with more than 250 employees. The share of value added is similar, though somewhat larger (40 percent), for firms with more than 250 employees. The higher capital intensity, on average, in larger firms explains this discrepancy. The existing large Swedish corporations are good at adapting to changes, but these adaptations have partly been about downsizing the number of employees since the turn of the millennium. Nevertheless, the existing large corporations clearly can no longer act as an engine for employment growth, and new firms must be founded and expanded to generate new jobs.

© THE AUTHORS AND STUDENTLITTERATUR

Table 5.5 The number of employees in the 20 public companies in Sweden with the most employees in 2000, along with a comparison with 2012 (rounded to the nearest hundred, including subsidiaries).

Company	2000	2012
Ericsson	37,900	17,600
AB Volvo	25,000	23,300
ABB	18,400	9,100
Volvo Car Corporation	18,300	15,600
Skanska	15,700	10,800
NCC	14,300	7,500
Saab (not Automobile)	13,300	10,900
Scania	12,100	12,000
SAS	10,000	4,000
Sandvik	9,700	11,300
AstraZeneca	9,500	6,200
SSAB	9,100	6,500
PEAB	9,000	12,600
Electrolux	8,200	2,000
SCA	6,400	5,800
Securitas	6,300	6,900
SKF	5,200	2,900
Holmen	4,200	2,900
Atlas Copco	2,400	4,700
Total in the above companies	235,000	172,600
Total in the private sector	2,406,000	2,746,000
Share in the 20 largest companies	9.8%	6.3 %

Note: Financial firms are not included. In addition to the largest public companies, Volvo Car Corporation has been included. Source: CM Partner, Nordisk Affärsinformation [Nordic Business Information], Statistics Sweden, own calculations.

Table 5.6 The size distribution of firms in the Swedish business sector in 2011 in terms of employees and value added (percent, excluding financial firms).

	Firm size			
	0–9	10–49	50–249	250–
Employees	23.5	22.2	18.4	35.9
Value added	24.3	18.2	17.3	40.1

Source: Heyman, Norbäck and Persson (2013).

Some of the large Swedish corporations are innovative. Successful large corporations can promote the emergence of new entrepreneurial firms through the division of labor. Small and new firms concentrate on the most risky and uncertain, and potentially the most radical, innovations, while large incumbent firms are principally engaged in less risky and incremental innovations (see more in section 6.3).[26] Because of their size, large corporations account for the lion's share of the aggregate spending on R&D (the entire business sector contributes almost 70 percent of Sweden's total R&D).

Large corporations often operate on the knowledge frontier in their respective industries, and the employees in their R&D departments have expert knowledge with regard to the latest technologies. As a result, they often generate new and competitive ideas that can serve as a foundation for new firms. Many of the most successful new firms are spin-offs from existing large corporations, when employees who have accumulated knowledge and experience start new firms.[27] Large corporations are also important as customers of and investors in the new firms. Spin-offs from existing large corporations tend to grow faster than other new firms do, perhaps because spin-offs can re-use valuable technology and industrial experience from the large corporations.

Spin-offs from large multinational corporations are seemingly less common in Sweden than in other comparable countries.[28] Meanwhile, large multinational corporations constitute an unusually large share of the Swedish economy. Few spin-offs from large multinationals will mean

---

26 Baumol (2004, 2010) and Norbäck and Persson (2009).
27 Klepper (2001); Andersson and Klepper (2013).
28 Andersson and Klepper (2013).

  © THE AUTHORS AND STUDENTLITTERATUR

few new companies (with good inherent growth potential), which will ultimately affect the development of the entire Swedish economy. Therefore, improving the interaction between the existing large, R&D-intensive corporations and new growing firms is a potentially important part of Swedish entrepreneurship policy.

5.6 Chapter Summary

In this chapter, we have learned the following:

- No clear-cut and indisputable empirical measure of entrepreneurship exists.
- In the empirical research, different kinds of "narrow" measures of entrepreneurship are frequently used, including the self-employment rate or related measures, such as the I EA index. At best, these measures are rough approximations, and, at worst, they are completely misleading.
- Broader measures of entrepreneurship, such as the GEDI, integrate a variety of different measures of entrepreneurship.
- Other indicators of entrepreneurial activity include the prevalence of high-growth firms, the extent of venture capital investments and the share of individuals who have created fortunes by starting and developing new and successful firms.
- Entrepreneurial activity in Sweden differs markedly depending on the measure used. Gauged with narrow measures of entrepreneurship, entrepreneurial activity in Sweden is on par with other wealthy countries. However, relatively few large Swedish companies have been founded since the Second World War.

The Role of Entrepreneurship in the Competence Structure

Entrepreneurship is crucial for economic development, but it is not the only factor that determines how the economy evolves. In this chapter, we will discuss other actors and their role in helping entrepreneurial activities reach their full potential. Together, these actors constitute a so-called competence structure, which consists of the unique and complementary skills that are required to efficiently exploit new knowledge and to sustain economic development. We will also highlight the differential roles of the new, small and large firms in a dynamic economy.

6.1 The Different Actors in the Competence Structure

The entrepreneur does not act in a vacuum; he is dependent on an array of actors to realize his ideas. These actors have skills that complement those of the entrepreneur. When they interact and form a suitable skill structure, new ideas can be generated, identified, selected and commercialized. A lack of skills or an important actor may significantly impede or prevent development. Identifying at least six types of actors, in addition to the entrepreneur, is possible:

1 *Inventors*. Entrepreneurs generally have a good overall understanding of how to exploit an opportunity, but they tend to lack highly specific knowledge regarding relevant technologies. Inventors may create the foundation for a firm through a patented invention or work to solve specific problems.

2   *Industrialists.* Two different kinds of skill sets are generally required
    to introduce and then further develop a new idea. Industrialists
    are needed to take the commercialization beyond the initial
    entrepreneurial stage and to organize the expansion of original ideas
    into large-scale operations.

3   *Skilled labor.* Economic development and growth requires skilled
    white-collar and blue-collar workers. The functioning of the labor
    market and the educational system is crucial in supplying firms with
    workers with relevant skills.

4   *Venture capitalists.* They finance firms and entrepreneurs with skilled
    capital in the early phases of development. They identify various
    entrepreneurs and their projects, determine whether and how much
    to invest and decide how it should be valued. They thereby provide
    industry experience, contacts and management skills. See Box 5.2.

5   *Actors in secondary markets.* These actors have skills similar to those
    of venture capitalists and serve a similar function, but they operate in
    a later stage in a firm's lifecycle. They assess firms' value, contribute
    capital and evaluate the competence of the owner(s) in different
    firms. They also help entrepreneurs and venture capitalists reduce or
    terminate their involvement as the firm moves into a more mature
    stage.

6   *Competent customers.* Consumption is the final goal of production,
    and, for growth to occur, the products produced must be what the
    consumers *de facto* demand. Some consumers—so-called competent
    customers—function as crucial sources of information regarding
    consumer needs and preferences. A product will not be better than
    what is demanded by the customers. A part of the entrepreneurial skill
    set thus involves choosing and cooperating with the right customers.

   © THE AUTHORS AND STUDENTLITTERATUR

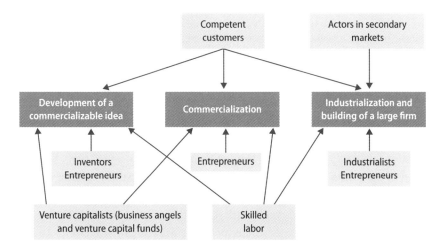

Figure 6.1 The competence structure: From a concept to a large-scale company.

Note: The figure attempts to capture, in a stylized manner, the phases during which the various actors in the competence structure participate in the industrialization process. Initially, the entrepreneur identifies potential opportunities in his interactions with competent customers. The inventors are involved to resolve technical problems. Sometimes, the process is initiated by an inventor whose idea is further developed by entrepreneurs. The need for skilled labor may already exist at this stage. The early commercialization phase mainly involves entrepreneurs and, to a lesser extent, skilled labor. In the industrialization phase, the industrialists are activated, which requires more skilled labor. The venture capitalists finance development in the early stages, while actors in secondary markets enter the process at a later stage. Source: Adaptation from Eliasson (1996) and Henrekson and Johansson (2009).

Figure 6.1 shows how the different actors contribute to the development process—all the way from a concept to full-scale industrialization. The figure is a simplification. For instance, industrialists and actors in the secondary market can be involved at a much earlier stage; actors can work alongside each other or overlap during different phases. The same person can also fulfill more than one role. For example, an entrepreneur may also be an inventor or act as an industrialist.

6.2 The Special Role of New and Small Firms

Many studies emphasize the importance of new and small firms for the development and commercialization of knowledge.[1] New and small firms should be particularly suitable for developing innovations for several reasons:

- As entrepreneurship is about judgmental decision making under uncertainty and is based on perceived opportunities, the exploitation of a perceived opportunity will frequently occur within a new firm. Selling an opportunity that others do not perceive or understand to large incumbent firms is impossible.[2]
- The owners of new and small firms are not solely motivated by the prospect of making money. Therefore, they may be prepared to make less than they would be compensated in a large firm for performing the same task. Hence, it will be cheaper for large firms to let the small firms work on research and innovation.[3]
- On the other hand, the owners of new and small firms may also make more money than if they had performed the same function as intrapreneurs in large firms.
- Large firms have created bureaucratic structures and procedures that are not always conducive for generating innovations. Measuring, checking and rewarding the innovative activities of employees is difficult, while controlling and paying for routine tasks is much easier.
- The optimal structure for controlling and coordinating routine tasks (which are necessary and account for a large share of the man-hours in large firms) often results in a bureaucratic structure that inhibits innovative activities among employees.[4]
- If a new and radical innovation fails, a large incumbent firm may lose prestige, which makes discontinuing projects that should be terminated difficult.

---

1 Acs and Audretsch (1987, 1990) were among the first to note the importance of small firms in this respect.
2 Foss and Klein (2012).
3 Baumol (2010).
4 Holmström (1989).

   © THE AUTHORS AND STUDENTLITTERATUR

- An incumbent firm that develops new products is likely to compete with itself, given that the new products will reduce the profits from the firm's existing product range. Therefore, large corporations that are required to maintain efficiency and profitability may tend to prioritize existing customers, suppliers and markets. An innovation could also require a new organizational or compensation structure.[5] Therefore, innovations in these firms will mainly aim to improve existing products or the firm's position in existing markets.[6]

New firms put competitive pressure on existing firms and push them to be more efficient. Frequently, new firms will also introduce structural changes and revolutionary innovations. The investors and employees of incumbent firms are often tied to existing technologies through extensive investments in physical and human capital, which lose value when radical innovations are introduced.

Therefore, introducing genuinely new products and production methods in large and mature firms may be difficult. As such, the level of innovation is often lower in markets in which mature firms do the lion's share of developing innovations.[7] Having small (and new) firms outside the large incumbent firms developing radical innovations is better, as larger firms can more easily close down these projects (by terminating contractual agreements with third parties) without suffering adverse consequences within the firm. This relationship tends to be particularly suitable in the biotechnology and pharmaceutical industries.[8]

In some industries, innovation is largely driven by the users (customers) rather than by large or small firms. This user role is particularly common in

---

5 Cullen and Gordon (2006).
6 A distinction is sometimes made between disruptive innovations and sustaining innovations. Disruptive innovations may at times be less efficient than the products that they replace, but they have different characteristics (smaller, portable, cheaper, etc.) that make them attractive (often in other market niches initially). See Christensen and Raynor (2003) or Sandström (2010) for a more thorough discussion and further examples.
7 Geroski (1995), Baldwin and Johnson (1999) and Audretsch (1995). According to calculations by Acs and Audretsch (1990), based on various datasets from the 1970s and 1980s, small American firms developed 2.4 times more innovations per employee than large ones. The research findings on this issue are ambiguous.
8 Baumol (2010, p. 207).

industries that produce technical appliances and scientific instruments. In these cases, competent customers operate as "user-entrepreneurs" in contrast to cases in which alert producers operate as entrepreneurs. Here, incumbent firms do not enter and take over until the users' ideas have been validated in the market as useful and in demand.[9]

6.3 The Different Roles of Large and Small Firms

An entrepreneur may choose to not commercialize his innovation and instead allow other actors with complementary skills develop it into a finished product that is manufactured and distributed at an industrial scale. During the 2000s, a school of thought developed arguing that the incentives to innovate are strengthened if the ownership of the developed ideas changes throughout the process—from the idea to finished product in the market. At first, business angels and venture capitalists play a central role, while larger, incumbent firms may become increasingly important at a later stage in the development process.

In general, we can imagine three different strategies for the commercialization of an innovation:

- *incumbent firms* develop innovations and commercialize them;
- *entrepreneurial firms* develop innovations and commercialize them, possibly supported by venture capital firms; or
- *entrepreneurial firms* develop innovations, possibly supported by venture capital firms, and then sell their innovations to incumbent firms, which commercialize them.

Economists Pehr-Johan Norbäck and Lars Persson have studied the three ideal cases above from a theoretical perspective, examining their effects on innovation incentives.[10] They find that the third commercialization method seems to be the most beneficial for developing commercializable innovations—in other words, entrepreneurial firms develop innovations,

9 von Hippel, Ogawa and de Jong (2011).
10 Norbäck and Persson (2009).

© THE AUTHORS AND STUDENTLITTERATUR

and incumbent firms commercialize them. Norbäck and Persson give three reasons for this finding.

First, incumbent firms that develop new products risk competing with themselves, which may reduce their willingness to develop new products. The entrepreneurial firm does not consider this risk. On the other hand, the entrepreneurial firm may instead take advantage of the incumbent firms' desire to protect their market positions by selling its innovation to one of them. Incumbent firms are not only interested in using an innovation but also want to prevent competitors from gaining access to it. This mechanism increases an innovation's value, thereby increasing the incentive for new firms to innovate.

Second, an entrepreneurial firm may benefit from, when possible, selling its ideas instead of commercializing them, as its market entry increases product market competition. Increased competition may drive down prices and profit margins compared with cases in which an incumbent firm had undertaken the commercialization.

Third, in terms of the commercialization of ideas, incumbent firms are presumed to be more efficient than smaller entrepreneurial firms. Large incumbent firms often have firm-specific assets that can be useful during the commercialization phase, such as marketing knowledge, distribution networks and complementary patents.[11]

Figure 6.2 illustrates how the commercialization process may playout when the entrepreneurial firm commercializes its idea compared to the case when the firm (or its strategic assets) is sold to an incumbent firm, which, in turn, performs the commercialization.

Therefore, both large and small firms are seemingly needed to ensure a successful innovation process. William Baumol aptly characterizes this interaction as "a symbiosis between David and Goliath."[12] A division of labor between large and small firms and their research activities has evolved. Large firms are typically better at R&D that aims to improve existing products, while small firms tend to produce radical innovations. Therefore, new technologies are often developed, implemented, commercialized and diffused in the form

---

11 Barba Navaretti and Venables (2004).
12 Baumol (2002a).

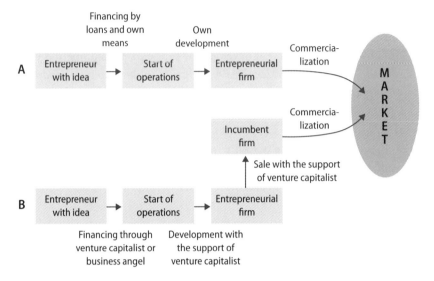

Figure 6.2 Commercialization of an idea by (A) a new entry and (B) a sale.
Source: Based on Norbäck and Persson (2009).

of new entrepreneurial firms. Many incumbent firms use acquisitions to gain access to new technologies.[13]

William Baumol has demonstrated the importance of small firms in the creation of many revolutionary American innovations, which often have been further developed and reached their full potential in large firms.[14] In a telling list of revolutionary American innovations developed by small firms, reproduced in *Table 6.1*, Baumol illustrates the importance of small firms for technological change and, ultimately, economic development. This list includes innovations such as the defibrillator, the microprocessor and the FM radio.

---

13 OECD (2000a, 2002).
14 Baumol (2004).

  © THE AUTHORS AND STUDENTLITTERATUR

Table 6.1 Important Innovations by Small American Firms during the 20th Century.

Air Conditioning	Heart Valve	Prefabricated Housing
Air Passenger Service	Heat Sensor	Pressure Sensitive Tape
Airplane	Helicopter	Prestressed Concrete
Articulated Tractor Chassis	High Resolution CAT Scanner	Programmable Computer
Artificial Skin	High Resolution Digital X-Ray	Quick-Frozen Food
Assembly Line	High Resolution X-Ray Microscope	Reading Machine
Audio Tape Recorder	Human Growth Hormone	Rotary Oil Drilling Bit
Bakelite	Hydraulic Brake	Safety Razor
Biomagnetic Imaging	Integrated Circuit	Six-Axis Robot Arm
Biosynthetic Insulin	Kidney Stone Laser	Soft Contact Lens
Catalytic Petroleum Cracking	Large Computer	Solid Fuel Rocket Engine
Computerized Blood Pressure Controller	Link Trainer	Stereoscopic Map Scanner
Continuous Casting	Microprocessor	Strain Gauge
Cotton Picker	Nuclear Magnetic Resonance Scanner	Strobe Lights
Defibrillator	Optical Scanner	Supercomputer
DNA Fingerprinting	Oral Contraceptives	Two-Armed Mobile Robot
Double-Knit Fabric	Outboard Engine	Vacuum Tube
Electronic Spreadsheet	Overnight National Delivery	Variable Output Transformer
FM Radio	Pacemaker	Vascular Lesion Laser
Free-wing Aircraft	Personal Computer	Xerography
Front-End Loader	Photo Typesetting	X-Ray Telescope
Geodesic Dome	Polaroid Camera	Zipper
Gyrocompass	Portable Computer	

Source: Baumol (2004).

No consensus exists regarding the belief that mainly small and new firms are responsible for the most radical innovations. Some scholars believe that large firms account for a larger share of radical innovations, at least in certain sectors with significant economies of scale.[15] However, the importance of small, non-radical—often referred to as incremental—innovations should not be underestimated. Every single innovation is perhaps not all that important, but, together, many small improvements to a product eventually result in far-reaching changes. Each incremental improvement in the capacity of computers that has been launched over time may seem marginal, but, taken together, these incremental improvements have resulted in computers that are exponentially faster, smaller and cheaper. As a result, computers are now used for completely different purposes than that for which they were originally developed.

SELL A FIRM OR INDEPENDENTLY DEVELOP IT?

Remembering that many entrepreneurial business ideas cannot easily be sold is important. If a business idea revolves around an imagined opportunity, which is largely based on the founder's tacit knowledge, the idea may only be truly valuable if the founder develops it within his own firm (see section 4.2 for a definition and discussion of tacit knowledge). Extensive anecdotal evidence also indicates that many truly influential technology firms have been entrepreneurial firms for an extended period of time.[16]

Even if codified knowledge (unlike tacit knowledge) can be transmitted relatively easily, another problem—referred to as Arrow's information paradox—arises for those who want to sell their firm to an incumbent firm.[17] This paradox comes into play when a potential buyer of the firm wants to obtain detailed information regarding the technology/product/business idea to assess its potential and, in turn, its economic value. However, once the seller has disclosed this detailed knowledge to the potential buyer, the latter possesses the desired knowledge and thus no longer has any reason to pay for it.

---

15 Tellis and Chandy (2000) and Pagano and Schivardi (2003) find that large European firms are more innovative than small European firms.
16 Horowitz (2010).
17 Arrow (1962).

          © THE AUTHORS AND STUDENTLITTERATUR

Furthermore, the incumbent firm may not always have the right skills and organizational structure to develop new products and innovations that are purchased externally. Organizational inertia also makes altering the inner workings of an incumbent firm difficult. In such cases, the innovation could be more efficiently commercialized in a new firm that can customize its organizational structure and the skills of its workforce based on the innovation.[18]

6.4 The Significance of Risk Capital

Empirical studies have highlighted the importance of venture capitalists. Studies have found that venture capital firms play an important role, particularly with regard to the success of new technology-based firms.[19] Venture capitalists not only function as passive financiers but also play a more active role in the development of new firms and the commercialization of ideas. American venture capitalists actively influence the strategic choices that the entrepreneurial firm makes, for example, by ensuring that the firm implements active personnel policies and efficient marketing strategies. Firms supported by venture capital also commercialize new products faster.[20] Similar evidence is also available for European venture capital firms.[21]

Researchers have also found that an innovation is more likely to be commercialized through an incumbent firm's acquisition of an entrepreneurial firm when the entrepreneur has received venture capital.[22] Venture capitalists possess solid knowledge of the actors in the market, and they facilitate an effective trade in knowledge assets between entrepreneurs and incumbent firms. Research has also shown that a sale is more likely when the entry costs are high, for example, when entry requires substantial marketing efforts, and when the idea has a high level of intellectual property protection.[23] If the idea is not protected, the original owner might pass on the idea to other actors after the sale. A sale without patent protection may also

---

18 Leonard-Barton (1992).
19 Gompers and Lerner (2001).
20 Hellmann and Puri (2002).
21 Bottazzi, Da Rin and Hellmann (2004).
22 Gans, Hsu and Stern (2002).
23 Gans, Hsu and Stern (2002).

be problematic, as a seller might find explaining the value of the innovation without revealing it difficult (Arrow's information paradox). Research has also shown that firms in industries with active venture capitalists have higher degrees of patent activity, which will facilitate future sales.[24]

Venture capital firms adopt three different (but not mutually exclusive) roles with regard to the firms in which they invest. They may act as investors, coaches or partners. Studies have examined the behavioral differences among venture capital firms in Scandinavia and in California. These studies have found that, even if many similarities exist between venture capital firms on both sides of the Atlantic, the American venture capital firms act more like partners, whereas Scandinavian venture capital firms act more like pure investors. Therefore, the American venture capital firms may seem more involved, committed and active than their Scandinavian counterparts.[25]

In addition to the formal venture capital market, an informal risk capital market, in which business angels play a particularly important role, exists (see Box 5.2). Business angels are wealthy private persons with experience in entrepreneurial venturing and/or business leadership, who have the time, dedication and capital to invest in new, promising business ideas. Through the business angel's network, the firm gains access to additional capital and skills.[26] Business angels are especially important in terms of contributing seed capital and knowledge at an early stage of the firm's lifecycle—when obtaining financing from traditional sources, such as banks and venture capital firms, is difficult. Ideally, a business angel contributes both additional financing and entrepreneurial skills.

In *Figure 6.3*, the main phases of a firm's development are described in more detail. Frequently, the entrepreneur does not have sufficient means to finance the firm's development until its full potential can be realized. Growth often requires changes in ownership during the development from an idea to full-scale production, which gives rise to incentive problems that must be handled.

A new firm that is based on a unique idea is normally founded by one or a handful of individuals. Especially in high-tech industries—or if the firm is

---

24 Kortum and Lerner (2000).
25 Berglund (2011).
26 Landström (2007) and Kerr, Lerner and Schoar (2010).

© THE AUTHORS AND STUDENTLITTERATUR

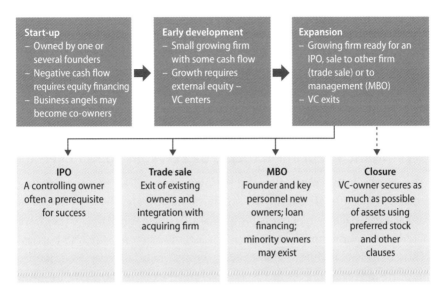

Figure 6.3 Central phases in the evolution of a firm. Source: Henrekson and Sanandaji (2016).

based on an untested idea—the risk is high, if calculating or estimating the risk is even possible. Even when the firm becomes successful, it usually takes a long time for the products to reach the market—and it takes even longer for the cash flow to turn positive. The shared risk is essentially incalculable, both for the founders and for the external stakeholders; it is genuinely uncertain. The returns on investment for new firms vary to an exceptionally high degree, and the probability that the entire investment will be lost is high. Three-quarters of American entrepreneurs who receive venture capital have a zero rate of return at exit. This risk profile, combined with low liquidity, means that the required rate of return will be high. If the return is not expected to be sufficiently high, the potential entrepreneur will not start a new firm.[27]

Creating the right incentives is exceedingly difficult as designing contracts that cover all contingencies is impossible. By the right incentives, we mean that the parties should strive to develop firms and innovations without wasting time, resources and skills—i.e., as efficiently as possible. When the parties are unable to write contracts that are sufficiently detailed to cover all

---

27 Hall and Woodward (2010).

possible outcomes, ownership and control must be specified *ex ante* between the parties involved. Innovative entrepreneurship is an activity in which the degree of uncertainty is unusually large, the value of assets is relation-specific and parties with vastly different interests must cooperate. To harmonize the incentives of the parties involved, a contractual tool is needed through which ownership and control can be conditioned on future outcomes.

SELF-FINANCING, DEBT FINANCING OR EXTERNAL EQUITY CAPITAL?

The entrepreneur must often use his own personal assets for financing because of asymmetric information, moral hazard and the high degree of uncertainty. Debt financing is problematic because the firms neither have fixed assets to mortgage nor a positive cash flow against which to borrow. Thus, banks are unable to finance risky entrepreneurial firms. Asymmetric information regarding the firm's potential and the risk of excessive optimism among founders/entrepreneurs also make obtaining debt financing more difficult.

However, few founders have enough capital to finance the firm until the cash flow turns positive or until the degree of uncertainty has declined sufficiently to make obtaining a bank loan possible. Therefore, many new firms may wither away prematurely because of a lack of capital for

Relation-specific assets: Assets with a specific value for certain actors in a specific context but without any alternative (or limited) use outside this context. A relation-specific asset, which is usually developed in a resource-intensive way, loses all or large parts of its value outside this context. For example, a certain production process requires buying custom-made equipment, and employees develop a highly specific set of skills for this purpose. If the production is discontinued, the specialized equipment and the developed skill set become worthless. The development of relation-specific assets requires trust between the parties and an agreement that prevents a stronger party from behaving opportunistically. Key employees must be able to ensure that they are not forced to leave the firm without receiving their fair share of the value that they have created. If no such trust exists, an entrepreneur and his financiers will likely be unable to develop the relation-specific assets necessary for building a successful firm.

© THE AUTHORS AND STUDENTLITTERATUR

development and expansion. Business angels are generally best suited to contribute equity capital during the initial seed phase. Uncertainty abates as more information becomes available regarding the business model's viability for the next phase of the firm's development. At this point, venture capital firms may consider financing the firm. Like business angels, they are not merely passive financiers; they also contribute other key inputs such as market expertise and network contacts, which increase the likelihood of the innovation's successful commercialization.

EXIT

When the firm has reached more solid ground—when its cash flow has stabilized, the risk has become calculable and forecasts regarding future growth and profitability can be made—the time has come for the venture capital firm to leave its ownership position, which can be achieved in a number of ways.

A first exit strategy involves an initial public offering (IPO). An IPO's success generally requires a controlling shareholder who has the incentive and ability to assume an active ownership role and to lead the firm in the medium run after the IPO. By giving enough stock options to management, usually the founder, these individuals become future major shareholders in the company if it is successfully developed, and an IPO can be more easily undertaken. Stock options also give the founder(s) strong incentives to remain in the firm and contribute to its development because he, in addition to securing ownership over a large part of the market capitalization created, has the opportunity to become a major owner of a public company in the future.

Today, selling the firm to another firm, normally a firm in the same industry, is the most common way of exiting. This is usually referred to as a *trade sale*. In this case, control over the firm is completely handed over to the buyer, and the entrepreneur/founder leaves the business, though with substantial financial assets that make starting new firms or acting as a business angel and/or venture capitalist possible.

If the firm performs really well, a third option involves the founder and other senior managers buying out the venture capital firm in a loan-financed buyout deal (a so-called management buyout or MBO), possibly in cooperation with a few private co-financiers with long-term perspectives.

In many cases, the firm does not develop according to the business plan, perhaps because the business idea does not reach its expected potential, the competition is tougher than initially forecast or the management—usually the founder—does not live up to expectations. Closing down or phasing out the firm may then be necessary. Successful commercialization is a long process, and skills and entrepreneurial talent are usually required to successfully generate and apply new knowledge.

6.5 Chapter Summary

In this chapter, we have learned the following:

- A successful commercialization process requires many unique and complementary skill sets. In addition to the entrepreneur, inventors, industrialists, skilled labor, venture capitalists, actors in secondary markets and competent customers are included in this so-called competence structure.
- A successful commercialization process often requires that firm ownership changes during the process from the inception of the idea to the finished product in the market.
- Large and small firms fulfill different roles in the innovation process and often complement one another. Large and mature firms tend to be better at incremental innovations that aim to improve existing products, whereas small and new firms are often better at developing radical innovations.
- Venture capital firms and business angels often play a decisive role by making a firm's development during the initial phases of its lifecycle possible. These actors not only contribute capital but also knowledge, experience and access to valuable networks.

© THE AUTHORS AND STUDENTLITTERATUR

Why Is Entrepreneurship Important?

In PART I, we discussed what entrepreneurship is, its function in the economic system and the different ways of measuring the degree of entrepreneurship. In this section, we shift our focus and ask what makes entrepreneurship so important. Why are so many people discussing the importance of entrepreneurship? Why are entrepreneurs referred to as key agents?

Chapter 7 addresses the crucial role played by entrepreneurship with regard to achieving economic growth and generating new jobs and employment. In chapter 8, the approach that we present in chapter 7 is pitted against the traditional view of the role played by the entrepreneur. In chapter 9, we discuss the research that seeks to prove the importance of entrepreneurship for economic development. In chapters 10 and 11, we present an analytical framework that shows how the extent of entrepreneurial activity in the economy is determined. These chapters provide a background for the next part of the book. Here, we introduce the concept of entrepreneurial rent, which is the compensation that the entrepreneur receives for exercising entrepreneurship.

The Importance of Entrepreneurship for Aggregate Economic Development

In the previous chapters, we discussed the concept of entrepreneurship, its function in the economic system and the different methods and metrics that have been used to quantify the extent of entrepreneurship. In the public debate, entrepreneurship is usually discussed in terms of its importance for the economic development of a country. In this chapter, we discuss why entrepreneurship is important and how it affects economic growth and job creation in the economy.

7.1 Entrepreneurship and Economic Growth

Basic economic models commonly assume that all individuals have perfect information about the economy in which they live and operate; however, this assumption does not reflect a reasonable approximation of reality. At any given time, no one knows all the prices and quantities that an economy offers, and no one knows all the available factors of production, their prices and all the production possibilities. In addition to a lack of information about present conditions, uncertainty regarding the future pervades. Most cases involve genuine uncertainty, as discussed by Frank Knight (see chapter 3). Even if an economic actor knows the current demand and the price of the product that she sells, she cannot know what conditions will be like tomorrow. New technologies, competitors, and legislation continuously change economic conditions, which affects actors' businesses. Furthermore, actors cannot insure themselves against every possible outcome and unforeseen problem that may arise in the future. For example, with respect to an innovation's introduction into a (new) market, accepting the premise of a known distribution of the potential outcomes and thus a calculable expected outcome is fundamentally impossible.

Therefore, unexploited opportunities will always exist, which has implications for the evolution and functioning of an economy.[1] An economy requires continuous experimentation—through examination, modification, renewal, and imitation—to find viable production and distribution methods. As Friedrich von Hayek once noted, information is not only important and incomplete (and thus expensive) but also *dispersed*.[2] Different individuals have information about different things. Even a country's most knowledgeable expert, economist or business owner is well informed only about a fraction of that country's firms and industries. Information is also frequently localized; a shopkeeper in Linköping probably knows more about the trade in her area than all the staff in Stockholm's consultancy firms combined. This telling example demonstrates the kind of tacit knowledge that cannot be captured and described in a superbly written analysis or consultant's report.

Because information in society is dispersed and fragmented, the economic decision-making process must be decentralized—which is one of Hayek's most important points. In fact, this idea constitutes the cornerstone of his criticism of the centrally planned economic systems in Eastern Europe.[3] As history has well documented, centrally governed states will fail to manage an economy comprising millions of workers and consumers, hundreds of thousands of firms and even more goods. Similarly, giant centralized corporations will not be able to efficiently focus on more than just a few markets.[4] Each actor in the economy possesses particular fragments of information, but no one has an overview of and control over all of it. Therefore, everyone should have the opportunity to act based on the information that she possesses.

A successful economy is driven by three fundamental processes:

- an identification process,
- a commercialization process, and
- a selection process.

---

1 Leibenstein (1968).
2 Hayek (1945).
3 Hayek (1989).
4 Some note that some large corporations are larger than the entire national economy of poor countries. Although true, this observation is not particularly informative. When markets in developed countries expand, specialized firms have the opportunity to grow large without controlling the market. For instance, Sweden's largest companies, Ericsson and Volvo, each employ less than half a percent of Sweden's labor force.

 © THE AUTHORS AND STUDENTLITTERATUR

The identification process is characterized by the ability to recognize (or generate) new ideas and innovations. The commercialization process is characterized by the desire and opportunity to introduce innovations in a market. In the selection process, less viable innovations are weeded out, and innovations of higher quality replace existing ones. Thus, economies are constantly subjected to transformation pressures. In a dynamic economy, existing products, firms and perhaps even entire markets will disappear, and new products and firms that are better and more efficient will continually replace them. Moreover, the birth of new markets and/or niches will serve as a natural laboratory, in which new ideas are tested against old ones, where the most successful ideas will survive while those lacking prospects will be phased out to free up resources. Joseph Schumpeter aptly called this process "creative destruction."[5]

THE IMPORTANCE OF COMPETITION

Competition in the marketplace can be considered a problem-solving process, through which valuable knowledge is sought, tested and accepted or rejected.[6] Through the interaction between buyers and sellers in a market, useful ideas (from the buyer's perspective) will survive and thrive, whereas impractical ideas are weeded out. In particular, competition in a marketplace serves three functions:

- *Identifying and testing knowledge.* The actors that are the most capable of identifying new valuable knowledge and successfully commercializing its inherent utility in the form of innovative products in the market will generate a profit and survive.
- *Disseminating knowledge.* Useful knowledge will be disseminated in an economy. Competitors will try to imitate (and perhaps improve) what has been proved successful in the market, successful ideas will be imitated in other markets, and satisfied customers will speak well of products to friends and family. Rising prices in a market work as a signal

---

5 See, for instance, Mantzavinos (2001) or Eliasson (1996) for an in-depth discussion.
6 See Kasper, Streit and Boettke (2012) for a comprehensive discussion regarding the role of competition.

of changing conditions, to which the market actors respond directly. Price changes disseminate information quickly even if the underlying causes are not necessarily known. A higher price for a certain type of raw material makes customers more interested in finding substitutes, and they will buy fewer products that use that raw material.

- *Correcting errors.* A well-functioning market with free entry and competition has a built-in self-correcting function that, through firms' income statements, shows what customers value. If knowledge and capital are not used in a value-creating way, a firm will reallocate the resources or exit the market. Failing firms also play an important role in the market by showing other actors what does not work and what is not sufficiently valued.

Assuming that market actors have perfect information in models and theories conceals the crucial role of the market. A market is so much more than supply, demand and a static equilibrium price. Rather, the market and the market process provide a mechanism with which to handle the information problems that characterize all existing economies. For this mechanism to function properly, actors must have the right incentives in the entrepreneurial discovery process, which requires that property rights be respected, that prices be set freely and that firms be allowed to make a profit or suffer a loss.

THE ENTREPRENEURIAL DISCOVERY PROCESS

The entrepreneurial discovery process, on which entire economies are based, is quite similar to the scientific research process (in an ideal case).[7] In science, a person begins with a problem that she wants to solve or understand. Based on the problem in question, hypotheses are formulated, which essentially amount to educated guesses. These hypotheses are then tested against "reality" to determine whether the hypotheses in question can be supported. In other words, science is nothing more than an ongoing process of testing hypotheses, whereby ideas are tested and either rejected or retained, thus

---

7 This idealized notion of science comes from philosopher Karl Popper. See Harper (1996), Sull (2004) and Berglund, Hellström and Sjölander (2007) for an in-depth discussion of the similarities between the scientific and entrepreneurial processes.

   © THE AUTHORS AND STUDENTLITTERATUR

contributing to an increased understanding and providing the basis for new ideas (to be tested). New problems and new attempts to solve these problems arise as hypotheses are tested. Hence, scientific work is an ongoing trial-and-error process that never ends.

The entrepreneurial discovery process follows the same logic. An entrepreneur never has access to perfect information, and she must make "guesses" regarding potential entrepreneurial opportunities. The opportunities that a potential entrepreneur perceives, or about which she "guesses," depend on the information available to her, i.e., previously acquired knowledge and her personal characteristics, such as her creativity, perseverance and risk aversion. An entrepreneur can test her idea using market research or consult experts in the area; however, the final test does not take place until the entrepreneur introduces her product in the market to test the opportunity that she believes to have uncovered. Based on the market response, the entrepreneur may reject the idea or modify it to better match consumer preferences and market demand.

Both the scientific and entrepreneurial processes are strategies in which one aims to orient oneself in a world filled with imperfect and incomplete information. Both processes have evolved to respond to this insufficiency; experimentation and testing serve as means of discarding mistakes and erroneous judgments and learning what works as the basis for finding a workable way forward. No endpoint or stationary equilibrium is ever reached in this ongoing evolutionary process, in which actors continuously test their way toward new and (hopefully) better solutions.

A SCHEMATIC MODEL

Figure 7.1 schematically illustrates the crucial importance of entrepreneurship and the market process for economic growth and increased prosperity. New entrepreneurial discoveries are identified or generated and are commercialized in the market, where a selection process takes place. This market process has both direct and more long-term indirect effects.[8]

There are two direct effects. First, new capacities and new structures develop if the entrepreneurial commercialization is successful, either through

---

8 Fritsch and Mueller (2004).

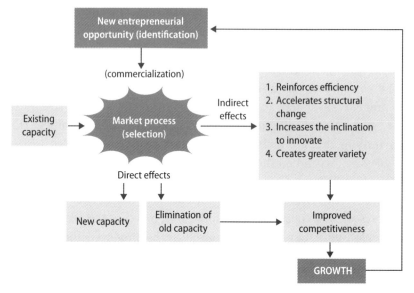

Figure 7.1 Entrepreneurship and growth. Source: Adapted from Fritsch and Mueller (2004).

establishment of a new firm or through the expansion of an existing firm. Second, obsolete capacity may be phased out. Specifically, new firms may replace old firms that are no longer viable, or unprofitable new firms may be forced to close down.

In addition to these direct effects, at least four indirect effects that affect the supply side arise during this process:

- a reinforcement of efficiency,
- an acceleration of structural change,
- an increase in the inclination to innovate, and
- an increase in the variety of goods and services offered.

These indirect effects are crucial for economic development in the long run.

In other words, entrepreneurship directly contributes to economic growth as successful firms expand, employ new workers and increase profits. Such a contribution is partly offset by the negative effect of the elimination or shrinkage of other firms on growth. Given that this new capacity allows more

 © THE AUTHORS AND STUDENTLITTERATUR

efficient operation and the production of more highly valued products, the net effect is positive. Moreover, this positive effect contributes to the indirect effects that drive sustainable growth in the long run. The scope and quality of the entrepreneurial activity determines how quickly and aptly an economy seizes the entrepreneurial opportunities that exist in a market economy.[9]

When an innovation is implemented, it almost invariably engenders chain reactions, which create new entrepreneurial opportunities in what Swedish economist Erik Dahmén has referred to as "development blocks."[10] Dahmén also distinguished between "competitiveness," which he saw as a static concept, and "development power," which is a dynamic concept. Translated to the terminology used here, development power can be said to measure an economy's capacity for entrepreneurial renewal. According to Dahmén, development power depends on firms' innovation potential, which is determined by the quality of the institutional framework.

Therefore, entrepreneurship often has a self-reinforcing effect. New discoveries and products generate new exploitable opportunities, which set a self-reinforcing and dynamic process in motion. In *Figure 7.1*, this process is illustrated by the arrow pointing from "growth" back to "new entrepreneurial opportunity," as entrepreneurship engenders new entrepreneurial opportunities. The emergence of new entrepreneurs also has a demonstration effect: the establishment of a firm sends a signal to other potential entrepreneurs to establish firms as well.[11] This analysis of the entrepreneurial process can be linked to our previous discussion regarding equilibrating and disequilibrating entrepreneurship (see *Figure 3.2* and *3.3*), in which one form enables the other.

THE IMPORTANCE OF NEW FIRMS

The indirect effects, which we discussed in relation to *Figure 7.1*, are often connected to new firms in particular; in practice, such a connection implies that an influx of new entrepreneurial firms is necessary for the development, renewal and transformation of an economy. Even if intrapreneurs can carry

---

9 Ovaska (2014).
10 Dahmén (1970).
11 Verheul et al. (2001).

© THE AUTHORS AND STUDENTLITTERATUR

out entrepreneurship in incumbent firms, new and (at least initially) small firms will inevitably be required to sustain a high degree of innovativeness. Although large firms are responsible for the bulk of R&D spending, smaller firms have proved to be much more innovative in certain industries, notably in ICT and other high-tech industries.

Other scholars, who have emphasized the key role of new firms, have also emphasized the importance of variety in relation to economic growth.[12] No new firm is ever identical to an existing firm, and thus, it has at least some unique features. The formation of new firms therefore contributes to some variety in supply and to a wider spectrum of methods of production, distribution and problem solving.

Hence, increased competition in a market unsurprisingly tends to occur via the emergence of new firms and an increase in the number of firms. However, an increased number of firms not only increases the competition for discovering new and exploitable opportunities but also (indirectly) creates increased opportunities for new firms to specialize and find their own niches. The way that competition affects the growth of cities is an illustrative example here. Indeed, increased competition, measured by the number of firms, has been shown to have a positive effect on the growth of cities.[13]

These indirect effects can arise even if the newly founded firms do not survive or grow. The existence of a competitive environment and the emergence of a selection process are the crucial elements. In fact, a competitive environment sometimes exists, even though no new firms have been founded and no explicit selection process has begun. If incumbents know that new firms can enter the market, potential competition—or market contestability—may be sufficient to maintain market discipline and innovativeness.[14]

Large firms with market power—based on either the possession of unique products or the protection of intellectual property rights (patents, licensing rights, trademarks)—are able to act monopolistically, which is likely to lower social welfare. Nobel Laureate George Stigler revolutionized his field of research by demonstrating that whether a firm acts monopolistically

---

12 Cohen and Klepper (1992).
13 Feldman and Audretsch (1999) and Glaeser et al. (1992).
14 See, for instance, Audretsch, Baumol and Burke (2001).

© THE AUTHORS AND STUDENTLITTERATUR

depends on its room for maneuver rather than its market share or size.[15] This room for maneuver is, in turn, a function of consumers' ability to switch to other products that meet the same needs and of the ability of new competitors to enter the market. When a large firm acts monopolistically, profit opportunities arise, which tends to attract competitors.

In addition, some kind of outside pressure always seems necessary to maintain efficiency in successful firms. Lacking contestants, firms tend to lose their edge over time, growing increasingly bureaucratic and inflexible and thus less attentive to value creation for their customers.[16] Even if a firm is using the most advanced production technologies, it can still suffer from production inefficiencies for a number of reasons: (i) a firm's management decisions are frequently based on habits, norms and standards rather than a maximization principle, which tends to result in inefficient decision making over time if the competitive pressure is low or non-existent, and (ii) employment contracts are always imperfect, particularly with respect to employee effort, which means that employees are able to underperform.

Both of these problems—that firms use their market power and that firms eventually lose their competitive edge—are considerably mitigated by the possibility for entrepreneurship and new firm entry. The crucial factor here is the *possibility* that markets are contestable—not whether a new firm actually enters the market. The risk of potential competitors taking over a market can often produce sufficient pressure on incumbent firms to maintain quality and abstain from excessive pricing. Microsoft is a case in point. Despite its extremely large market share in its industry, it has been forced to consider the threat of potential competitors when pricing its products.[17]

Therefore, whether possible improvements or innovations in production arise in existing or whether new firms enter the market is not pivotal. New firms that are outcompeted should not be considered an unnecessary waste of resources; instead, they should be regarded as a necessary investment—a part of the evolutionary process of the market economy. Because of the inherent uncertainty and perhaps because of psychological effects, too many entrants sometimes render new markets and industries inefficient. The earliest phases

15 Stigler (1968).
16 Leibenstein (1966).
17 Davis and Murphy (2000).

of the automobile industry, the computer industry and the IT sector in the late 1990s are three salient examples. The returns for those who become successful in these new industries are extremely high, but the likelihood of failure is great. Many firms have simultaneously entered new and promising industries, and few have survived. In the short run, this has resulted in crises and elimination. The industries soon rebounded, though only after incurring sizable costs in the form of an initial waste of resources.

The significance of competition for productivity growth has also been confirmed in a number of studies. For example, the OECD has found that a smaller portion (20–40 percent) of the growth in labor productivity occurs as a direct result of firms entering and leaving the market. However, new venture creation has a greater effect on total factor productivity (TFP), where a large part of the productivity increase results from new firms entering the market, as new firms that survive often do something innovatively different (and better) with the resources at their disposal.[18]

The relationship between entrepreneurship and growth operates not only directly but also indirectly through the effects of entrepreneurship on efficiency, transformation, innovation and variety in every firm, including established ones. Therefore, entrepreneurial activity is critical for productivity growth.

In the discussion above, we have shown the importance of new firms in general. In the previous chapters, we downplayed the importance of new (and small) firms and instead emphasized the importance of gazelles and high-growth firms. Of course, successful and rapidly growing innovative firms directly contribute to aggregate economic growth. However, new firms that grow at a slow pace, that do not grow at all or that fail to survive the competition also contribute to the economy through their effect on other firms.

7.2 Entrepreneurship and Job Creation

A priori, there are compelling reasons to presume that increased entrepreneurship also has a positive effect on employment, but the relationship between entrepreneurship and job creation is not as straightforward as one

---

18 OECD (2005).

   © THE AUTHORS AND STUDENTLITTERATUR

might think at first glance. New workers will not necessarily be hired when entrepreneurs found new firms or when existing firms expand by exploiting new opportunities. Rather, expansion can occur via a more intense use of capital. Therefore, for an incumbent firm, the number of employees may be reduced despite the increased value added. As we have seen, entrepreneurship involves finding new and more efficient combinations of factors of production. In the short run, the result of successful entrepreneurship comes mainly in the form of higher productivity. If the most efficient firms and if the firms with the highest labor productivity survive in the market, fewer employees will gradually be needed for any given production level.

However, starting a firm leads to employment for at least the person who starts the firm. Normally, a successful and expanding firm will sooner or later demand more labor, as workers (skilled and/or unskilled) are needed to complement the entrepreneurial function. Given that the number of firms is increasing, it is reasonable to believe that this increase implies an increased demand for labor.

The exploitation of entrepreneurial opportunities not only helps create new jobs but also destroys jobs. Although many new jobs will be created in new and growing firms, jobs will be lost in new firms that do not survive in the market and in old firms that are eliminated or downsized as other firms enter the market or expand. This is the employment effect of creative destruction. From an employment perspective, the net generation, i.e., the number of new jobs created minus the number of existing jobs lost, is what matters.

In fact, to understand the total effect of entrepreneurship on employment, an examination of its longer-term impact on competitiveness in the economy is required. Given that increased productivity and perhaps lower prices lead to increased production volumes, higher labor productivity does not necessary lead to lower employment. Instead, increased labor productivity is a prerequisite for the maintenance and expansion of a firm, which seems especially true for firms that operate in the global market. Available resources may also be channeled to other areas, where they can be put to better use.[19]

---

19 See Audretsch (2002) for a more thorough discussion.

© THE AUTHORS AND STUDENTLITTERATUR

The employment effects of entrepreneurship can be linked to the discussion illustrated in *Figure 7.1* regarding the direct and indirect effects of entrepreneurship. As shown in *Figure 7.2*, the employment effects can be divided into three phases:[20]

- a commercialization phase,
- a selection phase, and
- a final phase with long-run effects.

In the first phase (the commercialization phase), which occurs when a new firm is founded or when an incumbent firm expands, employment normally increases as a direct result of new or increased activity. In the next phase (the selection phase), employment decreases because older capacities have been scrapped or because the new firm is not competitive. In the third and final phase, employment increases once again because of the indirect supply-side effects of this process in the form of improved competitiveness. A favorable business climate today provides sustainable employment tomorrow because it helps maintain competitiveness by increasing efficiency, contributing to structural change, strengthening the inclination toward innovation and increasing variety in the marketplace.[21]

The final phase is the most important one for long-term job creation in the economy. The immediate direct effects of a new firm do not have the most significant positive effects on employment. Thus, an occasionally considerable time lag occurs before new firms and entrepreneurship have substantial effects on aggregate employment. In the short run, increased entrepreneurial activities are not expected to have a major impact on employment statistics, and it may take as long as six to seven years before the positive effects are discernible in the aggregate employment statistics.[22]

A specific mechanism by which entrepreneurship can be expected to reduce unemployment is its contribution to increased allocative efficiency in the labor market. In economic analyses, unemployment is largely viewed as a matching problem. The economy cannot quickly and cost-efficiently

---

20 Fritsch and Mueller (2004).
21 Fritsch and Mueller (2004) and Carree and Thurik (2006).
22 Fritsch and Mueller (2004).

© THE AUTHORS AND STUDENTLITTERATUR

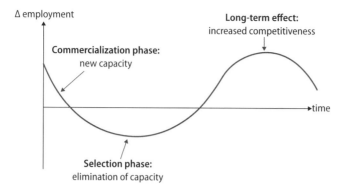

Figure 7.2 Entrepreneurship and employment.
Note: The exploitation of entrepreneurial opportunities not only creates new jobs but also destroys jobs. Jobs are created in new and growing firms, but they also disappear in the new firms that do not survive and in existing firms that are eliminated or downsized when new firms enter the market and competition is intensified. The employment effects of entrepreneurship can be divided into three phases. In the commercialization phase, when a new firm is founded or an established firm expands, employment increases as a direct result of new or increased activity. In the selection phase, employment declines because older capacities have been scrapped or because the new firms have not survived. In the final phase, employment increases again because of indirect supply-side effects that improve competitiveness. Source: Based on Fritsch and Mueller (2004).

find the equilibrium at which all resources are fully utilized. Heterogeneous workers and employers are searching for the best possible options in a world characterized by imperfect information and incomplete knowledge, which means that many job seekers remain unemployed for a long period. Consequently, entrepreneurship may reduce unemployment through a potentially very important mechanism, as one of the main functions of entrepreneurship is to (re)allocate existing and available resources in a world characterized by imperfect information and (frequently high) transaction costs.

Self-employment also functions as an alternative route into the labor market, not least because it offers a way of circumventing rules and agreements that inhibit the demand for certain types of labor. Such regulations include the minimum wage, standard rate compensation policies in unionized industries, regulations for working hours and mandated labor security. However, not all self-employment constitutes entrepreneurship according to the definition used in this book (section 4.1).

A high rate of unemployment may very well have a positive effect on the self-employment rate. For example, a high level of regional unemployment can induce many people to feel compelled to start their own firms in order to generate an alternative source of income. Thus, a high unemployment rate increases the level of necessity self-employment; accordingly, the correlation between unemployment and self-employment can be either positive or negative.[23] The relationship between the level of unemployment and necessity self-employment is expected to be positive, and in this case, causality goes from unemployment to new venture creation. With regard to opportunity-based entrepreneurship, the correlation with unemployment is instead expected to be negative, and causality runs in both directions: a low level of opportunity-based entrepreneurship leads to more unemployment, and depressed conditions imply fewer entrepreneurial opportunities. Nevertheless, some of those who are pushed into necessity self-employment because of high unemployment may become entrepreneurs (see *Table 4.1*).

7.3 Chapter Summary

In this chapter, we have learned the following:

- Because information in society is dispersed and fragmented, the economic decision-making process must be decentralized to be efficient.
- A successful market economy is supported by an identification, commercialization and selection process.
- The market process has a direct and indirect effect, and it affects a country's economic development and growth. Entrepreneurs play a crucial role in ensuring that this process is efficient.
- Entrepreneurship may directly contribute to economic development and growth as successful firms expand, employ new workers and increase profits.

---

23 See the various GEM reports for further discussion. For instance, Minniti, Bygrave and Autio (2006), Bosma and Levie (2010) and Singer, Amorós and Moska (2014).

   © THE AUTHORS AND STUDENTLITTERATUR

- In the long run, indirect supply-side effects arise from a well-functioning market process with associated competitive pressures that secure efficiency, accelerate structural change, increase the inclination to innovate and produce greater variety. This is the most crucial mechanism for an economy's development in the long run.
- The relationship between entrepreneurship and job creation is complex and far from obvious. Jobs will be lost when firms fail because of competition. In the long run, successful entrepreneurship results in increased competitiveness and helps maintain a high and sustainable level of employment. As such, it often takes a long time for employment statistics to reflect the positive effects of entrepreneurship.

CHAPTER 8

Entrepreneurship in Mainstream Growth Theory

In the previous chapter, we saw that entrepreneurs play a central role in economic growth. In this chapter, we juxtapose this view with how the entrepreneurial function is discussed in mainstream economic growth theories. Do entrepreneurs and the entrepreneurial function play a prominent role in growth theory, or is entrepreneurship marginalized?

8.1 Traditional Growth Theory and Entrepreneurship

A detailed analysis of the mechanisms in the growth theories developed in mainstream neoclassical economics during the postwar period clearly shows that the aspects emphasized in this book thus far are largely absent from these theories. Traditional growth theories attribute the economic growth that occurs in an economy to the accumulation of different inputs, such as labor and capital. By postulating mathematical relationships between different inputs and production, conclusions regarding the optimal savings ratio and the maximum rate of growth, given a certain input, can be drawn. According to these theories, growth results from the interaction among investments, population growth and consumers' propensity to save. During the first three decades of the post-war period, growth policy was greatly inspired by these theories, investments were promoted through favorable tax treatment and other measures (e.g., tax deductions and allowances for accelerated depreciation), and labor supply was encouraged through subsidized childcare and separate (instead of household) taxation combined with progressive taxation, which provided strong incentives for married or co-habiting households to have two income earners.

In this standard neoclassical theory, growth does not depend on the exploitation of untapped opportunities, as they are simply assumed to not exist. All factors of production and production possibilities are exploited, and they will always be exploited optimally. If the level of investment rises, thereby increasing the capital stock, growth will automatically follow. This basic theory ignores the renewal function, which entrepreneurship research has found to be crucial, and it essentially classifies firms, business ideas and activities as givens and does not consider the fact that someone has furnished these ideas or created these firms. How capital is organized, structured and used is a non-existing problem, and managing and controlling production becomes trivial, as capital is assumed homogeneous. Instead, the main problem involves determining the optimal amount of capital (and thereby the savings rate). Qualitative aspects, the purposes for which capital is to be used, and the ways in which firms should be organized are not addressed in this theory.[1]

Hence, the traditional neoclassical approach postulates an unambiguous and precisely defined relationship between inputs and production. However, empirical evidence has shown that changes in the capital stock and in the labor force can account for only a small fraction of total economic growth, perhaps as little as 20 percent. The remainder of the growth has been attributed to technological change, which remained unexplained in first-generation models.[2]

An entrepreneur-oriented perspective considers the reality that someone must combine available or new factors of production and thereby create a supply of goods and services, which may then lead to growth and increased social welfare. This process does not happen automatically. For the elegant mathematical production functions to capture what really happens, entrepreneurs must be able to discover, create and develop potential opportunities with the available resources. In fact, because the theory

---

1 MIT professor Paul A. Samuelson, the most influential economist of the post-war period, has coined the term the "shmoo"-view of capital, where capital is infinitely elastic and entirely fungible so that it may be reallocated at no cost (Foss et al. 2006). Shmoos are identical and fungible characters in an American cartoon for children.
2 Solow (1956, 1957). The unexplained part was aptly named the Solow residual in honor of Robert Solow, the MIT economist who developed the seminal neoclassical growth model. Solow was awarded the Nobel Prize in 1987 for his contributions to growth theory.

  © THE AUTHORS AND STUDENTLITTERATUR

assumes that no untapped opportunities exist, it implicitly assumes that the most brilliant entrepreneurs imaginable exist and that they pursue the most socially value-creating ventures available.

8.2 New Growth Theory, Knowledge Capital and R&D

Concurrent with the rise of the knowledge society, traditional growth theory has expanded to incorporate investments in knowledge capital and the development and diffusion of new technologies.[3] Knowledge capital is linked to single individuals, where it is usually termed human capital, or to firms, where it is usually termed structural capital. Structural capital enables human capital to function in firms. Firms own structural capital, and it remains with them when people leave. In addition to proprietary software, processes, patents, and trademarks, such capital includes a firm's brand, organization, information system, and proprietary databases.

In addition, firms are assumed to benefit from the general development of a country or industry. Today, many scholars argue that R&D, innovation and technological change drive a country's economic growth. The theoretical foundation for this notion was developed by Paul Romer and Robert Lucas at the University of Chicago in the 1980s.[4] These growth theories are commonly denoted endogenous because technological change, which is assumed to explain long-term growth, is determined within the model. In previous models, technological change was determined outside the model, remaining unexplained. As such, the first-generation theories are usually denoted exogenous.

The R&D sector is central in endogenous growth models. Not only does it produce both firm-specific knowledge and publicly available knowledge, R&D activity in combination with capital accumulation and the growth of labor input also determines the rate of growth. The amount of useful new knowledge produced is determined by the amount of labor allocated to the R&D sector (including universities), the size of society's knowledge stock and the productivity of R&D workers. The size of the knowledge stock is then assumed to affect productivity growth.

---

3 This section and the following section draw on Braunerhjelm, Eklund and Henrekson (2012), chapter 2).

4 The seminal papers are Romer (1986, 1990) and Lucas (1988).

© THE AUTHORS AND STUDENTLITTERATUR

PART II WHY IS ENTREPRENEURSHIP IMPORTANT?

Knowledge is undoubtedly crucial for economic growth. The great leaps in human material development—such as the First Industrial Revolution in the late 18th century and the Second Industrial Revolution a century later—were based on new knowledge, new technologies and revolutionary innovations. The same applies to the ongoing ICT revolution. Nonetheless, the empirical effect of investments in knowledge (measured as R&D or education) on economic growth is unclear. Some studies find a positive relationship, while other studies find weak, or even non-existent, support for the hypothesis that investment in R&D results in more rapid growth. The simple correlation between R&D investments and growth for the OECD countries in the 2000s is actually weakly negative (see *Figure 8.1*). However, at a lower level, such as the industry or firm level, the results are more robust and generally positive, especially with regard to private R&D investments. Generating positive effects from government-financed R&D in the business sector is difficult, while publicly funded basic research appears to have positive effects, even if the time lag is often substantial.[5]

The weak correlation between research and growth in Sweden has been referred to as "the Swedish paradox."[6] Astrid Kander and Olof Ejermo have examined this paradox, and they argue that finding a direct relationship between R&D and growth is difficult, as there is no reason to believe that there is a direct mechanical relationship between R&D and growth. Instead, an unfavorable ecosystem for entrepreneurship can render the relationship weak or non-existent.[7] Furthermore, they find that the relationship is weak primarily in rapidly growing industries.

Knowledge-based growth models examine how and how much knowledge (measured in various ways) is produced, which partly explains this relatively weak relationship. They do not explain how knowledge is diffused and transformed into economically valuable goods and services, and the explanatory factors that are measured and included in these models (e.g., R&D expenditure as a share of GDP, the share of the population with a tertiary education) do not necessarily capture the mechanisms that are most relevant for the growth and transformation of economies.

---

5 Bergman (2012), Sala-i-Martin (2002) and Svensson (2013).
6 Edquist and McKelvey (1998).
7 Kander and Ejermo (2009) and Ejermo, Kander and Henning (2011).

  © THE AUTHORS AND STUDENTLITTERATUR

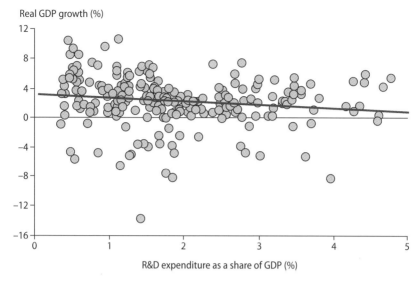

Figure 8.1 The relationship between annual GDP growth and R&D expenditure in 33 OECD countries, 2001–2009. Source: Braunerhjelm (2012).

These shortcomings have inspired researchers to conduct empirical studies that have shown that knowledge and R&D should be supplemented with entrepreneurial activities, competition and mobility across industries and firms in order for economic growth to be realized.[8] Institutions— laws, regulations and standards—that structure the economic and social interaction of the agents who transform knowledge into goods and services are also crucial for growth.

While modern growth theories have taken important steps toward integrating technological change and some of its determinants, they ignore the crucial role of entrepreneurs. R&D alone is insufficient. Rather, as with capital and labor, someone must apply and combine the results from R&D investments with other factors of production to generate growth. In reality, no mechanical relationship exists between increased R&D spending and more rapid growth; new ideas and inventions are just the first step in the

8 See, for instance, Holcombe (1998), who claims that "entrepreneurship is the engine of economic progress," and Baumol (2002b). Another mechanism is the mobility of human capital (Moen 2005).

innovation and commercialization process. For R&D investments to benefit the economy at large, someone must be able and willing to exploit new knowledge—for example, by commercializing new products or introducing new production methods. Entrepreneurs play a crucial role in this context.

Neither Henry Ford nor Bill Gates invented the technologies on which they relied to build their successful companies. However, they exploited the available resources and available knowledge in novel and value-creating ways. They were entrepreneurs, and their exploitation of new knowledge—rather than the new knowledge itself—generated growth. Focusing solely on R&D with respect to growth ignores the need for entrepreneurship and the commercial application of new knowledge. An increase in the amount of knowledge and inventions results in economic growth only if they can be put to good use in the form of innovations, which are mainly generated by entrepreneurial firms. An economy that allocates a large part of its resources to R&D but lacks an equivalent level of entrepreneurial capacity to exploit the new knowledge and inventions generated by R&D cannot be said to have used its scarce and most sophisticated resources efficiently. New firms and business ideas are necessary to take full advantage of the commercial potential that results from the development of new knowledge.

This distinction is useful for explaining why some countries are marred by stagnation and others are stuck in underdevelopment. A country can experience weak technological change not only because new knowledge is not generated but also because the new knowledge is not applied or utilized in the business sector. For example, on the one hand, the Islamic civilization of the 12th century seemingly suffered from a lack of new inventions, but the knowledge that was available was fully used and exploited. On the other hand, the Soviet Union and the Roman Empire are usually noted as examples of societies that produced new knowledge and generated many inventions but did not effectively convert the new knowledge into valuable goods and services because of an unfavorable entrepreneurial climate.[9] Another example is Central America before the arrival of the Europeans, whose inhabitants had invented the wheel but only used it in small toys and for ritual purposes.[10]

---

9 Mokyr (1990) and Baumol (2002b).
10 Diehl and Mandeville (1987).

 © THE AUTHORS AND STUDENTLITTERATUR

8.3 New Growth Theory and Entrepreneurship

First-generation knowledge-based (endogenous) growth models were modified in the early 1990s to include a specific type of entrepreneur.[11] These models claimed to capture Schumpeter's creative destruction. At best, this claim is only partially true. Models of this kind analyze specific and distinct types of innovation and entrepreneurship. They most closely approximate R&D in large pharmaceutical companies, which shares relatively few similarities with entrepreneurship and innovation more generally. Consequently, the conclusions drawn from these models with respect to economic policy are not readily applicable to innovation and entrepreneurship, not least because of the underrated role and importance of small and new firms. These models are also unable to capture the growth that emanates from organizational improvements and tougher competition, which accelerates both technological development and the diffusion of technology between firms via imitation.

The criticism leveled against newer endogenous growth models takes various forms, but it is mainly directed at how knowledge is disseminated and transformed. While the weakness of earlier exogenous growth models was that knowledge was treated as "manna from heaven," knowledge-based models are unable to explain how knowledge is applied and disseminated. The transformation of R&D-generated knowledge into economically valuable goods and services is now assumed to work efficiently; thus, this transformation becomes exogenous in such models. Furthermore, in these models, the utilization of new knowledge is not associated with any cost to the firms. This shortcoming likely explains why the empirical literature does not find unequivocal support for the hypothesis that investments in R&D—and to some degree in education—have positive effects on growth.

However, the most recent empirical studies have identified some of the mechanisms that are particularly important for the dissemination of knowledge and its transformation into economically valuable commodities. Among these mechanisms, we find entrepreneurship, high-tech clusters and labor mobility.[12] In this new growth theory, the importance of knowledge

---

11 Important pioneers among these so-called neo-Schumpeterian model builders are Segerstrom (1991), Aghion and Howitt (1992) and Cheng and Dinopoulos (1992).
12 See Braunerhjelm (2011, 2012) for a more extensive discussion.

spillovers (i.e., the ideas and knowledge disseminated or exchanged between firms in different sectors and areas of application) is often emphasized. The knowledge generated within an organization will also benefit other firms and organizations in the long run. Nevertheless, how knowledge spillovers operate in practice is analyzed only rudimentarily in most theoretical models.[13] Such models focus on firms and usually assume that the number of firms remains unchanged. However, knowledge and ideas are available in and developed by individuals, not firms themselves; the number of firms is hardly constant over time, and even if the number of firms were relatively constant, new firms would replace exiting firms over time.

Entrepreneurs may also be an important piece of the puzzle in these expanded theories and models. An innovation's estimated value may differ significantly between different individuals, and only a very small proportion of all inventions and ideas will ultimately result in profitable innovations. For example, research has shown that only an estimated one to two percent of all the inventions that originate from the most advanced and expensive university research generate significant economic returns.[14] Therefore, the individuals or firms that have generated new knowledge may believe that this knowledge has no commercial value, whereas others may judge it differently. Furthermore, competent individuals may be willing to leave a (large) firm and bring new knowledge or a business idea to other firms, sectors and regions, if such a move is practical and legally possible. (Of course, in such cases, the firm has been unable to fully protect itself against such actions through patents or other types of intellectual property rights protection.) Individual knowledge may also be made useful and further disseminated in an economic system through the creation of a new firm.[15] For example, Xerox and Apple were started because the founders of these firms did not have the support and requisite resources to pursue their ideas about photocopiers and computers in the firms in which they were employed.[16] Other important channels for

---

13 See, for instance, Acs et al. (2009), Braunerhjelm et al. (2010) and Audretsch and Thurik (2004) for further discussion.

14 Carlsson and Fridh (2002).

15 See Audretsch (1995). For start-ups based on research at Xerox, see Chesbrough and Rosenbloom (2002).

16 Audretsch and Thurik (2004).

    © THE AUTHORS AND STUDENTLITTERATUR

> **Cluster**: A cluster is a geographic concentration of interconnected firms that compete and cooperate to produce related products. Typical examples include Silicon Valley outside San Francisco and Kista in Stockholm. Clusters stimulate innovation, learning and knowledge spillovers as people move between firms in a cluster.

the dissemination of knowledge in the economic system include incumbent firms' acquisitions of start-ups that have generated new knowledge or that employ competent key individuals.[17]

ALTERNATIVE APPROACHES

Over the past few decades, an alternative approach to endogenous growth models has been developed: the evolutionary economics approach. In this tradition, interacting dynamic processes govern the ways in which economies or industries evolve. Most prominent among these are the mechanisms that ensure variation in product space, selection (market competition), and knowledge transmission over time (routines). A routine is a pattern of behavior that occurs repeatedly but that is subject to change if conditions change.[18] The evolutionary approach emphasizes the central role of the continuous selection of firms and products that appear in the market. Many different models have been developed in this tradition; however, they are vague with respect to policy conclusions and are more concerned with determining how industries and technologies evolve over time than with identifying policies that promote growth and social welfare.[19]

A parallel, and somewhat overlapping, research strand has aimed to integrate newer endogenous growth models with insights emanating from industrial organization research. For instance, such research has focused on how entry barriers, strategic R&D and strategic collaboration influence innovation and growth.[20] The findings of this research suggest that

---

17 See Ghio et al. (2015) for a research survey on knowledge spillovers and entrepreneurship.
18 See Orsenigo (2009) for a survey.
19 Nelson and Winter (1982) provide a seminal contribution. See also Acs et al. (2009).
20 Acemoglu, Aghion and Zilibotti (2006), Aghion et al. (2004, 2006) and Howitt (2007).

competition and innovation interact and affect both innovation and new firm creation. Therefore, entry barriers should be low to stimulate efficiency and productivity.[21] How low entry barriers affect existing firms depends on where the firm is located in terms of technology—more technologically advanced firms are expected to increase their investments in innovation to respond to potential competition, while less sophisticated firms are expected to reduce or discontinue their innovation activities if the threat is deemed too costly to address. In the literature, this is referred to as the escape–entry effect or the discouragement effect.[22]

R&D, inventions and new knowledge generation seemingly cannot be equated to entrepreneurship. However, new knowledge does create opportunities for entrepreneurial discoveries.[23] Entrepreneurs can be considered agents who transform new knowledge into business opportunities, and they may realize these opportunities by, for example, creating new firms, which will contribute, in turn, to the dissemination of knowledge in the economy. This process contributes to growth and development, even if entrepreneurs are not those who originally produce and develop new knowledge.

The model outlined above may be called "linear," whereby a scientific discovery leads to an invention that is developed into an innovation, which is ultimately exploited by an entrepreneur. This linear model is illustrated in *Figure 8.2.* A real-life example that illustrates this model is the scientific research that led to the discovery of the possibility of splitting atoms. This research made building a test reactor (invention) possible, which ultimately resulted in a commercially viable nuclear reactor that was then used to generate electricity for the electricity market (innovation).[24]

However, reality is often more complex. Many innovations do not directly originate from a new invention or discovery; instead, they are based on existing knowledge or finished products, which are adapted or improved over time to (better) meet market demands. Most innovations

---

21 Schmitz (1989) makes an interesting theoretical contribution in positing that the mechanism that drives growth consists of entrepreneurs who imitate other firms, which results in greater competition, more innovation and a higher rate of growth.

22 Aghion and Griffith (2005).

23 See Holcombe (1998, 2003).

24 Kasper, Streit and Boettke (2012).

© THE AUTHORS AND STUDENTLITTERATUR

Figure 8.2 The linear model of innovation.

do not entail radical changes based on new technological breakthroughs; rather, they are incremental, i.e., small, step-by-step adjustments based on imitating existing products or services. A successful economy also results from continual innovations based on a smaller amount of knowledge of the particular circumstances concerning time and place.

The problems and impediments that need to be overcome to successfully exploit an innovation do not have to be directly linked to the discovery in question. For an entrepreneur, finding the right suppliers, organizational structure, financing, logistics and distribution systems, and employees is imperative. If he fails in this task, the commercialization process will be unsuccessful, regardless of the quality of the invention or innovation. Determining the best way to commercialize an innovation normally requires tests and experimentation in the market.[25]

8.4 Conclusions Regarding the Leading Growth Theories

In the new generation of growth theories, the focus has shifted from the accumulation of factors of production to the role of knowledge and R&D activities. Even if these theories are more realistic and have more explanatory power than first-generation models, they still lack a dynamic perspective and an understanding of the importance of entrepreneurs. The conclusions of these theories have greatly influenced discussions on economic policy in some unfortunate ways. Such discussions have tended to overly focus on the rate of R&D investments, the share of an age cohort that has obtained a college degree, the number of patents filed per capita, or other indicators of a country's knowledge stock and the inputs that may contribute to the growth of that stock. However, weak economic development does not necessarily result from a low rate of R&D investment, too few people graduating from college or a low rate of patenting per capita or per firm. An increase in

---

25 Kasper, Streit and Boettke (2012).

R&D investments, students graduating from college and patents does not automatically translate into a high rate of economic growth. Weak economic performance may indicate that the knowledge generated is not used or that the new knowledge is not disseminated to other parts of the economy. Therefore, the main problem may be an unfavorable entrepreneurial climate rather than low levels of investment in education or insufficient R&D.

However, education, R&D and patenting are still relevant. The point here is that these factors alone cannot drive economic development; investment in R&D may be necessary, but it is far from sufficient. A high rate of R&D investment does not guarantee that new products or services will be successfully commercialized, which is a necessary condition for the expected effect on economic growth to be realized. For example, by examining only the patenting rate, one cannot learn whether commercialization has been profitable, or even whether the patent holders have initiated a commercialization process.[26] Only some registered patents are exploited, and the lion's share of the economic value flowing in comes from a small fraction of these patents.

Figure 8.3 presents a more fruitful way to illustrate the role of R&D and new knowledge. First, new knowledge and inventions must be developed into innovations in order for them to be exploited and commercialized. Entrepreneurs play a crucial role in such development. Innovations may then lead directly and indirectly to economic growth. They have not only a direct impact through the increased value added from successful innovations but also an indirect impact through entrepreneurs' contributions to knowledge spillovers, such as when new knowledge is exploited in a different industry or in another geographical area. However, existing products and firms become obsolete when new entrepreneurial opportunities are discovered or created, which has a dampening effect on the economy in the short term. In the longer run, the resources that are freed up may be used in better and more efficient ways in new firms.

When new methods, technologies or products are introduced, new questions and ideas are generated, which helps (other) entrepreneurs discover new opportunities that result in subsequent innovations. Even if an innovation is a commercial failure, it contributes new knowledge, which

---

26 Braunerhjelm (2008) and Svensson (2012).

   © THE AUTHORS AND STUDENTLITTERATUR

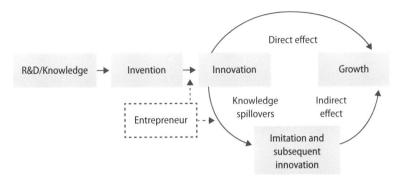

Figure 8.3 Knowledge, innovation and growth.

may ultimately lead to more successful innovations. Therefore, such failures do not necessarily constitute a waste of resources from a social perspective; instead, they are an integral part of an economy based on experimentation and selection. However, the important point here is that imitation and subsequent innovations do not occur automatically; an active entrepreneur, who acts as the driving force of this process, is a necessary element.

An innovation with the potential to increase growth does not have to be a new physical product, such as a photocopier or a computer. Organizational and business-related innovations, such as improvements in a firm's production, sourcing and distribution methods and business model, may be just as important. Wal-Mart, H&M, Zara and IKEA forcefully illustrate this point.

8.5 Chapter Summary

In this chapter, we have learned the following:

- Traditional growth theory, so-called exogenous growth theory, lacks an entrepreneurial perspective. Models based on this theory focus on the amount of inputs, such as labor and capital.
- In newer growth theories, so-called endogenous growth theories, knowledge, R&D and innovation are emphasized as important explanations for economic growth. In early endogenous growth models, the entrepreneurial function was completely absent.

- In some cases, recent endogenous growth theories include entrepreneurs, though in a restricted and stripped-down way.
- For R&D and new knowledge to enhance social welfare, someone must exploit the new knowledge in a productive manner. Here, entrepreneurs play a crucial role. The entrepreneurial function is neither simple nor mechanical, and it is not automatically activated.

© THE AUTHORS AND STUDENTLITTERATUR

The Importance of Entrepreneurship— The Empirical Evidence

In the previous chapters, we have discussed how the role of entrepreneurship is viewed and why entrepreneurship is expected to be important for economic development. We have argued that successful entrepreneurship contributes to both economic growth and job creation. In this chapter, we will present the most important empirical studies that assess its importance in these respects.

9.1 Entrepreneurship as an Object of Measurement

Although strong *a priori* reasons and prevailing experience strongly support the importance of the entrepreneurial function and the individual entrepreneur, proving their significance using state-of-the-art empirical and econometric methods is nevertheless a delicate task, as measuring entrepreneurial activities in a clear-cut manner is difficult.

The elusive nature of entrepreneurship also explains why many scholars have chosen to emphasize other aspects, even when they have studied entrepreneurship and innovation. This particularly applies to empirical research that uses standard econometric methods, but it also holds true in neoclassical theory, which requires formulating problems with a high degree of mathematical stringency. As we have already noted, the start-up rate or self-employment are frequently used as measures of the entrepreneurial activity in a country or region. Again, these measures of entrepreneurship are far from ideal, as entrepreneurship is not defined by a specific type of firm or employment form. Not all new business owners or self-employed individuals are entrepreneurs, and not all entrepreneurs are new business owners or self-employed individuals.

Since the early 1990s, an increasing number of scholars have begun showing an interest in the relationship between the rate of entrepreneurship and various economic outcome variables, which has led to the publication of several good empirical studies. The key findings of these studies are presented in this chapter.[1]

OTHER METHODOLOGICAL PROBLEMS

Even if a relationship or a correlation can be identified, establishing that the relationship is causal may still be difficult. Does a causal relationship actually exist, or does some other underlying factor that is not present in the analysis affect both the outcome variable (for example, growth or employment) and entrepreneurial activity? Do more entrepreneurs contribute to increased growth, or does increased growth lead to more entrepreneurs entering the market? If causality is present, it probably moves in both directions and contributes to a self-reinforcing process between entrepreneurship and growth, which makes distinguishing one effect from the other difficult. Similar methodological difficulties exist with regard to finding a causal relationship between entrepreneurial activity and job creation. The more aggregated the data, the more difficult distinguishing the components that drive the processes will be.

9.2 Narrow Measures of Entrepreneurship

Even though most of the empirical research on the importance of entrepreneurship actually analyzes the importance of self-employment and business ownership—which the narrow measures of entrepreneurship capture—briefly showing the results from this research may still be worthwhile. Not only will this overview provide the reader with an idea of how this research has evolved and been shaped, but it will also present the difficulties of finding clear-cut results. Research that uses better and more comprehensive measures of entrepreneurship exists, though it is far less common. This research is presented in section 9.3.

---

1 Other and more comprehensive surveys include Carree and Thurik (2010), Braunerhjelm and Wiklund (2006) and van Praag and Versloot (2007).

          © THE AUTHORS AND STUDENTLITTERATUR

GROWTH

When analyzing the effect of entrepreneurial activity, many scholars use the measure of entrepreneurial activity developed by the GEM, which we presented in chapter 5. This measure, referred to as TEA, is defined as the share of working-age individuals (aged 18–64) who are either involved in the process of starting up a company or are active as owner-managers of companies less than 42 months old (3.5 years). One study examined 36 countries and found that the degree of entrepreneurship had a significant positive impact on the growth rate in developed economies.[2] Other scholars have found that no country with high entrepreneurial activity, measured as TEA, simultaneously has low growth.[3] Other studies have found that between one-third and one-half of the cross-country differences in growth can be explained by the difference in entrepreneurial activity that is measured as TEA.[4]

With regard to the importance of new and smaller firms for economic development, a number of empirical analyses have found a positive relationship between small firms and growth when other factors, such as investments, employment, R&D and internationalization, have been considered.

First, these analyses established that small and new firms grow faster than older and larger firms do. This relationship has been found in a number of studies, thus rejecting Gibrat's Law, which maintains that the growth rate of a firm is independent of its size.[5] At the firm level, the empirical research has thus found that small firms, on average, grow more rapidly than larger firms do. At the same time, small and young firms are the least likely to survive. In addition to elimination, the influx of new firms and the testing of new ideas are thus vital components of dynamic economies.

Finding a relationship between different narrow measures for entrepreneurial activity and growth at the national level is more difficult. Sometimes, only certain industries that are considered more innovative are analyzed. In the early 1990s, scholars were already claiming that a strong positive relationship existed between economic growth and the share of small

---

2 Galindo, Méndez Picazo and Alfaro Navarro (2010).
3 Reynolds et al. (2002).
4 Reynolds, Hay and Camp (1999) and Zacharakis, Bygrave and Shepherd (2000).
5 See, for instance, Hart and Oulton (1996) or Almus and Nerlinger (2000). See Davidsson and Delmar (2002) and Daunfeldt, Elert and Lang (2012) for the Swedish case.

firms in the economy.[6] Based on a sample of 45 countries at different phases of development, one study established a strong covariation between growth and small firms, but it was more cautious with regard to the causal relationship.[7] Scholars have also found that entrepreneurial activity in the form of new firms and market dynamics positively relates to growth. In addition, in this case, causality could not be firmly established, but it likely goes in both directions (i.e., it may very well be that high growth also encourages more people to start firms).[8]

Although the rate of self-employment is often a directly misleading measure of entrepreneurship, it has frequently been used in the empirical literature. As we noted in chapter 4, the relationship between entrepreneurship and self-employment may be negative. Scholars have found a positive relationship between growth and self-employed individuals for 20 OECD countries from 1982–2002. The effect is much stronger in the latter part of the period. Other studies have also found positive relationships. The direction of causality has also been examined, and increased self-employment has been found to lead to increased growth.[9] However, other scholars find no support for the hypothesis that self-employment has a positive impact on growth.[10] In addition to these two perspectives, other studies suggest that an "optimal" level of self-employment exists; more self-employed individuals can have either a positive or negative impact on the economy depending on this optimal level.[11] In other words, the results seem contradictory.

The ideas that we have presented regarding the importance of the entrepreneur in transforming knowledge and inventions into innovations— and eventually contributing positively to growth—also receive empirical support. As we have already noted, countries that spend a great deal of resources on R&D and generate new knowledge may still experience little

---

6 Levine and Renelt (1992).

7 Beck, Demirguç-Kunt and Levine (2005). Regarding causality, see also Carree and Thurik (1999) and Braunerhjelm (2011).

8 Klapper et al. (2010).

9 Acs et al. (2009) and Braunerhjelm et al. (2010).

10 Blanchflower (2000). However, his method has been criticized by Carree and Thurik (2010).

11 Carree et al. (2002) and Hartog, van Stel and Storey (2010).

  © THE AUTHORS AND STUDENTLITTERATUR

growth if the level of entrepreneurial activity is low. Research has shown that a high proportion of start-ups or self-employed individuals in the economy indicates more opportunities for new knowledge to result in new, innovative products.[12]

JOB CREATION

The empirical studies do not offer an unambiguous picture regarding the importance of entrepreneurship in creating jobs. As we have concluded above, theoretically, the relationship between entrepreneurship and employment can be either positive or negative. However, as we have already mentioned, the main problem is that no good empirical measure of entrepreneurship exists to estimate its effect on job creation at the aggregate level. Many studies have used narrow measures for entrepreneurship and have examined the relationship between new venture creation and employment/unemployment For good reason, scholars have argued that the empirical results are contradictory. For example, some studies find a positive relationship between new venture creation and unemployment, whereas other studies find a negative relationship. Moreover, some studies find no statistically significant relationship at all.[13]

Obtaining different results is also possible if one contrasts trends over time in a single country to cross-country comparisons at a particular point in time. Many empirical studies find that new venture creation is positively correlated with the rate of unemployment over time, which indicates that the growth rate of necessity self-employment is higher in bad times than the growth rate of opportunity entrepreneurship in good times. However, when comparing countries, one often finds a negative relationship between the rate of unemployment and the degree of new venture creation, i.e., unemployment tends to be higher in countries with low start-up rates.[14]

---

12 Block, Thurik and Zhou (2013).
13 Fritsch (2011) offers a survey. Evans and Leighton (1990) and Reynolds (1994, 1999) find a positive relationship; Audretsch and Fritsch (1994) find a negative relationship; and Carree (2002) finds no relationship.
14 Parker (2009).

The importance of self-employment in relation to aggregate employment/ unemployment has been thoroughly analyzed. For example, one study has found a relationship between an increase in the share of self-employed individuals and declining unemployment in 23 OECD countries between 1984 and 1994.[15] Other studies have modeled and tested the relationship between self-employment and unemployment in both directions and have found evidence of both negative and positive effects. One study concludes that the negative effect—that self-employment reduces unemployment— dominates the positive effect.[16] The OECD has also concluded that increased self-employment has become an important source of job creation in many OECD countries.[17] In this context, the OECD mentions Germany and Canada in particular.

The importance of small firms for employment has also been examined. Based on data for Sweden in the early 1990s, small firms have ultimately been recognized as particularly important.[18] However, this conclusion has been called into question. The crisis in Sweden in the 1990s was exceptionally serious and this pattern has not been repeated in subsequent and less dramatic recessions. Between 1984 and 1993, the employment share of small firms (1–9 employees) increased by approximately 20 percent both in the overall economy and in the manufacturing sector, but the employment share of small firms has declined since then.[19] Other critical voices have also denied the important role of small firms. For example, one study argues that the importance of small firms is overrated and that statistical problems make interpreting the results difficult.[20]

In addition to measurement problems and the uncertain direction of causality, finding empirical support for the contribution of new firms or self-employment to job creation is difficult because the lasting effect on employment takes some time to materialize (compare the discussion in section 7.2). Many previous studies only examined the relationship in the

---

15 Audretsch and Thurik (2000).
16 Thurik et al. (2008).
17 OECD (2000b).
18 See Davidson, Lindmark and Olofsson (1996) and Braunerhjelm (2006) for the employment contribution of small firms.
19 Henrekson, Johansson and Stenkula (2012).
20 Davis, Haltiwanger and Schuh (1996). Davidsson, Lindmark and Olofsson (1998) responded to this critique.

          © THE AUTHORS AND STUDENTLITTERATUR

short run and thus overlooked the potentially important long-term effect of entrepreneurship. For instance, support for this view can be found in studies that conclude that new venture creation in the 1980s cannot explain changes in employment in the 1980s but can explain those that took place in the 1990s.[21] New studies also suggest that positive effects exist; however, any tangible positive effects of increased self-employment on the level of employment can only be observed after a delay of several years.[22]

Overall, new research still seems to reveal that new firms and self-employment are positive for long-term employment, but, over time, these dynamics cause this relationship to increase the volatility in the labor market. Recent research also shows that the gross flows of labor— that is, the in- and outflow of labor from different employers—tend to be larger in newer, smaller and heavily specialized firms and in firms that experience rapid growth in productivity and employment.[23] The relationship is not (only) about the short-term effect of the creation of new firms. In the long run, employment across the entire economy (including large incumbent firms) benefits from a high rate of new venture creation.[24]

ENTREPRENEURSHIP AND REGIONAL DEVELOPMENT

Above all, entrepreneurship should perhaps be regarded as a regional phenomenon, and its impact should thus be particularly pronounced at the regional level and in regional statistics, both with regard to employment and economic growth. As described above, the main problem is that scholars often use the rate of new venture creation and self-employment as measures of entrepreneurial activity. A number of studies have examined the impact of new firms and self-employment at the regional level, and they have concluded that new firms and self-employment, combined with the level of knowledge in the region, contribute to higher growth, employment and prosperity from a regional perspective.

For example, scholars have found a positive correlation between the rate of new firm formation (as a percentage of the labor force) and employment

---

21 Audretsch and Fritsch (2002).
22 Carree and Thurik (2008).
23 Reynolds (1999) and Audretsch (2002).
24 Fritsch and Noseleit (2013)

growth in a number of regions in the United States.[25] Another result shows that only new firms with at least 20 employees in large and densely populated regions have a long-term positive impact on employment.[26] Other scholars have found that the number of new firms (as a proportion of the population) help explain regional-level growth in Germany.[27] Numerous state-level studies in the United States have shown that business dynamics (approximated by in- and outflows of firms in the market) have a positive effect on productivity and employment. In Europe, similar results have been found for a number of countries, including Spain and Germany. However, until the 1990s, different measures of entrepreneurship had not been shown to have positive effects on regional growth.[28]

The size of the employment effects—as well as the size of the growth effects—may also be linked to the population density of a region or a city. Some studies show that the positive impact of new venture creation will be greater when population density is high.[29] Cities with many and various types of firms offer a better breeding ground for growth and the diffusion of knowledge.[30]

9.3 Other Measures of Entrepreneurship

Entrepreneurship and innovation have undoubtedly played a crucial role in various historical leaps in the development of national economies. For example, the Second Industrial Revolution in the late 19th century was marked not only by major technological breakthroughs—mainly electricity and the combustion engine—but also by the emergence of new firms and industries that were based on these radical breakthroughs. This period was characterized by institutional reforms, which included both a knowledge upgrade (including compulsory schooling) and improved possibilities for the diffusion of knowledge and the conversion of new knowledge into valuable goods and services (for example, increased competition and limited

---

25 Acs and Armington (2004).
26 Acs and Mueller (2008).
27 Audretsch and Keilbach (2004).
28 Braunerhjelm (2008).
29 Fritsch and Falck (2002).
30 Carree and Thurik (2006) and Glaeser (2012).

© THE AUTHORS AND STUDENTLITTERATUR

risk taking through joint-stock companies). This period, much like today, witnessed growing internationalization, whereby trade volumes increased, cross-border investments grew and people travelled between countries far more than in the past because of the rapid extension of railway systems and the introduction of transoceanic steamship traffic.

In this flourishing environment, Joseph Schumpeter wrote his pioneering works, in which he declared that the entrepreneur was the market economy's main engine and agent of change and, in turn, the main driving force behind industrial transformation, dynamism and economic growth. William Baumol recently argued that entrepreneurial and radical innovations and the direct and indirect effects of subsequent knowledge spillovers explain more than 90 percent of economic development since the 18th century.[31] The United States Department of Commerce estimates that nearly three-quarters of total growth during the post-war period in the United States can be derived from technological innovations.[32] Based on these insights, innovations should be just as central as the price mechanism in economic theory and education.

The lack of any firm conclusions regarding the importance of entrepreneurial activity based on the rate of self-employment or other narrow metrics of entrepreneurial activity in empirical studies is hardly surprising. Entrepreneurship may be of various qualities and may be channeled in different ways—not all forms of entrepreneurship are equally positive for the overall economy and most business owners are not entrepreneurial. We have emphasized the importance of high-growth firms and high-impact entrepreneurship (HIE), and we have referred to the most successful entrepreneurs as super-entrepreneurs—i.e., individuals who have created a personal fortune of at least one billion dollars by starting and growing firms. Research has also shown that ambitious entrepreneurs—i.e., entrepreneurs who want to grow—play a greater role in growth than business owners in general.[33] Studies have also found a positive relationship between innovative entrepreneurship and growth based on quality-adjusted patent data for 22 countries.[34]

---

31 Baumol (2010, chapter 5).
32 Rai, Graham and Doms (2010).
33 Wong, Ho and Autio (2005), Valliere and Peterson (2009) and Stam et al. (2009).
34 Salgado-Banda (2007).

THE IMPORTANCE OF HIGH-GROWTH FIRMS

In chapter 4, we noted that not all entrepreneurial activities are equally valuable for society. Numerous scholars have analyzed the job creation effects of rapidly growing firms—gazelles. One study found that the top 10 percent of the fastest growing firms founded in the United States from 1977–1978 contributed 74 percent of all the jobs created (by firms founded in that period) over the following eight years.[35] In another study, the researchers found that all new net jobs in the United States in the 1990–1994 period were created in a few rapidly growing firms.[36] Examining 100 small firms in the United Kingdom at a particular time, one scholar reports that the four that grew most rapidly generated half of all the jobs created by those 100 firms.[37]

Therefore, only a small proportion of firms seemingly have great potential for rapid growth. In chapter 5, we noted that high-growth firms have been shown to be crucial for employment growth and to be responsible for a large proportion of all new jobs in the economy. Recent research has also shown that many phenomena that are linked to entrepreneurship follow a so-called power law distribution. This implies that most firms have few owners and little invested capital, do not create much employment beyond the owner(s) and do not make significant profits; by contrast, a few firms create most of the new jobs, make large profits, and so on.[38]

Scholars have also studied the top ten percent of the fastest growing firms in Sweden and the ways in which they have contributed to employment creation.[39] Regardless of how they analyze the outcome (time period, type of growth, type of business entity), and contrary to the findings of studies in the United States and the United Kingdom, they find that the bulk of new employment generation in Sweden cannot be attributed to a small elite of high-growth firms.

---

35 Kirchoff (1994).
36 Birch, Haggerty and Parsons (1995).
37 Storey (1994, p. 113).
38 Crawford et al. (2015).
39 Davidsson and Delmar (2003).

 © THE AUTHORS AND STUDENTLITTERATUR

9.4 Final Reflections

In this chapter, we have concluded that trying to establish and quantify the importance of entrepreneurship for economic growth and job creation presents significant methodological difficulties. However, both statistical and econometric methods improve over time, and the empirical support for the central role of entrepreneurship in economic development gradually grows stronger as new studies appear.

Securing widespread and staunch recognition of the importance of entrepreneurship for job creation and increased prosperity in the public debate and economic policy discussions probably requires more empirical evidence than that which has been presented so far. The continued development of more and better empirical indicators of entrepreneurship that are in line with the definition in this book is necessary; that is, these indicators should include ability and willingness of individuals

- to discover and create new economic opportunities;
- to introduce their ideas in the market under uncertainty, making decisions regarding the localization, product design, use of resources, institutions and reward systems; and
- to create value, which often, though not always, means that the entrepreneur aims to expand the firm to its full potential.

9.5 Chapter Summary

In this chapter, we have learned the following:

- Empirically showing the importance of entrepreneurship for economic growth and job creation is difficult, as no entirely satisfactory empirical measure of entrepreneurship exists.
- Most of the empirical research on the importance of entrepreneurship uses narrow measures of entrepreneurship, such as the effect of self-employed individuals or small or new firms on the economy. Even if positive effects may be demonstrated based on this research, no conclusive results exist.

- Some studies use more adequate and encompassing measures, and these studies have identified some positive effects. However, few studies of this kind exist.
- Future research has ample opportunity to conduct better empirical analyses on the importance of entrepreneurship for economic development.

© THE AUTHORS AND STUDENTLITTERATUR

CHAPTER 10

Supply of and Demand for Entrepreneurship

In the previous chapters, we have concluded that entrepreneurship plays a key role in the economic system but that it is a highly complex phenomenon. In addition, entrepreneurial activity is not ordained by nature. A great deal of entrepreneurship is channeled through start-ups, but start-ups are not created automatically. Someone must be willing to start a new firm, and those who already own a firm and see the potential for expansion must be both willing and able to realize this potential. In this chapter, we present an analytical framework that helps us to study the determinants of entrepreneurship. Within this framework, we discuss the possibility of analyzing entrepreneurship in terms of supply and demand, and thus the existence of a market for entrepreneurship services in which supply and demand can be equilibrated.

10.1 Entrepreneurship as a Factor of Production

Several approaches can be used to incorporate the entrepreneur and the entrepreneurial function into economic theory. Each approach has advantages and disadvantages. One possibility involves starting out with an ordinary production function and then letting the traditional factors of production—labor and capital—and the newer factors—human capital and knowledge/technology—be complemented by an additional factor of production: entrepreneurship. When land was, relatively speaking, a more important factor of production, economic theory commonly included it as a separate factor of production in addition to capital and labor.

A factor of production is essentially nothing more than a good or a service that a firm needs to produce new goods or services. Viewing entrepreneurship as such a factor comes quite naturally. Obviously, a great number of other, non-traditional, factors of production can be added, for example, organizational/structural capital and ownership control. A more detailed breakdown into different kinds of human and physical capital is also possible. What a suitable breakdown looks like depends on the question analyzed.

Hence, one way of understanding the determinants of entrepreneurship—similar to how the use and the price of other factors of production are usually analyzed—involves distinguishing between the supply side and the demand side of entrepreneurship. Established and well-functioning factor markets often exist for capital and labor. Here, supply and demand meet, and the factor prices are determined. Nobel Laureate Theodore Schultz has forcibly argued that identifying the marginal product of an entrepreneur is possible. The marginal product is how much the production increases at the margin if the entrepreneurial effort in a firm increases. This concept should be relevant since an entrepreneur's abilities clearly benefit a firm and its production.[1] Therefore, Schultz asserts that a supply, a demand and a market for entrepreneurs exist—or that establishing them is possible.

However, this book has shown that discussing a market for entrepreneurial efforts or entrepreneurs is difficult. A general problem is that entrepreneurship is more difficult to define and quantify than other factors of production. Yet, measurement difficulties do not imply that entrepreneurship is less relevant than other factors or that a market cannot exist. With regard to the problem of measuring entrepreneurship, two diametrically opposed views exist. On the one hand, economists David Audretsch and Max Keilbach argue that empirically measuring entrepreneurship is not any more difficult than measuring other factors of production.[2] As is the case when measuring capital, labor and knowledge, simplifications and assumptions are necessary to obtain a tractable empirical measure. Audretsch and Keilbach argue that empirically using the number of start-ups as a macro-level approximation of an economy's entrepreneurial activity is feasible. On the other hand, William Baumol, in stark contrast to Audretsch and Keilbach, argues that

---

1 Schultz (1980).
2 Audretsch and Keilbach (2004).

    © THE AUTHORS AND STUDENTLITTERATUR

"entrepreneurship is hard to define and therefore impossible to measure statistically."[3]

As a factor of production, entrepreneurship differs in several crucial ways from capital and labor. There exist very few markets where one can buy and sell entrepreneurial services. For example, a firm may find employing or hiring people to make entrepreneurial decisions in the same way as it contracts other workers difficult. Entrepreneurship is not a mechanical or routine activity. Imitating a successful entrepreneurial firm is usually more difficult than one might think, whether it involves giving someone a task to fulfill the entrepreneurial function or becoming an entrepreneur oneself. Therefore, an entrepreneur is not the supplier of a directly substitutable service that can be bought and sold in an established market.

One may argue that every single opportunity and entrepreneur is unique, and each opportunity is uniquely tied to a particular entrepreneur. As such, many individual markets exist for entrepreneurs—perhaps as many markets exist as there are potential entrepreneurs. However, even if every entrepreneur is a unique individual, several different individuals should be able to exploit a particular entrepreneurial opportunity, even if replacing a specific entrepreneur with somebody else to pursue the same opportunity may sometimes be difficult. In other words, substitutability may be low.[4]

In addition, the productivity of a potential entrepreneur may be—and generally is—connected to the form of ownership. An entrepreneur whose firm is acquired or an entrepreneur who is an employee of a firm from the outset, i.e., an intrapreneur, does not have the same incentive that he would have had, if he had owned the firm. Some venture capital firms specialize in supporting new entrepreneurial firms, but this support involves high transaction costs.[5] Therefore, the same person commonly both supplies and demands entrepreneurial services. An individual perceives (discovers or creates) an opportunity and wants to be the one to realize it. This is the case for many entrepreneurial business owners; the business owner demands his own services as an entrepreneur.[6]

---

3 Baumol (2002b, p. 56).
4 Casson (2003).
5 See Kerr, Nanda and Rhodes-Kropf (2014) for a discussion of how venture capitalists select entrepreneurial projects.
6 Baumol (2010) and Ricketts (2002).

Box 10.1

The Principal–Agent Problem

When gains can be made through specialization, a relationship will likely develop in which agents act on behalf of a principal. Examples of such relationships abound: a lawyer who gives advice to his client, a doctor who examines a patient or a business leader who acts on behalf of a firm's owners. In this context, we are particularly interested in cases in which management acts on behalf of firm owners. The principal–agent problem concerns how to achieve correspondence between the interests of the principal (the owners) and the agent (management). The principal primarily finds preventing the agent from acting in accordance with his own interests difficult because of asymmetric information. For example, the owner finds closely observing what management does and how hard they work difficult. In addition, management's informational advantage gives them the opportunity to pursue their own goals, such as increased status and improved career opportunities, instead of maximizing the value of the business, which tends to be the owners' goal.

Moral hazard is the second important reason that the principal finds preventing the agent from acting in accordance with his own interests difficult. Moral hazard arises when one party takes more risks because someone else bears the burden of those risks. A classic example is when an individual has purchased insurance against theft, thereby reducing the incentive to take precautions that reduce the risk of theft. In turn, the likelihood of theft increases. When thefts increase because of moral hazard, insurance premiums go up.

The principal-agent problems (see Box 10.1), which arise because of asymmetric information, moral hazard and imperfect contracting, are central to entrepreneurship as a factor of production. Principal-agent problems refer to problems that may arise when a principal (e.g., an owner) delegates decision making to an agent (e.g., a hired management team or a professional board of directors); the agent has incentives to not behave in full conformity with the principal's interests. These problems are aggravated when the principal finds observing and controlling the agent's behavior difficult.

   © THE AUTHORS AND STUDENTLITTERATUR

Unlike capital and labor, entrepreneurship services are very difficult to procure through explicit contracting. For the decision making, risk taking and efforts to take full effect, they generally must be linked to a significant ownership share (sometimes 100 percent). The entrepreneur is almost invariably unable to sell his services to others at a price that corresponds to their actual value, nor does he have access to perfectly functioning capital markets. Therefore, the investment must largely be financed by his own resources, which further impedes the creation of an external market for entrepreneurial services.

The emergence of markets for entrepreneurs or entrepreneurial effort is made even less likely because entrepreneurial ability is a heterogeneous characteristic; potential entrepreneurs are not equally skilled, and they do not have skill sets in the same areas. Not only will the ability and marginal productivity vary considerably between different entrepreneurs, these variations will also be unknowable in advance.

Marco Caliendo and Alexander Kritikos have tried to assess who have the potential to be a successful entrepreneur.[7] They find that using tests or interviews to predict successful entrepreneurs does not work. According to Stanford professor Edward Lazear, such predictions are also difficult because the people who ultimately become entrepreneurs tend to be good at and have experience in several different areas rather than being exceptionally skilled in one or two areas.[8] According to Lazear, entrepreneurs are "jacks-of-all-trades" rather than niche specialists. For example, we now know that the marginal product of Ingvar Kamprad's entrepreneurship services has been extremely high and has far exceeded the marginal product of an "average" entrepreneur. Kamprad's entrepreneurship *ex post* arguably proved to be one of the most productive in the world during the post-war period. However, the important question is whether it could have been possible, using an extraordinarily well-crafted test, to identify the young Kamprad's exceptional entrepreneurial talent.

To counter this argument, somebody could perhaps mention that the markets for conventional factors of production, such as labor and capital, are highly fragmented and that they actually consist of many different

---

7 Caliendo and Kritikos (2008).
8 Lazear (2005).

markets. However, there is strong support for the far greater heterogeneity and uncertainty in the assessment of potential entrepreneurs. As emphasized by Israel M. Kirzner, the exercise of entrepreneurship is an open-ended process. The level of productivity is gradually revealed only after the process is under way, i.e., when the entrepreneurship is actually exercised.[9] The same conclusion follows from Sarasvathy's effectuation view of how entrepreneurship is carried out (see chapter 3). Therefore, the exercise of entrepreneurship is a highly individual activity that is based on subjective valuations and assessments that are extremely difficult to buy and sell at a market price in an established market.

10.2 The Determinants of Entrepreneurial Activity

The entrepreneurial activity in the economy obviously depends on a variety of factors. For the sake of simplicity, entrepreneurial activity can be said to depend on four factors that are linked both to the economy as a whole and to single individuals:[10]

- entrepreneurial competence,
- access to both financial and human capital,
- entrepreneurial opportunities, and
- willingness.

These four factors determine the supply of and the demand for entrepreneurs and entrepreneurial effort. As we will argue below, the supply of entrepreneurs is linked to potential entrepreneurs who have skills and capital, while the demand is associated with the presence of opportunities. The willingness to pursue entrepreneurship will act as a selection mechanism for whether one eventually chooses to become an entrepreneur.

---

9 Kirzner (1997). Kirzner's analysis is greatly inspired by von Mises (1949).
10 The following discussion draws on OECD (2005), Verheul et al. (2001) and Lundström and Stevenson (2001).

    © THE AUTHORS AND STUDENTLITTERATUR

ENTREPRENEURIAL COMPETENCE

An unavoidable restriction for the prevalence of entrepreneurship is the stock of *entrepreneurial ability* or *competence* among the working-age population.[11] Whether this ability or competence is innate or something that individuals can learn is a debated issue.

Today, few scholars believe that entrepreneurship is only determined by innate traits. Instead, many scholars argue that people may be born with greater or lesser *potential* to develop into successful entrepreneurs. Whether and to what extent this innate potential is developed depends on the environment. Some people have an innate potential, but having such potential does not necessarily ensure that they will develop it. Therefore, even if we were able to perfectly measure the innate traits, that would be insufficient to determine whether a particular individual would become an entrepreneur or how successful this person would be. However, some people are seemingly more likely to develop into successful entrepreneurs.[12]

Many scholars have also discussed whether entrepreneurship can be taught. The ability to learn entrepreneurship may be either about "studying" (reading) how to be a successful entrepreneur or about "practicing" entrepreneurship and thereby developing one's entrepreneurial skills. No consensus exists in this area. For example, Edward Lazear asserts that entrepreneurial decision making is so domain-specific and context-dependent that general education will not make much difference.[13] A Swedish study found that students who had undergone a special entrepreneurship program in high school were more likely to start firms but that these firms were not more likely to survive than firms that were started by people who had not participated in the program.[14] Other studies have found that entrepreneurship programs may positively influence the development of non-cognitive entrepreneurial traits, such as self-discipline, social skills, motivation, work ethic, perseverance, reliability and emotional stability.[15]

---

11 Frequently, the term "ability" is used for innate traits while "competence" is used to denote traits acquired through learning.

12 Gartner (1988).

13 Lazear (2005).

14 Elert, Andersson and Wennberg (2015).

15 Rosendahl, Sloof and van Praag (2014).

© THE AUTHORS AND STUDENTLITTERATUR

As we have already noted, the entrepreneurial ability seems to be present, at least to some extent, in most people,[16] which is completely in line with the view that few people have the potential to become truly successful entrepreneurs. Regardless of whether entrepreneurial ability is innate or learned (or a combination of the two), it is a prerequisite for initiating and developing successful entrepreneurship.

CAPITAL

To start or develop a firm, one needs capital. Active entrepreneurship often requires someone who is willing to contribute resources to start and grow a firm. This "someone" is frequently the entrepreneur himself. The more uncertain the project and the harder it is to appraise, the greater the share of the financing that must consist of equity infusion. Because of asymmetric information and moral hazard, an entrepreneur may find locating external financiers difficult. The entrepreneur knows more about the project than potential financiers do, and the latter must handle the risk that the entrepreneur exaggerates the potential of the project or manages their resources in a careless or incompetent manner. Incentive problems of this kind are inevitable, and designing contracts that cover every contingency is practically impossible. Therefore, the entrepreneur's significant equity contribution is usually necessary to obtain additional loan and/or equity financing from external parties. A significant equity investment by the entrepreneur also strongly signals that he believes in his project.

As we have already discussed, venture capital firms contribute external equity financing, but they rarely invest in the earliest so-called "seed phase." Personal wealth or relatives and friends who provide equity financing are normally prerequisites for new entrepreneurial projects. Empirical research has also documented a positive relationship between a person's wealth and his propensity to become an entrepreneur.[17]

Therefore, an entrepreneur must generally invest his own financial resources and thus also become a capital owner, in the form of (partially)

16 Baumol (2010).
17 See the contributions in Landström (2007) and Cumming (2012) for in-depth discussions regarding the financing of small companies by business angels and venture capitalists.

© THE AUTHORS AND STUDENTLITTERATUR

owning his own firm. When it is linked to ownership, the supply of entrepreneurial effort cannot be separated from the supply of capital; the choice will be to offer a "basket" of entrepreneurial effort and equity financing. By contrast, a capital owner does not have to be an entrepreneur, and most capital owners are not entrepreneurs. Through their ownership, financial risk taking becomes an integral part of entrepreneurship, even if, in the strictest sense, an entrepreneur assumes the financial risk in his role as a capital owner.

An individual who possesses entrepreneurial ability/competence and has access to capital is a qualified entrepreneur.[18] In reality, only qualified entrepreneurs can be part of the supply of entrepreneurs and take advantage of the entrepreneurial opportunities that exist in the economy. A non-qualified entrepreneur is not doomed to refrain from entrepreneurship, and he may ultimately qualify by, for example, acquiring capital (by saving money or by attracting external investors).

On the one hand, Israel Kirzner and Joseph Schumpeter have argued that the entrepreneurial function in itself does not require capital.[19] Kirzner asserts that a truly talented entrepreneur cannot be completely "unqualified." The lack of personal financial resources surely presents an additional transaction problem, but, according to Kirzner, a skilled entrepreneur is always able to somehow obtain the required resources, which he considers part of the entrepreneurial ability. On the other hand, Frank Knight argues that it is almost inevitable that an entrepreneur will invest in his firm.[20] In other words, Knight asserts that the financing function and the entrepreneurial function cannot be separated. Several economists, including Murray Rothbard, have criticized both Kirzner and Schumpeter for ignoring or downplaying the importance of financing.[21] Rothbard argues that the "capitalist–entrepreneur"—the entrepreneur who contributes the necessary financial resources himself—is crucially important for the economy. "Entrepreneurial ideas without money are mere parlor games," says Rothbard; entrepreneurs without capital cannot get past the idea phase until they receive financing.

---

18 Casson (2003).
19 Kirzner (1973, 1997) and Schumpeter (2004 [1934]).
20 Knight (1921).
21 Rothbard (1985).

Those who are unable to contribute the requisite capital themselves rarely attain the requirements to become qualified entrepreneurs.[22]

If a potential entrepreneur is unable to muster the financial resources required to start his own firm, then another option is to sell his business idea. However, as we noted in chapter 4, selling a business idea is not always possible, even if it is codified in the form of an approved patent. A large part of the knowledge needed to carry out the venture is likely tacit knowledge, meaning that it is linked to particular individuals and is difficult to transfer to another person by writing it down or verbalizing it. In addition, an information asymmetry exists between the buyer and the seller. Moreover, the value of the idea is unknown until the idea has been commercialized in the form of an entrepreneurial project. The value of a business idea is also subjective and can differ significantly between economic actors. As a result, a potential entrepreneur finds selling an idea that he is convinced will be successful difficult unless the other party makes the same positive assessment.

In the case of intrapreneurship, new business opportunities are launched inside an incumbent firm. Here, the funding usually comes from internal resources, which means that the intrapreneur does not need to contribute his own capital. However, many innovations are commercialized most efficiently in new firms, and the principal–agent problem implies that intrapreneurs do not have the incentive to act optimally; intrapreneurs do not necessarily receive any part of the capital value that results from successful intrapreneurship. This argument speaks against the efficiency of intrapreneurship.

If the intrapreneur had instead been the owner of his firm, he would have been both the principal and the agent, which would have eliminated the problem. One way of remedying or at least alleviating this problem involves using some kind of a stock option program that rewards the intrapreneur in a way that at least partially mimics direct ownership. Perfectly designed, such a program would make the intrapreneur behave *as if* he were the owner of the project. In reality, achieving a full concurrence between the interests of the intrapreneur and those of the firm owners is difficult, but stock options can increase the alignment of interests considerably compared with wage compensation for the intrapreneur.

---

22 See Parker (2009, chapters 7–9) for an in-depth discussion regarding entrepreneurship and financing.

© THE AUTHORS AND STUDENTLITTERATUR

ENTREPRENEURIAL OPPORTUNITIES

For a qualified entrepreneur (a person with entrepreneurial abilities and access to capital) to actually become an entrepreneur, exploitable *opportunities* must exist or be created. Alternatively, entrepreneurs must believe that they have discovered opportunities that can be exploited. As long as resources can be (re)allocated in novel ways—with an expected return that exceeds existing options—entrepreneurial opportunities will exist. The opportunities will depend on the ease of entry and/or expansion and the conditions of the macroeconomic environment. New opportunities will constantly arise as new knowledge and new information are developed, discovered or disseminated. Entrepreneurial opportunities are the result of macro-factors (e.g., demographic changes, level of education, preferences, and regulatory frameworks) and micro-factors (e.g., the alertness of the individual entrepreneur, subjective judgments and interpretations of the surrounding environment).

The demand for entrepreneurial effort arises because of the presence of entrepreneurial opportunities. This demand is *indirect*—in this case, one usually refers to derived demand. Because unexploited opportunities can always generate excess returns for a firm if an entrepreneur discovers/creates/ experiences these opportunities (for example, in the form of new goods and services), an indirect demand for entrepreneurial effort will always exist.

WILLINGNESS

Joseph Schumpeter argues that three difficulties reduce a person's willingness to become entrepreneur:

- resistance to new tasks,
- resistance based on the human mind, and
- resistance from others in the surrounding environment.

When discussing resistance to new tasks, Schumpeter refers to the fact that people tend to be reluctant to take on new tasks—which is a defining feature of entrepreneurial activity—as neither information about previous outcomes nor a tested regulatory framework on which to rely exists. One is thus forced to rely more on intuition than on regular optimization strategies.

The human mind also has an inherent tendency to shun what is new. People have a certain reluctance to try out new things and would rather just carry on with "business as usual" to save energy and avoid possible frustration. Schumpeter draws a parallel to science, where the leading scholars in a field tend to adhere to a certain paradigm and are reluctant to modify their approach or methodology.[23]

The third and last form of resistance comes from the surrounding environment. Political or legal restrictions may hamper or even prevent innovations (see the discussion on institutional entrepreneurship in section 4.4). However, above all, Schumpeter argues, other people may condemn or frown upon a person who is different and tries something new, which results in a social pressure that stifles one's willingness to become an entrepreneur. Generally, competitors also have a vested interest in maintaining the *status quo*. Therefore, they will do their best to discourage innovative entrepreneurs.[24]

As such, a potential entrepreneur must *want* to exploit an opportunity. Here, individual psychological factors such as self-confidence, stress tolerance and risk aversion will play a role. The presence of role models and an entrepreneurial spirit that encourages entrepreneurial initiatives may also have a positive effect on one's willingness to become an entrepreneur. For example, Sweden is home to the so-called "Gnosjö spirit," which is important in encouraging entrepreneurial initiatives in and around Gnosjö in the Swedish province of Småland.[25]

Those who want to become entrepreneurs should also have a strong internal locus of control—that is, the belief that he largely controls the factors that determine whether or not plans will be realized.[26] In addition, economic factors will play a crucial role in one's willingness to become an entrepreneur. If an individual perceives that the cost of becoming an entrepreneur is greater than the utility ("the profit"), then whether this person perceives an opportunity and has both the ability and the requisite capital does not matter. Perhaps an alternative option, typically regular employment, provides better compensation. Perhaps the expected profit, or utility, of becoming an

---

23 Cf. Kuhn (1962).
24 Schumpeter (2004 [1934]) and Knudsen and Swedberg (2009).
25 Johannisson (1984, 2004).
26 Rauch and Frese (2000).

© THE AUTHORS AND STUDENTLITTERATUR

entrepreneur is not estimated to be sufficiently high relative to the personal effort and the risk to which the individual must expose himself. A potential entrepreneur must always balance the risk of failure and the possibility of success. How are these outcomes valued and how likely are they to occur? The higher the expected return of a project and the lower the risk aversion of the potential entrepreneur, the higher the likelihood of the project being implemented.[27]

One can imagine an individual who loves taking risks or who is driven by things other than making money—for instance, by working independently without superiors or simply dreaming of becoming the best in his trade—or someone who wants to become an entrepreneur even if the compensation is less than the salary he could obtain otherwise. Some studies on the self-employed show that only the 25 percent most well-paid of the self-employed earn more as self-employed individuals than as employees.[28] On the one hand, 25 percent may seem low, but, on the other hand, self-employed individuals generally have significantly more possibilities than employees to reduce their taxable income. Hence, more than 25 percent of the self-employed have more room for consumption as a self-employed individual than as an employee.

However, most self-employed individuals are not entrepreneurial. Even when examining the returns on innovations, studies show that they are generally low. One study showed that a full 60 percent of all innovations had negative returns, but this study also found that six percent of all innovations had a return of at least 1,400 percent.[29]

Attempting to become an entrepreneur can be compared to participating in a lottery, although the entrepreneur believes that he, through his own effort, can influence his chance of drawing a winning lottery ticket. The average return on investment is negative, but a few extremely valuable prizes are won. The chance of making huge profits explains why many people choose to become entrepreneurs. Therefore, in addition to the level and variance of the expected returns, the chance of getting one of these mega-rewards— despite the low probability—will lure people into entrepreneurship.[30]

---

27 Kihlstrom and Laffont (1979).
28 Hamilton (2000).
29 Åstebro (2003).
30 Baumol (2010) and van Praag (2009).

© THE AUTHORS AND STUDENTLITTERATUR

One can draw parallels to Edward Lazear's and Sherwin Rosen's tournament theory, which explains highly progressive wage ladders in hierarchical organizations.[31] According to this theory, a very well-paid position, such as CEO, incentivizes other employees in the firms to work diligently, as they may have a chance of being promoted to that position in the future. The same phenomenon prevails in many competitive sports, where the possibility of success encourages individuals to devote a large part their waking hours to training, although very few athletes succeed in becoming highly paid superstars. Alfred Marshall, arguably the most influential economist of his time, highlighted the phenomenon in the late 19th century: "If an occupation offers a few extremely high prizes, its attractiveness is increased out of all proportion to their aggregate value" because "young men of an adventurous disposition are more attracted by the prospects of a great success than they are deterred by the fear of failure" and "the social rank of an occupation depends more on the highest dignity and the best position which can be attained through it than on the average good fortune of those engaged in it."[32]

If one also considers the non-pecuniary motives behind entrepreneurship, then becoming an entrepreneur does not necessarily seem irrational, even if the average monetary compensation is less than that of the best option as an employee.

A SCHEMATIC ILLUSTRATION

All the factors described above will determine the supply and demand for entrepreneurs and entrepreneurial effort. The supply depends on competence and capital—that is, the factors that are the basis for what we call qualified entrepreneurs. Therefore, supply will be linked to the general competence level in the economy, but factors such as attitudes and the degree of risk aversion among individuals will also play a role. These traits differ depending on the individuals' age, gender and ethnic origin, which means that the demographic makeup will influence the supply of entrepreneurs. The demand

---

31 Lazear and Rosen (1981).
32 Marshall (1961[1890]). Today, Marshall would probably have written "young people," but the view on the abilities and inclinations of women was very different when he was writing in 1890.

© THE AUTHORS AND STUDENTLITTERATUR

Figure 10.1 Supply, demand and the selection of entrepreneurs.

Note: The level of entrepreneurial activity is measured as the number of entrepreneurs at the intersection between the supply of and demand for entrepreneurs. Demand is a function of existing entrepreneurial opportunities. Demand is indirect (derived) and is influenced by factors such as new technologies, industry structure and macroeconomic conditions. Supply depends on both individual and societal factors, such as access to capital and attitudes toward risk taking and business ownership. Source: Based on OECD (2005).

depends on the presence of created, discovered or perceived opportunities. Along with a subjective assessment of the business climate and future prospects, factors such as new technologies, differences in preferences among consumers, the industry structure and the macroeconomic development will influence demand.

The level of entrepreneurial activity will ultimately depend on the willingness of potential and qualified entrepreneurs to become entrepreneurs and start new firms or expand existing ones to take advantage of the available opportunities. If an individual believes that the expected profit of becoming an entrepreneur is inadequate relative to other options or insufficient based on the risk involved, then he will use his entrepreneurial talent to a lesser degree or choose to become or remain an employee. The expected level of compensation relative to the risk will act as a selection mechanism. *Figure 10.1* provides a schematic illustration of this process.

© THE AUTHORS AND STUDENTLITTERATUR

10.3 Is There a Market for Entrepreneurship?

If we allow ourselves to make additional explicit and implicit simplified assumptions, constructing a more "traditional" supply and demand diagram is possible, as shown in *Figure 10.2*. The x-axis indicates the number of active entrepreneurs, and the y-axis indicates the entrepreneurs' expected compensation. For readers familiar with the analytical methods in neoclassical economics, explaining the extent of entrepreneurial activity in the economy in this manner is not far-fetched. However, keeping in mind that this model—as with all models—is a simplification is important. By linking the theory of entrepreneurship to the model of supply and demand, the analysis can be more formal and apply the same economic mechanisms/regularities that hold true for other factors of production. This approach has also resulted in several contributions.[33]

The demand curve represents the presence of entrepreneurial opportunities in an economy at a certain point in time and given the economy's structure and level of development. The demand curve is negatively sloped to reflect that the entrepreneurs' expected compensation will be lower the greater the number of active entrepreneurs. The demand function is implicitly based on the assumption that a given number of entrepreneurial opportunities can be discovered or created and that the entrepreneurial activities of others have a negative impact on the feasible return of an individual potential entrepreneur. From a dynamic perspective, one additional entrepreneurial activity may actually give rise to new entrepreneurial opportunities for both the entrepreneur himself and for other entrepreneurs—see *Figure 7.1* in chapter 7. In the dynamic case, an increase in the number of entrepreneurs will shift the demand curve outward because of the increase in the number of entrepreneurial opportunities that arise when new entrepreneurs enter the market. As such, entrepreneurial compensation is not necessarily negatively related to the number of entrepreneurs. Claiming that the number of opportunities is fixed is also contradictory if one simultaneously argues that opportunities are subjectively created and thus essentially infinite.

The supply curve, with a positive slope, represents the supply of qualified entrepreneurs. The higher the expected compensation, the greater the number

---

33 See, for instance, Casson (2003), Schultz (1980) and Holmes and Schmitz (1990).

© THE AUTHORS AND STUDENTLITTERATUR

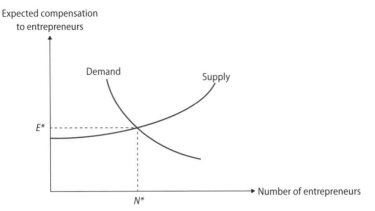

Figure 10.2 Supply of and demand for entrepreneurs.

Note: With the aid of a number of simplified assumptions, constructing a traditional supply and demand diagram for entrepreneurs is possible. This figure illustrates the market for entrepreneurs, but the supply and demand graph must be used with great caution, as elaborated in the main text. Source: Based on Casson (2003).

of individuals interested in becoming entrepreneurs. The supply curve starts with the salary that a potential entrepreneur would have received had he not chosen to become an entrepreneur. No one wants to be an entrepreneur if the compensation is lower than this reservation wage, which corresponds to the entrepreneur's opportunity cost. In real life, of course, this wage varies between individuals. As we discussed in the previous section, individuals may have reasons other than monetary compensation for wanting to become an entrepreneur. Hence, some people may venture into entrepreneurship even if the expected compensation is lower than the reservation wage.

The supply curve is initially relatively flat, representing the employees who are most eager to become entrepreneurs, while the curve gradually steepens to reflect that higher returns will be required to induce additional individuals, who value their leisure highly or have other well-paid options, to become entrepreneurs. One can also imagine that a stronger entrepreneurial culture and more positive attitudes regarding entrepreneurship influence and potentially flatten the supply curve.

Where the supply and demand curves intersect, a form of equilibrium is attained, with a certain level of entrepreneurship (N^*) and the entrepreneur's corresponding compensation (E^*). Analyzing entrepreneurship in this way is clearly a (somewhat misleading) simplification; however, as long as we are aware of the simplifications, it can show that the relationship between supply, demand and compensation also applies to entrepreneurship. A change in the level of entrepreneurship may depend on changes in supply or demand, and entrepreneurial compensation at equilibrium will react differently to different types of shocks. The analysis will also depend on how steep or flat the supply and demand curves are—that is, how sensitive supply and demand are to changes in entrepreneurial compensation.

OBJECTIONS

One must remember that real-world relationships are more complex than what one may infer from this static graph. For example, in this model, every entrepreneur is assumed to receive the same compensation in equilibrium (E^*). This conclusion is misleading, even in equilibrium. The leverage of entrepreneurial effort, when combined with other factors of production, varies across industries and firms. Even more importantly, entrepreneurial ability differs between individuals, which will have an impact on the amount of the compensation. The model can be interpreted as saying that entrepreneurial compensation in a particular industry or for a particular type of entrepreneur is the same, but this interpretation is also a simplification. It is the expected return that is the same, given the entrepreneurs' ability, access to capital, industry, etc. The variance is also considerable compared with that of employee compensation. In reality, as we have already noted, some will get a very high return on their entrepreneurship, whereas others earn nothing or even get a strongly negative return if all or part of their own concomitant equity investment is also lost.

The derivation of supply and demand curves for entrepreneurs (or entrepreneurial effort) requires additional assumptions, which are unrealistic with regard to entrepreneurship. The curves cannot be drawn unless one assumes that known and quantifiable entrepreneurial opportunities exist and that economic agents respond to them in predictable ways. However, a key characteristic of entrepreneurial activity is that assessing its outcome in advance is impossible. As a result, the entrepreneur himself is often the only person who demands the entrepreneurship services supplied. He is the only one who is able or willing to assess the services offered, and he must start

© THE AUTHORS AND STUDENTLITTERATUR

his own firm for the demand to be realized. Therefore, many people may argue that the use of supply and demand diagrams is both contradictory and misleading. However, in addition to their expository value, these diagrams are valuable from an explanatory perspective because we are forced to simplify matters and make assumptions that run counter to the very definition of entrepreneurship to draw these supply and demand curves.

10.4 Final Reflections

In this chapter, we have presented an analytical framework to study the determinants of entrepreneurship. Four factors have been identified as crucial for the degree of entrepreneurial activity: entrepreneurial competence, access to capital, entrepreneurial opportunities and the willingness to exploit these opportunities.

We then identified the conditions that need to be met to conceptually identify the supply of and demand for entrepreneurs. The analysis clearly showed that the market structure is vastly different from the structure of conventional markets. As a result, except in exceptional cases, no external market for entrepreneurship exists. The same person usually both supplies and demands his entrepreneurial services; the person who discovers or creates an opportunity typically both wants and needs to realize its commercial potential by starting his own firm.

For the entrepreneur to fully benefit from his entrepreneurial effort, managerial decision making and risk taking need to be linked to a significant ownership share in the venture. The entrepreneur cannot sell his services to someone else at a price that corresponds to their expected value. First, an external part cannot assess the prospective entrepreneur's ability, including his business idea, with sufficient precision. Second, the entrepreneur's incentives are weakened if he becomes an employee. Demand is indirect and is influenced by factors such as new technologies, industry structure and macroeconomic conditions. Supply depends on both individual and social factors, such as access to capital and cultural attitudes regarding risk taking and business ownership.

10.5 Chapter Summary

In this chapter, we have learned the following:

- An economy's entrepreneurial activity depends on four factors: entrepreneurial competence, access to capital, opportunity and willingness.
- Discussing a market for entrepreneurs is difficult. Normally, the same person both supplies and demands entrepreneurship services.
- The demand for entrepreneurship services arises because of the presence of entrepreneurial opportunities, and it is influenced by factors such as new technologies, industry structure, macroeconomic conditions and individual subjective assessments of the surrounding environment.
- Supply depends on both individual and social factors, such as access to capital and attitudes towards risk taking and business ownership.

© THE AUTHORS AND STUDENTLITTERATUR

The Entrepreneur's Compensation and Entrepreneurial Rents

In the previous chapter, we discussed the determinants of entrepreneurship and the supply of and demand for entrepreneurs. In this chapter, we expand on this analytical framework and analyze compensation for the exercise of entrepreneurship, which we refer to as entrepreneurial rent. We will discuss entrepreneurial rent in both the short run and long run and from individual and social perspectives.

11.1 Economic Rents and Entrepreneurial Rents

As the entrepreneur has a specific function, she will receive compensation for exercising this function, just as employees and capital owners receive compensation for their inputs. An employee receives a salary, and labor will be compensated (in the case of perfect competition and assuming that capital and labor are the only inputs) in terms of its marginal contribution to the firm's revenue. Technically, this contribution is known as the marginal revenue product of labor (MRP), which is defined as change in revenue caused by the change in output produced by the last unit of labor employed (marginal product of labor · marginal revenue). Similarly, capital owners will receive compensation (a risk-adjusted rate of return), which, in the long run, corresponds to capital's marginal revenue product.

The *risk-adjusted rate of return* includes the return exceeding the risk-free rate of interest (customarily defined as the interest rate on government bonds), which is what an investor demands to be willing to invest in a risky project instead of investing in secure government securities. The more risky the project, the greater the return an investor will require to invest in the project. A few projects have very high rates of return *ex post*, while most

Rate of return *ex ante*: the compensation that an investor expects to receive.
Rate of return *ex post*: the compensation that an investor actually receives.

projects develop only modestly or are terminated, which often implies that investors lose their entire investment.

To complete the analysis, let us introduce the entrepreneurial function and its compensation. The surplus generated in a successful, entrepreneurial new or incumbent firm will be higher than the profit that corresponds to the risk-adjusted market rate of return. This additional profit will be called the *entrepreneurial rent.*[1] It results from the entrepreneur's actions when she actively discovers or creates opportunities and makes decisions about how to combine factors of production and how to allocate resources across activities.

The total profit generated must be divided between the entrepreneur(s) and the capital owner(s), and the entrepreneur's compensation will then formally be determined by the contract between these two parties. The entrepreneur may receive a direct share of any profit after the other factors of production have received their share. She may also receive a regular "entrepreneur's wage," with or without a performance-related component. The entrepreneur may also be granted the right to choose how to use the other factors of production, given that the other factors are offered compensation that is contracted in advance (loan interest rate, hourly wage, rent for facilities). The entrepreneur will thus be able to claim the entire surplus that may materialize in a firm by combining the other factors of production in a novel way.[2]

If the entrepreneur and the owner are the same person, which is typically the case in small or new entrepreneurial firms, the division of the total compensation is not an issue. However, if the person who fulfills the entrepreneurial function is not a shareholder or only owns a small share of

---

1 Readers who do not feel comfortable using the term "rent" in this context might consider using "entrepreneurial profit"—a return above the risk-adjusted market rate of return. However, the connection to what we later refer to as economic rent and quasi-rent will not be as clear.
2 Shane (2003).

© THE AUTHORS AND STUDENTLITTERATUR

the firm, then large portions of the return attributable to entrepreneurship will accrue to others, giving rise to a potential incentive problem.

In practice, the entrepreneur's compensation will be classified as either capital income (dividends or capital gains) or labor income, and it will then be taxed according to the rules that apply to these types of income. However, from a conceptual perspective, this classification is irrelevant.

DIFFERENT KINDS OF ECONOMIC RENTS

The entrepreneurial rent closely relates to what is referred to as an economic rent in economics, which also goes by the name of *Ricardian rent* after economist David Ricardo (1772–1823). Ricardo defined rent as the return to a factor of production exceeding the level necessary to ascertain its supply (for example, the risk-adjusted market rate of return to a capital owner). An economic rent can result from a quantity constraint on the supply side. For example, a hotel located on an attractive beach may charge prices that result in a return in excess of the risk-adjusted market rate of return. Nature supplies the economy with a fixed stock of attractive beaches; therefore, even in the long run, competing hotels cannot offer the same service and thereby drive down the rate of return. Another example is a unique piece of art, where the supply of that particular piece in its original state is also given.

Closely linked to this concept are so-called quasi rents, also called *Marshallian rents* after economist Alfred Marshall (1842–1924). Quasi rents are economic rents that eventually disappear because the supply is adjustable in the long run, while it is fixed in the short and medium run. A typical example is the housing stock in a town, which is very nearly fixed in the short run, as new construction only represents a few percent of the total stock. However, in the long run, the supply may vary.

Government interventions and regulations may also give rise to economic rents. By giving monopoly privileges to a specific firm in a certain industry, this firm may, without fearing competitors, charge higher prices and thereby make higher profits than what would have been possible otherwise. This so-called monopoly rent is an example of an economic rent that is created through government intervention rather than through natural limitations. Another example is the introduction of patent and licensing regulations that can induce firms to charge higher prices than what may have been possible otherwise. Given that patents and licenses are granted for a limited period, these supernormal returns are quasi rents that can be obtained in the short and medium run; however, they will disappear in the long run.

Should an economic rent be regarded as an equilibrium phenomenon or as a Schumpeterian disequilibrium phenomenon? An economic rent may arise and persist in equilibrium based on government regulations or natural limitations, but it can also arise and possibly persist because of an entrepreneurial discovery or activity—and then be referred to as an entrepreneurial rent. A summary of the different types of rent is presented in *Table 11.1*.[3]

Table 11.1 Rents in equilibrium and disequilibrium.

	Equilibrium rents	Schumpeterian disequilibrium rents
Economic rent (Ricardian)	Arises as a result of resources in absolutely fixed supply.	Arises as a result of an entrepreneurial discovery or creation that requires a resource whose supply is fixed (unique competence, organizational advantage that cannot be imitated, patent, copyright, locational advantage, etc.).
Quasi rent (Marshallian)	Arises as a result of resources in fixed supply in the short or medium run.	Arises as a result of an entrepreneurial discovery or creation that requires a resource whose supply is fixed or highly constrained for some significant period of time (organizational superiority, creation of a strong brand name, etc.).

Source: Lewin and Phelan (2002).

WHY DO ENTREPRENEURIAL RENTS ARISE?

When using the term entrepreneurial rent, we refer to compensation in excess of the profit that corresponds to the risk-adjusted market rate of return that an entrepreneurial firm can generate through an innovation (i.e., a form of Schumpeterian disequilibrium rent). An entrepreneurial rent arises as a result of entrepreneurial insight or a specific entrepreneurial skill. Entrepreneurial rents may also arise even if every actor knows the

---

3 See, for instance, Lewin and Phelan (2002, p. 221–245), Alvarez (2005, p. 133–135) or Rumelt (2005) for an in-depth discussion on entrepreneurial rents and economic rents in general.

   © THE AUTHORS AND STUDENTLITTERATUR

potential value of an innovation in advance, as the entrepreneur may have a unique ability to combine other factors of production to ensure that all or part of the innovation's potential value is actually realized. Knowing that a commercialized innovation can generate an entrepreneurial rent is insufficient; being able to implement that commercialization is also necessary.

Hence, entrepreneurial rents arise when entrepreneurs successfully combine resources in new ways or, in other words, when they create innovations. The quantity constraints that form the basis for entrepreneurial rents primarily originate in the limited entrepreneurial ability and effort that the economy supplies. Because the supply of entrepreneurs is limited and qualified entrepreneurs constitute a heterogeneous group, entrepreneurial rents do not have to be temporary. Even if potential entrepreneurs may enter and compete with existing firms, not all entrepreneurs have the same abilities or opportunities.

Conceptually, the entrepreneur's short-run compensation can be considered a "monopoly" on information or superior knowledge, which contributes to the firm's superior performance. However, stressing the differences between monopoly rents and entrepreneurial rents is important. Despite their similarities, these are two distinct phenomena. A monopolist can take advantage of her unique position to acquire resources at the expense of others (consumers in particular) and to prevent innovations by potential rivals. An entrepreneur contributes her unique competence to the development of the firm by creating and/or discovering and exploiting new opportunities, which ultimately benefits society. According to the calculations of Yale professor William Nordhaus, the entrepreneur, on average, receives less than five percent of the increased value generated by entrepreneurial activities. The rest primarily accrues to consumers in the form of lower prices and products of higher quality.[4]

---

4 Nordhaus (2005). Baumol (2002b) estimates that roughly 80 percent of an innovation's value goes to parties who are not directly involved in its creation and exploitation.

11.2 Entrepreneurial Rents in the Short and Long Run

Entrepreneurial rents are conceivably reduced or even eliminated in the long run. The differences between various entrepreneurial activities may be significant; some entrepreneurial rents may disappear quickly, while others persist for a long time. Entrepreneurial rents that are likely to disappear rather quickly generally come from activities that are relatively easy to imitate and when the knowledge or ability—in practice or based on proprietary rights—is not linked to a specific person or organization. In this case, the relevant knowledge is easily transferable at low cost and thus may rapidly spread across the economy. Such entrepreneurial rents are quasi rents with relatively short lifespans. Ordinarily, imitating rivals enter the market, which increases supply and lowers price.

However, certain activities are difficult to imitate and may be based on an entrepreneur's unique traits. The critical knowledge can thus be considered tacit. For example, only one Ingvar Kamprad and one Richard Branson exist, and entrepreneurial services of Steve Jobs' caliber cannot be purchased at a specified market price in any market. Activities that initially seem easy to imitate may prove to be much more complex and hard to imitate, thus requiring particular entrepreneurial skills to be realized.

Every firm can also be regarded as a unique combination of employees and entrepreneurs with different innate abilities, learned skills and experiences. This combination may give rise to a distinctive entrepreneurial firm, which cannot be imitated in the market at a reasonable cost and thus cannot be replicated.[5] In such cases, the entrepreneurial rent is Ricardian and thus even persists in the long run.

ISOLATING MECHANISMS AND IMITATION

Richard Rumelt discusses various forms of what he calls "isolating mechanisms," which make protecting entrepreneurial rents from being taken away by imitators possible.[6] Patents are an obvious example of such a formal mechanism. Not all innovations can be protected through patenting, but many other mechanisms exist:

---

5 Ricketts (2002) and Wu (1989).
6 Rumelt (2005).

 © THE AUTHORS AND STUDENTLITTERATUR

- **Response lags in competitors' behavior**. Competitors always take some time to observe, evaluate and implement countermeasures.
- **Tacit knowledge**. The information required to successfully imitate an innovation is often more difficult to access and absorb than one might think because of a significant element of non-codifiability. This element makes imitating an innovating firm not only more difficult but also more costly.
- **Economies of scale**. Increased competition can result in the market price being pushed down below cost, which is unprofitable for imitating firms (and for the innovating firm).
- **Learning costs** (for potential competitors). If imitation requires learning and experience, imitating firms with less experience will be a step behind, and it will take time before competitors are able to challenge the innovating firm. This point is partially related to the first point above.
- **Buyer switching costs for product/firm/supplier** (for the end user). If the buyer's costs that are associated with switching to another product or supplier are high, imitating rivals will find competing with the firm that introduced the innovation difficult, even if imitating competitors improve the product (somewhat).
- **Network products**. If the innovation is a network product (where the utility of the product is increasing with the number of users), imitating rivals will have a hard time competing with the innovating firm (if this firm has built a sufficiently large customer base), even if imitating competitors improve the product (somewhat).
- **Reputation**. If demand for the product is linked to the good reputation of the firm's product and if the reputation is a function of how long the product has been in the market, imitating rivals will find competing with the firm that introduced the innovation difficult.
- **Buyer evaluation costs** (for the end user). For customers, evaluating and choosing between numerous alternatives may be costly. A cost-minimizing strategy involves doing what "most people" do and selecting the market-leading product. This strategy means that new competitors find gaining market shares difficult, even if imitating competitors manage to offer a slightly better product.
- **Advertising and channel crowding**. Promoting oneself and creating a good image for one's product may be cheaper when operating alone and

being the first one in the market, while doing so becomes increasingly difficult and expensive when many competitors are fighting for attention.

The aforementioned points imply that imitating competitors may find achieving success difficult if they simply imitate the entrepreneur or merely improve the product/innovation slightly. To succeed, imitating competitors must generally improve the product/innovation substantially. Hence, competition and imitation lead to continual improvements, and imitating competitors must be, to some extent, entrepreneurial to succeed. Entrepreneurial breakthroughs create an incentive for new entrepreneurial improvements.

PRICE FORMATION, FACTOR PRICES AND ENTREPRENEURIAL RENTS OVER TIME

William Baumol argues that price setting for entrepreneurial firms' innovative products is a kind of intertemporal price discrimination.[7] Initially, when an innovation is commercialized and competition is weak or non-existent, demand will be inelastic, and the price (and thereby the entrepreneurial rent) will be high. As imitating competitors establish themselves in the same market, demand becomes more elastic, and the price (and thereby the entrepreneurial rent) will fall.

Entrepreneurial rents are not simply reduced or eliminated by increased competition from new entrants, which leads to falling market prices. Entrepreneurial rents can also be reduced by rising prices for raw materials, intermediate inputs and other factors of production. For instance, those who supply inputs to the firm will notice that the firm makes an "excess profit" and want to get a share of the entrepreneurial rent. Some part of the above-normal return tends to "trickle down" to the other factors of production (labor, capital, land, intermediate inputs) that the entrepreneur has combined in a more value-creating way than before. For such profit sharing to occur, a supplier or an employee must have a certain degree of market power, or imitating competitors must push up the price of inputs and wages for those who possess critical inputs or skills.

---

7 Baumol (2010).

   © THE AUTHORS AND STUDENTLITTERATUR

Price discrimination: When firms charge different prices to different buyers because of their different willingness to pay. In using this strategy, firms can increase their profits. A typical example is student discounts. **Intertemporal price discrimination** refers to a strategy in which the price varies over time. For instance, a product can initially have a high price, which the most eager customers are willing to pay, or it may be more expensive to fly during high seasons or rush hours.

This situation can also be analyzed as a so-called hold-up problem, where the entrepreneur creates entrepreneurial rents by combining factors of production and making certain investments that cannot be easily undone. Realizing profit opportunities depends on, among other things, the suppliers of inputs, who do not necessarily depend on the entrepreneur to the same extent. Therefore, the suppliers can take advantage of their power position and seize a portion of the entrepreneurial rent.[8]

In other words, part of the entrepreneurial rents will, in the long run, be transformed not only into lower prices for consumers but also into higher salaries for employees as production volumes increase and/or new competitors enter the market. As a result, entrepreneurial rents in a particular firm or type of production are reduced or even eliminated.

TWO GRAPHICAL ILLUSTRATIONS

This process is illustrated graphically in *Figure 11.1*. In the figure, the evolution of the rate of return generated by *one* entrepreneurial opportunity is presented. When an opportunity is exploited at t_0, a return—which can be denoted an entrepreneurial return—above the risk-adjusted market rate or return accrues to the entrepreneur. Over time, the entrepreneurial return—and hence the entrepreneurial rent—will decline, and the return will approach the risk-adjusted market rate of return. Eventually, the entrepreneurial rent may be fully eliminated. One can also imagine a situation in which the return at

---

8 See Malcolmson (1997) for a discussion of hold-up theory.

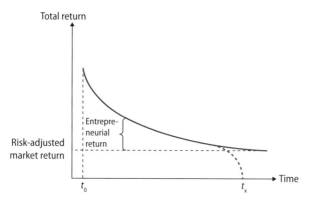

Figure 11.1 Entrepreneurial rent from the exploitation of an entrepreneurial opportunity.

Note: Entrepreneurial rent (in $) = entrepreneurial return (%) · capital (in $), where entrepreneurial return = actual return − risk-adjusted market return. The entrepreneur's compensation will be classified as capital income, capital gains and/or labor income, and it will thus be taxed according to the rules that apply to these types of income. A successful exploitation of an entrepreneurial opportunity creates a return on the invested capital that (greatly) exceeds the risk-adjusted market rate of return. Imitating competitors and the introduction of new and related products generally leads to the entrepreneurial rent eventually falling and ultimately being entirely eliminated.

some point in the future (t_x) falls to zero when new innovations are introduced that make the exploited opportunity obsolete or, in other words, worthless. For example, the world's best manufacturers of CDs or analog cameras will continue to receive a certain entrepreneurial rent even if competitors do their best to imitate them. The entrepreneurial rent only vanishes when CDs or analog cameras become obsolete due to superior digital alternatives.

However, on a more aggregate level, entrepreneurial rents will not vanish because new entrepreneurial opportunities are continuously discovered and created in a dynamic economy. When these opportunities are successfully exploited, new entrepreneurial rents arise.

The entire course of events can be illustrated as in *Figure 11.2*. Initially, the economy is in an experimentation phase, in which several firms test and modify potential entrepreneurial opportunities with varying results. Eventually, one firm has a breakthrough in the form of a successful discovery and exploitation of an innovation (or all the firms might fail). This successful exploitation will result in a return that exceeds the risk-adjusted market rate of return; the successful firm obtains an entrepreneurial rent (the

© THE AUTHORS AND STUDENTLITTERATUR

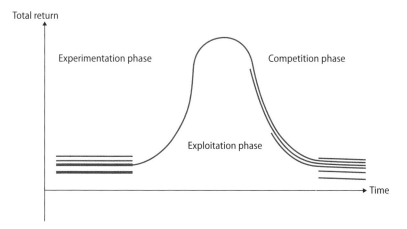

Figure 11.2 Experiments and competition for entrepreneurial opportunities.
Source: Knudsen and Swedberg (2009).

exploitation phase). The increased rate of return and the innovation attract imitating rivals, and the market enters the competition phase, during which the total return is pushed back to "normal" levels and the entrepreneurial rent is eliminated. A new experimentation phase ensues to pursue new entrepreneurial rents. The duration of the exploitation phase depends on the presence and the extent of isolating mechanisms.

11.3 The Entrepreneurial Rent from the Perspective of the Individual

Entrepreneurial rents may be very high because the entrepreneur does something unique and, in some cases, something exceptionally value-creating and difficult to imitate. If entrepreneurial activity were a costless process of alertness, then entrepreneurial rents might be considered a windfall gain, i.e., a reward that is received without any direct correlation to one's own input or compensation that is not proportional to the individual's—in this case, the entrepreneur's—effort. Coincidence or sheer luck may play a crucial role.

Still, no entrepreneurial rents are certain. The entrepreneur may have incorrect information, or she may have misinterpreted the available information. Ultimately, the economy is characterized by risk and uncertainty, and fully certain profits are rarely up for grabs. Therefore, viewing entrepreneurial rents as windfall gains is misleading. Nevertheless, many economists tone down the importance of risk and uncertainty and consider entrepreneurial rents a form of arbitrage profit—i.e., a risk-free profit that originates from the entrepreneur's utilization of misalignments in market prices for inputs and/or the final products. Alternatively, they interpret entrepreneurship as the kind of innate alertness attributed to entrepreneurs by Kirzner (Mark I), which neither assumes uncertainty nor has an opportunity cost.

Even though the future is uncertain and non-entrepreneurs and entrepreneurs cannot precisely predict how factors, such as demand, the price of inputs and other economic variables, will evolve, describing positive entrepreneurial rents as the product of pure luck is also misleading. Making informed decisions under genuine uncertainty requires competence and experience. The degree of uncertainty is often reduced over time, and the rents that result from an entrepreneurial project are neither definitive nor predetermined; they instead depend on continued efforts that require the input of entrepreneurial talents and skills.[9]

However, one should not disregard that even a certain degree of luck and fortunate circumstances, which have not been included in an entrepreneur's calculations, may partially explain the size of the entrepreneurial rent. However, this luck factor is conditional. The potential entrepreneur must act and actually realize her entrepreneurship. A luck factor can only become operative in projects that are actually carried out, and entrepreneurship is risky and demanding. Entrepreneurial rents are not a question of luck in the sense of profits falling into the entrepreneur's hand as "manna from heaven." Someone who does not actively look for opportunities and tries to realize these opportunities in the form of an activity within the framework of a firm will have zero probability of becoming a member of a group in which, *ex post*, someone has been exceptionally "lucky."

9 Alvarez (2005, p. 24–25).

   © THE AUTHORS AND STUDENTLITTERATUR

Perhaps a soccer analogy can further clarify this issue. Good teams are often declared lucky. Luck was arguably involved when Cristiano Ronaldo kicked the ball, which then bounced off a defending player, changed direction and thus completely fooled the goalkeeper. However, for this "luck" to come about, Ronaldo had to actively attempt to end up in a position where it was possible (or was considered reasonable) to hit the goal; it also took courage and determination to actually kick the ball.

11.4 The Social Function of the Entrepreneurial Rent

In mainstream economic theory, an economic rent is what a factor owner is paid minus what she would have demanded for supplying the factor in question. Does this definition imply that many entrepreneurial rents are unjustified and serve no purpose? No. The entrepreneurial rents that persist in the long run can be considered compensation for the unique and non-replicable competence that these entrepreneurs contribute. The entrepreneurial rent cannot be considered an example of over-compensation similar to an ordinary monopoly rent.

At first sight, it may be tempting to view entrepreneurial rents that will vanish in equilibrium as a waste that serves no purpose. When a product is mature and the production technology is well known and widespread, the same economic activity will occur without the necessity of any entrepreneurial rent. For example, a new product may initially have a high price, which then falls over time; eventually, the product may not provide more than compensation at the going market rate for the labor, capital and other inputs required for its production. Initially, the product is allegedly sold at an "excess price," which accrues to the entrepreneur as a rent.

This reasoning is flawed; the entrepreneurial rent cannot be regarded as unnecessary, undeserved or unfair. Most entrepreneurial rents will likely disappear over time. However, the analysis above neglects to consider that the individual entrepreneur's quest for a high return in the form of an entrepreneurial rent leads to a product's development and marketing in the first place. The fact that the entrepreneurial rent has vanished when equilibrium is reached is irrelevant. Entrepreneurial rents or the expectation of entrepreneurial rents are necessary to induce a sufficient number of people to devote themselves to entrepreneurship.[10] Even a low probability of an extremely high entrepreneurial rent may serve as a strong incentive for many people to expend entrepreneurial effort. From the individual's economic perspective, investing in risky entrepreneurial projects may only be warranted if the high likelihood of extensive losses is offset by a very high rate of return (compared with the risk-adjusted market rate of return) if successful.[11]

Instead of equating entrepreneurial rents to monopoly rents, which should be opposed, entrepreneurial rents should be viewed as providing the necessary incentives for innovative activities. The temporary entrepreneurial rents compensate the entrepreneur for her exploitation costs, which are costs that imitators do not have to incur. Considering all the losses associated with failed entrepreneurial ventures, the average return on innovative activities is modest, perhaps even negative. Blocking the "upside" of successful entrepreneurship, for example, by means of highly progressive taxation of entrepreneurial income, would impede and thus reduce the extent of productive entrepreneurial activity.

A tradeoff exists between the need for a sufficiently long exploitation phase (and the chance to generate entrepreneurial rent) and a quick start of the diffusion phase (in which knowledge is disseminated and benefits society, which corresponds to the competition phase in *Figure 11.2*). Without an exploitation phase, no innovative activities will occur. However, without the diffusion phase, society cannot benefit from the full potential of an innovation. On the one hand, disseminating and benefitting from new knowledge is crucial for economic growth and prosperity. On the other hand, the more rapid diffusion of new knowledge results in a shorter exploitation phase, which, in turn, weakens the driving forces behind developing new knowledge.

---

10 Defining "a sufficient number" involves a normative element. Even if productive entrepreneurship creates social value by definition, people who have this talent can create even more social value if they expend their effort on other pursuits (wage employment, parental leave, studies, philanthropy, etc.). However, for the most successful entrepreneurs—e.g., Ingvar Kamprad and Sam Walton—such alternative pursuits would unlikely be preferable from a social perspective.
11 Rumelt (2005).

© THE AUTHORS AND STUDENTLITTERATUR

This tradeoff is most clearly apparent with regard to patent law. Patents are a way of stimulating innovation by legally stipulating a predetermined duration for the exploitation phase, while the patent's scope and duration determine the extent and speed of the diffusion phase. However, patents do not necessarily put an end to diffusion. Through licensing and royalty contracts, knowledge diffusion can take place during the term of the patent. When properly designed, patent law does not slow down the creation, exploitation and diffusion of new valuable knowledge—it just guarantees the innovator/ entrepreneur a sound level of compensation if successful. This does not imply that the existing patent system is optimally designed.[12] Many analysts claim that filing for patents in the United States has become too easy, which arguably has led to socially harmful barriers to competition. For example, in their influential book *Innovation and Its Discontents*, economists Adam Jaffe and Josh Lerner argue that "the role of patents in the U.S. innovation system has changed from fuel for the engine to sand in the gears."[13]

Entrepreneurial rents also function as a signal to decision makers in other parts of the economy, sending the message that reallocating resources and putting them to more efficient use elsewhere would be profitable. As resources are reallocated to the activities that have high entrepreneurial rents, these rents will begin to fall. When no further reallocation is necessary, the entrepreneurial rent has been eliminated, and it thus no longer serves as a signal. Although entrepreneurial rents may not exist in equilibrium, they are not necessarily superfluous. Only analyzing and comparing static equilibria can be dangerous because the entrepreneurial function may then appear unnecessary.

From a social perspective, the presence of and search for entrepreneurial rents will thus contribute to the continuous structural changes that are required to generate economic growth. If no potential entrepreneurial rents existed, no one would be willing to assume the role of the entrepreneur and agent of change in the economy. The entrepreneur is needed for economic development, and entrepreneurial rents are a prerequisite for entrepreneurship's emergence and implementation. If entrepreneurial rents did not exist, firms would continue producing existing goods and services,

---

12 Baumol (2010).
13 Jaffe and Lerner (2004).

while the willingness and the ability to search for new products would be wiped out. From a social perspective, the entrepreneur's compensation can be regarded as a compensation for the generation and exploitation of new or unique knowledge.

The capital values created in firms controlled by people such as Swedish entrepreneur Jan Stenbeck, Microsoft's Bill Gates and Amazon founder Jeff Bezos are not return on invested capital, nor would the same wealth have been created by these people investing money in the stock market and becoming employees in other companies. These entrepreneurial rents instead represent a return to a completely different factor of production, namely, entrepreneurship.

11.5 Chapter Summary

In this chapter, we have learned the following:

- The surplus arising in a new or established successful entrepreneurial firm will be higher than the profit that corresponds to the risk-adjusted market rate of return. We refer to this profit as entrepreneurial rent.
- Most entrepreneurial rents will disappear in the long run, but various isolating mechanisms ensure that entrepreneurial rents persist in the short or medium run.
- From the individual perspective, entrepreneurial rents may be considered a composite compensation for exercising entrepreneurship. They are potentially very high. Even if luck plays a certain role with regard to the presence and size of the entrepreneurial rents, these rents are definitely not certain or predetermined.
- From a social perspective, the presence of and search for entrepreneurial rents contribute to the continuous structural change required to bring about economic development.
- The lack of entrepreneurial rents in equilibrium does not suggest that they do not serve a key function.

© THE AUTHORS AND STUDENTLITTERATUR

PART III

Entrepreneurship and Economic Policy

So far, we have consistently emphasized the importance of entrepreneurship for innovation, renewal, economic growth and job creation. We have also noted that entrepreneurs do not automatically aim for these noble things. Even if other factors, such as social recognition and media attention, also influence their desire to become an entrepreneur, the pursuit of profits plays a part that is impossible to ignore. When entrepreneurs search for and attempt to create entrepreneurial rents, entrepreneurs are largely governed by the incentives—the reward structure—that prevail in the environment in which they exercise their entrepreneurship. These incentives are essentially determined by the institutional structure of the economic system. Good institutions or favorable rules are prerequisites for encouraging entrepreneurial efforts and for channeling entrepreneurship in ways that are productive for society.

So what are the essential rules of the game? In the following three chapters, we will identify and analyze the most important institutions in this context and discuss how they should be designed to promote productive entrepreneurship. The analysis is limited to the institutions that the political decisions may directly or indirectly affect. In chapter 12, we discuss the basic principles for analyzing policy measures. In chapter 13, we discuss a number of policy measures in more detail and what conclusions one may draw from economic research regarding the effects of these measures. Chapter 14 is devoted entirely to analyzing the effects of taxation.

Entrepreneurship and Economic Policy—Basic Points of Departure

When entrepreneurs are searching for and seeking to create entrepreneurial rents, they are influenced by the reward structure that they encounter. This structure is primarily determined by the economic system's institutional setup.[1] In this chapter, we discuss what we consider the most important starting points for an analysis that aims to identify the key institutions and policy measures to facilitate the emergence of an entrepreneurial economy.

12.1 Small Business Policy versus Entrepreneurship Policy

Entrepreneurship is both elusive and multidimensional. In policy discussions, entrepreneurship has often been considered synonymous with self-employment or small business ownership, and since politicians and journalists began realizing the importance of entrepreneurship, the debate has often focused on what we would prefer to refer to as a policy for small firms. We must distinguish between small firms and entrepreneurship, but we also must distinguish between small business policy and entrepreneurship policy.[2]

Small business policy refers to a policy that aims to support small firms (including self-employed individuals) using various means. Support for small firms can be justified in several ways. From a macroeconomic perspective, one may want to support the positive effects (externalities) that one considers associated with a greater number of small firms, such

---

1 For an excellent review of different kinds of institutions and the reasons why institutions play such a crucial role in a country's development, see Kasper, Streit and Boettke (2012).
2 Lundström and Stevenson (2005) discuss the difference between SME policy and entrepreneurship policy at great length.

as increased employment, higher growth and more innovations. From a microeconomic perspective, one may want to compensate for the competitive disadvantages of small firms relative to large firms, notably fewer opportunities to exploit economies of scale as well as various cost and information disadvantages.[3] Small business policies often include the creation of different public agencies and programs to support the establishment of small and new firms.

In policy discussions, both a relatively small and a relatively large share of small firms are used to justify why small firms should be supported and why more small firms should exist. If the proportion, on the one hand, is relatively small (over time or compared with other countries), this category of firms is argued to be neglected and requiring additional support. If, on the other hand, the proportion is relatively large (over time or compared with other countries), this large proportion will serve as evidence of the need to stimulate small firms because of their considerable socio-economic significance. Regardless of the size distribution of firms, one can argue that small firms should be given special treatment.

Small business policies aim to influence *quantitative* aspects of business activity, such as the number (or percentage) of self-employed individuals, small and new firms or the size distribution of firms. More firms or more self-employed individuals are always considered desirable, as such numbers allegedly indicate a higher level of entrepreneurial activity. However, this is an overly narrow view of entrepreneurship. An economy may actually suffer from too many small firms or too many self-employed individuals. Attempting to identify an "optimal" level for the rate of self-employment or business ownership and to steer the economy toward this level is not to be recommended. Determining an "optimal" level is practically impossible, and even if such a level did exist, it would still vary over time and between regions and industries.

Because it is difficult or even impossible for politicians and bureaucrats to predict who will become a (successful) entrepreneur, attempting to support a particular group or a particular type of firm is also misguided. A system based on special benefits and regulations for selected categories usually becomes extremely complicated, with extensive rules, exemptions

3 See, for instance, Storey (2003) or van Stel, Storey and Thurik (2007).

© THE AUTHORS AND STUDENTLITTERATUR

and exemptions from the exemptions. In turn, significant administration and information costs often result, which may make things worse for the very type of firm that the measures intend to benefit. For instance, small firms are disproportionally affected by an increased regulatory burden, as high fixed costs are relatively more expensive for small businesses.[4] Pontus Braunerhjelm and Johan Eklund have shown that an increased administrative burden weakens the incentive to start a new firm. They find that new venture creation decreases by three percent if the administrative burden is increased by ten percent.[5] In addition, cumbersome administrative systems encourage unproductive and destructive entrepreneurship by introducing extensive lobbying efforts. Once politicians begin to grant favors to a certain group, good arguments for increasing the number of beneficiaries will abound.

Unless a significant market failure exists that may be identified and corrected (or mitigated) by economic policy, being skeptical of targeted support is warranted. A policy that aims to promote entrepreneurship should have a broader approach. It should aim to support an economic system that encourages individuals to pursue productive entrepreneurship and business growth, irrespective of the type of firm. The economic and business policies should, as much as possible, not seek to influence the "natural" development of firm size, business growth or firm type through targeted subsidies or tax deductions. Market forces and the profit motive alone should determine, to the greatest extent possible, how the business sector develops.[6]

Economic development—as well as the social welfare that it entails—normally benefits from a situation in which the rules encourage and reward productive entrepreneurship regardless of type or individual characteristics. A well-designed entrepreneurship policy facilitates productive entrepreneurship activities and makes creating and exploiting valuable knowledge possible. Whether such activities involve a high or low proportion of self-employed individuals or small firms is of minor importance. The policy should instead focus on more *qualitative* aspects. A policy that favors entrepreneurial firms with potential to become high-impact (HIE) or rapidly growing firms is preferable to a policy that aims to maximize the number of

---

4 EU (2007, 2008).
5 Braunerhjelm and Eklund (2014).
6 Holtz-Eakin (2000).

firms or the share of business owners.[7] This preference corresponds well with the OECD's conclusions that all-encompassing institutional/macroeconomic measures are preferable to various targeted microeconomic measures.[8]

Instead of attempting to persuade as many people as possible to start a firm, one should encourage the *right* people to start or expand firms. Unemployed individuals who start firms to make a living may be valuable. However, these livelihood firms have a slim chance of becoming high-growth firms that create value and opportunities to make a living for more people than the unemployed individual himself.[9] Leading and developing a high-growth firm is a complex and highly demanding task that requires access to networks and a complementary competence structure, which unemployed people rarely have. Successful entrepreneurship requires that the entrepreneur's ideas be tested in the market. Chance and luck may play a role, but only those who subject their ideas to a market test can benefit from luck or chance. Encouraging entrepreneurship across the board is not the same as encouraging as many people as possible to become self-employed individuals or to start their own firms.

In recent years, many countries have changed the approach of their business policies—away from a small business policy, which is more focused on quantity, to a more qualitative entrepreneurship policy.[10] *Figure 12.1* schematically illustrates the crucial differences between small business policy and entrepreneurship policy.

Quantitative objectives are advantageous because they are relatively easy to evaluate. Many studies that attempt to evaluate government programs are based on quantitative measures. For instance, one may assess whether a specific program has led to an increase in the number of firms in the industry, region or individual category. Many scholars prefer quantitative variables because they are more amenable to—or are a prerequisite for—empirical analysis. However, quantitative analysis risks committing the classic mistake of searching in the easiest places—a strategy reminding of the story of the

---

7   Shane (2008, p. 162).
8   OECD (2007a).
9   Autio, Kronlund and Kovalainen (2007).
10   In some cases, scholars have begun to talk about high-growth entrepreneurship policy, that is, a policy aimed at stimulating high-growth firms (Stam et al. 2012).

   © THE AUTHORS AND STUDENTLITTERATUR

Figure 12.1 Small business policy versus entrepreneurship policy.

drunkard who looks for his lost keys under a streetlight because of the light, even though he lost his keys in the darkness of the park.

The more qualitative aspects of entrepreneurship are much more difficult to address analytically and are thus more difficult to evaluate. Therefore, analyzing and evaluating entrepreneurship policy is a more delicate task. Entrepreneurship policy seeks to increase the propensity for innovation, growth and employment, and, by extension, social welfare. Weak development in these areas indicates that the entrepreneurship policy needs to be changed.

Small business policies may be in direct opposition to entrepreneurship policies. Policy measures that aim to make being self-employed or owning a small firm more favorable may prevent or impede the expansion of firms, even when socially desirable. For example, measures that seek to reduce the regulatory burden for firms smaller than a certain size will reduce the inclination to expand beyond this threshold. In Germany, many firms choose to not have more than 49 employees, as the administrative cost based on the design of the regulatory framework rises sharply for firms with 50 employees or more.[11] In France, trade unions' influence on firm management and the cost of dismissal increase as soon as the number of employees exceeds 49. Italy and Portugal have a similar limit at 15 employees.[12]

Although the purpose of such legislation is well intended—wanting to assist small firms, which often suffer more from different regulations—one should not lose sight of an ever-present side effect: obstacles for growth are created for firms with high growth potential. If finding suitable phase-out

---

11 Autio, Kronlund and Kovalainen (2007).
12 See Andersson and Henrekson (2015) and the references contained therein.

rules or compensating high-growth firms in other ways is impossible, one should be wary of this type of small business policy. Existing firms may find recruitment more difficult if potential workers prefer to be (or remain) self-employed.

In addition, small business policies may suffer from "dilution" when well-meaning policymakers try to give "something to everyone." For example, Finland has the greatest number of firms backed by public venture capital per capita in the world. An array of governmental institutions and agencies have handed out small amounts of money to a large number of firms. On average, each firm receives less than what Indian firms receive, despite Finland's far higher wage costs and price level.[13] This case shows that focusing on the qualitative aspects of entrepreneurship is preferable to attempting to stimulate firm formation and self-employment in general, regardless of the underlying entrepreneurial ambition.[14]

However, the strong arguments against a targeted small business policy should not be interpreted as an indirect argument in support of policies that favor big business. The framework for economic and industrial policy should promote competition and business activity across the board. It should not be designed to favor certain kinds of firms, industries or firm sizes or to legitimize entrenchment and weak competition. University of Chicago professor Luigi Zingales aptly opines that business policies should be pro-market, not pro-business. Pro-business proponents maintain that the government should encourage and support specific firms and industries through subsidies, tax incentives or other favorable actions. Pro-market proponents oppose this view, instead asserting that the government should create a level playing field on which every economic agent can compete on equal terms. When the buyer/consumer is no longer the one who decides whether a firm succeeds or fails, firms will devote more effort and resources to ensure that they receive benefits from the public sector and less effort in creating value for their customers. Such behavior not only decreases firms' productivity but also creates fertile ground for corruption and clientelism.[15]

---

13 Autio, Kronlund and Kovalainen (2007, p. 80).
14 Stam et al. (2012) and Autio, Kronlund and Kovalainen (2007).
15 Zingales (2012).

　　　　　© THE AUTHORS AND STUDENTLITTERATUR

Clientelism: A system in which those in power offer services and privileges to their "clients" in exchange for the support of the latter.

The fundamental objective of entrepreneurship policy is to create a dynamic economy that motivates potential ambitious entrepreneurs to start and develop firms. This policy should encourage renewal and growth, regardless of whether the development occurs in new or incumbent firms and whether these firms are large or small. This policy should ultimately support a country's ability to develop knowledge, new ideas and solutions to pressing problems to strengthen its competitiveness and thereby create the best possible conditions for increased social welfare.[16] Such a policy rewards

- education,
- knowledge transfer,
- competitive pressure, and
- incentives for entrepreneurs.

In chapters 13 and 14, we will return to the actual contents of such a policy.

12.2 Basic Preconditions for Economic Policy

Researchers have discussed several factors that may influence entrepreneurial activity. These factors range from labor market regulations to the size of the public sector. Economic policy may affect the entrepreneurship activity in five different ways by influencing:[17]

- the demand for entrepreneurship,
- the supply of entrepreneurship,
- the supply of resources and knowledge,
- preferences for entrepreneurship, and
- the decision-making process of potential entrepreneurs.

---

16 Cf. Hart (2003) and Danish Government Platform (2005).
17 Audretsch et al. (2002).

We will not systematically structure the discussion on entrepreneurship policy based on these five aspects. A certain economic policy measure or institutional reform will normally affect every aspect, at least to some degree. We will note the cases in which only a certain aspect is affected.

To be efficient, the economic policy does not necessarily have to affect the total number of entrepreneurs in society; altering the distribution between unproductive and productive entrepreneurship may be just as important. If policies can help channel unproductive entrepreneurship into something socially productive, then economic development can be substantially improved.[18]

A PASSIVE OR ACTIVE STATE

One generally harbors one of two perspectives on the role of the state and the economic policy vis-à-vis entrepreneurship. A passive perspective regarding the role of the state implies that the state should primarily maintain a regulatory framework and infrastructure to facilitate entrepreneurial activities. Alternatively, one may advocate a more active role for the state—i.e., that the state should actively step in and support or subsidize, for instance, R&D or a specific type of firm. Those who believe that the state should play a more active role argue that the price mechanism and the profit motive are insufficient means of incentivizing entrepreneurs. Therefore, the economic policy arsenal should contain various support programs that aim to strengthen the driving forces of entrepreneurship. In the next chapter, we discuss the commonly recommended measures in more detail.

Irrespective of one's active or passive approach to the state and economic policy, fundamental freedoms and rights must be respected and the protection of private property rights must be guaranteed for productive entrepreneurship to thrive. The capitalist market economy works best in systems that are characterized by political freedom. The exploitation of entrepreneurial opportunities includes gathering and using valuable information, and political freedom encourages the exchange of information

---

18 Baumol (2002b).

 © THE AUTHORS AND STUDENTLITTERATUR

in general. People who grow up in free systems also tend to exhibit greater initiative and self-confidence, which are some of the traits that foster entrepreneurial ability.[19]

RULE OF LAW AND PROPERTY RIGHTS

Closely linked to political freedom is the rule of law. This implies that not only citizens but also the government and its agencies are subject to the law, and the law is rooted in the public consciousness; it is universal and is aligned with what is generally believed to be right and wrong. Moreover, sanctions and penalties must be meted out by autonomous, disinterested courts that follow the established procedures.

In Sweden, the legal status of women was for a long time equal to that of minors. For example, until 1863, 25-year-old unmarried women were not given full legal rights like male adults. Before 1863, the Supreme Court could confer such rights on unmarried women in rare cases. Widows' legal status was comparable to that of adult men. A widow generally had the same right as a man to enter into contractual agreements. A widow was allowed to manage her property and her inherited property as long as her children's share of the inheritance was secured. Given these conditions, prominent women entrepreneurs were unsurprisingly lacking in early Swedish history. Nevertheless, several exceptionally successful female entrepreneurs left a mark at that time. An outstanding example is Christina Piper, who was presented in chapter 5 (Box 5.1).

Private property rights are crucial for the exercise of productive entrepreneurship. These rights go beyond the right to use an asset and the right to compensation should the asset be expropriated. One can discuss four fundamental dimensions of private property rights:[20]

- the right to use the good,
- the right to earn income from the good,
- the right to transfer the ownership of the good to others, and
- the right to the enforcement of property rights.

---

19 Shane (2003, chapter 5).
20 Kasper, Streit and Boettke (2012).

The right to use is the right to employ the asset as one pleases and the right to develop that asset. The right to earn income from the asset closely relates to the first dimension and ensures the right to the proceeds generated by the property. The right to transfer the ownership concerns the contractual freedom to transfer all or part of the property rights by sale, gift giving or renting. The right to enforcement refers to protection from the state and other individuals who are illegally encroaching on property rights. Effective property rights presuppose that the police and the judicial system will assist the individual if he were to be the victim of, for instance, theft or vandalism. In other words, the state makes a commitment to protect people against encroachments on their lawful property.

If people perceive that property rights are strongly protected, then they can also expect that they will become lawful owners of the potential profits from exploited entrepreneurial opportunities. If the rule of law prevails and the judicial system is efficient and objective, entrepreneurs are more willing to embark on long-term projects because the basic rules of the game can be expected to remain unchanged. Similarly, entering into agreements and carry out transactions with other parties on a strictly professional basis is less risky. In a well-functioning society characterized by the rule of law, in which the four basic dimensions of property rights are guaranteed, greater specialization and division of labor are possible. Therefore, entrepreneurs can more easily exploit their ideas without having to internalize the entire value chain—in other words, they do not have to do everything themselves. Access to external risk capital and complementary skills can also be gained based on contractual agreements.

Strong property rights encourage innovations because the right to future proceeds is secured *ex ante*. The return on innovations is also often protected by specific complementary institutions, such as patent law and trademark and copyright protection.[21] The incentives for potential entrepreneurs to exploit innovations are significantly weakened if the control of the entrepreneurs' assets and their future return is weak or uncertain. Formal property rights that do not include the right to use, the right to proceeds and the right to transfer

21 The research literature on the importance of property rights for economic development is overwhelming. For overviews, see Besley and Ghatak (2010) and Waldenström (2006).

 © THE AUTHORS AND STUDENTLITTERATUR

are meaningless.[22] In countries with weak property rights, entrepreneurs will also be less willing to reinvest profits in their firms.[23] Clearly defined and enforceable property rights are also a necessary condition for the emergence of well-functioning financial markets. In the poorest countries, an overwhelming majority of the population lacks formal property rights to their assets. Therefore, they cannot trade these assets outside a narrow circle of relatives and close friends, and, without a title, property cannot be used as collateral for loans or be used to increase access to financing.[24]

If the support for and enforcement of property rights is weak, the levels of unproductive or destructive entrepreneurship may increase. Organized crime syndicates and the emergence of a mafia are telling examples of innovative responses to the shortcomings in (or lack of) a formal institutional framework. However, these activities do not necessarily lower social welfare, given the institutional shortcomings of the economic system in which they emerge. If the state does not protect one's property, the local mafia boss's protection may be preferable to no protection at all. The developments in Somalia, Iraq and Syria in recent years are sad cases in point.[25]

12.3 Is There an Optimal Economic Policy Mix?

Regardless of how one chooses to classify and systematize different policy measures, assessing their impact and relative effectiveness is no easy task. Apart from the potential difficulty of measuring the qualitative aspects of entrepreneurship, various measures tend to interact. Policies may be complementary and thus mutually reinforcing, but they may also counteract one another.[26] Measures that are introduced simultaneously in different areas—for completely different purposes—may also affect entrepreneurial

---

22 Rodrik (2007, p. 156).

23 See, for instance, Johnson, McMillan and Woodruff (2002), who analyze newly founded firms in post-communist countries.

24 De Soto (2000).

25 Bandiera (2003) and Milhaput and West (2000).

26 Orszag and Snower (1998), who examine the complementarity between different measures to combat unemployment, is an interesting parallel example. They show how the effect of a certain policy measure may be affected by the implementation of completely different measures.

activity.[27] As the effect on entrepreneurship depends on the entire spectrum of economic policy measures, in practice, distinguishing and identifying the effective measures is very difficult. Quantifying the impact of these measures is even more difficult.

As always, the context also plays role. Various countries' political, economic and cultural systems differ considerably. Each country has a unique set of characteristics. The system of a particular country cannot be perfectly replicated or imitated through well-reasoned political decisions. However, comparing the economic policies of different countries and trying to find best practices is not wrong or pointless. Such a comparison may provide useful guidance and contribute forceful arguments for value-creating policy measures.

At the same time, one tends to disregard the importance of context when comparing countries. A certain factor may be more or less relevant in different countries depending on the circumstances and the general institutional setup in this country. Even when the formal institutions are identical in two countries, the outcomes may still be different. Informal institutions (such as social and cultural factors) also influence the outcome and may impact how the formal institutions ultimately affect the economic actors.[28] Unless informal institutions comply with formal institutions, the latter are unlikely to fulfill their intended function and provide a sound structure for people's behaviors and interactions. For instance, if individual freedom and private property rights are not culturally recognized and embedded, formal institutions that allegedly guarantee individual freedom and private property rights become largely ineffective. In this case, the institutions *de jure* and the institutions *de facto* differ.[29] Another example of a disconnect between *de jure* and *de facto* is the case of countries that have high income taxes, but where aggregate income tax revenue is low because of numerous loopholes and outright evasion. Similarly, in some countries, the level of *de jure* employment protection is high, but it can easily be circumvented by using temporary employment contracts (or by bribing the government official who is commissioned to enforce compliance of the law in question).

---

27 OECD (2007a).
28 See, for instance, Li and Zahra (2012).
29 Acemoglu, Johnson and Robinson (2005).

© THE AUTHORS AND STUDENTLITTERATUR

In other words, no "optimal" economic policy is valid for every country. In addition, even if a certain economic policy mix may be optimal for a particular country, this mix will probably change over time as the economy evolves and the views and preferences of the people adjust. An attempt to rank policy measures based on their relevance provides some kind of guidance at best, but it could also prove directly misleading for an individual country.[30]

No single, time-invariant measure can or should be used to encourage entrepreneurship in an economy. One can try to find common features across countries based on suitable empirical methods, but one should be wary of hastily drawing sweeping conclusions. Although many scientific studies might have concluded that one measure is (the most) important, the measure in question still may not be the most suitable one for countries that are not covered in the studies.

Matters are further complicated by the time dimension. Several studies have shown that many policy measures have negligible effects on entrepreneurial activity in the short run.[31] Such inertia could be due to cultural factors or high transaction and transformation costs. Given the logic governing politics, muster political support for institutional reforms may be difficult when a considerable lag exists before any positive effects become apparent.

In reality, the policy mix will never be optimal. The political sector is not guided by an altruistic, omniscient, omnipotent and enlightened ethos, which resolutely aligns its economic policy with the most recent scientific findings. Political considerations, self-interest and rent seeking implies that society will never attain (or perhaps never even strive for) an imagined optimum. Moreover, major changes in the regulatory framework will invariably give rise to unintended consequences that are impossible to predict.

Motivated by the discussion above, we will not rank different economic policy measures according to their relevance. Instead, in the following two chapters, we will present a smorgasbord of measures that various studies have identified as important. As always, there are tradeoffs, and clear-cut answers cannot always be provided, which is also true for entrepreneurship policy.

---

30 Cf. the discussion in Rodrik (2007), Boettke and Coyne (2009) and Lundström and Stevenson (2005).
31 Acs and Szerb (2007).

Nevertheless, a policy that encourages and facilitates the emergence of a successful and prosperous entrepreneurial economy should be based on the following four basic premises:[32]

1 Starting a firm and expanding its operations in line with its inherent potential should be easy. As a corollary, closing down a failed business should not be overly difficult.
2 Productive entrepreneurship activities should be rewarded.
3 Non-productive and destructive entrepreneurship should be discouraged or penalized.
4 Leading firms, including large mature corporations, should have incentives to continue to innovate and grow. This presupposes openness to trade and an efficient competition policy that keeps winners "on their toes," so that they remain innovative and dynamic in order to maintain their leading position. No one should be able to live off historical achievements.

Every measure discussed in the following two chapters should be seen in the light of these four basic elements.

12.4 Chapter Summary

In this chapter, we have learned the following:

- Distinguishing between small business policy and entrepreneurship policy is necessary. Small business policies aim to support small firms and self-employed individuals using different means. Entrepreneurship policies aim to encourage productive entrepreneurship and business growth regardless of the type of firms—new, established, large or small—in which they take place.

---

32 Baumol, Litan and Schramm (2007).

© THE AUTHORS AND STUDENTLITTERATUR

- Small business policies may conflict with entrepreneurship policies. If using targeted instruments (e.g., reducing the regulatory burden only for firms that are smaller than a certain size), policymakers inadvertently discourage rather than stimulate growth.
- A basic prerequisite to ensure that economic policymaking operates as it should is ensuring the rule of law, including property rights and freedom of contract.
- Deriving some kind of optimal, economic policy mix that works in every context is not feasible.

CHAPTER 13

Entrepreneurship and Economic Policy—Measures

In this chapter, we will discuss a number of concrete policy measures and the findings of economic research regarding the effects of these measures. The chapter begins with a discussion of the value of policy measures that directly target individual companies and entrepreneurs. We then move on to discuss the significance of various institutions.

13.1 Direct Measures

The ultimate causes of economic growth are not increased inputs of the traditional factors of production (land, labor and physical capital) or human capital. Instead, economic growth results when entrepreneurial activity is encouraged and channeled into productive areas and when economically valuable knowledge is transformed into demanded goods and services within the framework of profit-making firms. Therefore, if one wants to stimulate economic growth, directly stimulating or subsidizing the supply of traditional inputs is misguided. Instead, one must create an institutional environment in which productive entrepreneurship is rewarded. This does not imply that the incentives for work and investments in physical and human capital are unimportant—weak or faulty incentives in these areas also have a major direct and indirect impact on the incentives for entrepreneurial efforts.

Long-term economic development will largely depend on the quality of new entrepreneurial firms and on how well the market selection process works. Entrepreneurship cannot be planned or mandated, but an environment—an "ecosystem"—can be created in which successful entrepreneurs are more likely identified and chosen through a market-like selection process. Because the elimination of less efficient firms is both a natural and a necessary element in a dynamic economy, a sensible strategy would generally avoid supporting companies that were threatened with closure to prevent or postpone their exit from the market.

SUBSIDIES TO NEW FIRMS

Possible direct measures should focus on encouraging the creation of new enterprises. However, helping create new companies through subsidies is a double-edged sword, as it distorts the market selection process. If established firms are forced to liquidate because of the entry of new firms that receive government support, the selection process is impaired. To be efficient, any support to new companies must be temporary and designed such that the selection process is distorted as little as possible.

Nevertheless, all types of support will have the negative side-effect that entrepreneurial efforts are devoted to designing the firm and the orientation of its activities so that it becomes eligible for support. This means that the entrepreneur uses some of her talent and energy to live up to the criteria that will lead to the firm receiving subsidies, instead of focusing on creating as much value for customers as possible in the most cost-efficient way. A social cost therefore arises when companies spend resources to compete with each other in the "political market" to get government support. If substantial profit opportunities arise in the political market, then entrepreneurs will be attracted to that market. Targeted support is a source of entrepreneurial rents, and if the support is not economically justified – for example, that it corrects a market failure – it gives incentives for unproductive entrepreneurship in the form of rent seeking.

Therefore, support for firms easily leads to rent seeking and the redistribution of wealth rather than the creation of additional value.[1] A classic example in Sweden is the direct support to call centers that are located in rural and northern Sweden. For a time during the 1990s, this support was so extensive that all costs, including wages, were covered for several years. When the support period expired, companies often closed down their existing locations and reemerged elsewhere to become eligible for a new round of location subsidies. Regulations and poorly designed subsidy schemes tend

1 Murphy, Shleifer and Vishny (1991).

© THE AUTHORS AND STUDENTLITTERATUR

to have the unfortunate consequence that the entrepreneurs who are best equipped to exploit the regulatory framework drive out the entrepreneurs who would have been most adept at creating social value.[2]

A support program may also target specific firms (for example, small firms), self-employed individuals, certain industries (ICT, biotechnology), certain regions (poor regions, sparsely populated regions) or specific groups (women, immigrants, ethnic minorities, the unemployed). This kind of targeted support may be justifiable because of its backing of firms that are considered particularly important for entrepreneurship and innovation or because it will benefit people who are under-represented as business owners (women, young people). When certain groups or firms receive various types of support, the ones ineligible for support will be at a disadvantage. As a result, potential entrepreneurs who do not belong to the targeted categories may refrain from starting or expanding their firms, which distorts the selection process and renders it less efficient.[3]

13.2 Indirect Support—Institutional Conditions for Productive Entrepreneurship

How should economic policy be designed to create an environment that encourages productive entrepreneurship as much as possible? A basic prerequisite is a macro policy that is characterized by fiscal and monetary stability. If inflation is high and volatile, if public finances are fragile and if the exchange rate is unstable, exploiting entrepreneurial opportunities is more difficult. Even potentially highly profitable entrepreneurial projects may be thwarted by crises that originate from macroeconomic imbalances.[4]

The pertinent micro-oriented policy measures cover a wide array of issues. A good starting point involves revisiting *Figure 10.1* in chapter 10, which depicts the most important determinants of the supply, demand and the selection of entrepreneurs: opportunities, competence, capital and willingness. These

---

2 See also the discussion in Chilosi (2001) regarding entrepreneurship and the Eastern European countries.

3 van Stel and Storey (2004).

4 Several studies show such an effect. For example, in a study on transition economies, McMillan and Woodruff (2002) find that entrepreneurial activity increases much faster in countries with a lower rate of inflation.

factors are influenced by the economic policies of a country, region and/or local community. We will discuss eight important institutional areas—except taxes, which will be analyzed in the next chapter—and the ways in which their design affects the driving forces for productive entrepreneurship:

1 regulations concerning savings and capital formation,
2 regulation of product markets,
3 regulation of financial markets,
4 regulations in the labor market,
5 the social insurance system,
6 bankruptcy law,
7 research, education and the diffusion of knowledge, and
8 attitudes and cultural perceptions.

13.3 Savings and Capital Formation

As we discussed in chapter 10, the availability of equity capital is crucial for both the establishment and the expansion of firms. The more uncertain a project, the greater the required equity share. Even when readily available collateral makes the firm eligible for bank financing, the bank still requires a significant equity share of the total investment to grant a loan. A substantial equity investment by the entrepreneur is a way for her to signal that she believes that the project has a high likelihood of success, which makes obtaining external financing easier. A great deal of scientific support shows that an individual's private wealth position both influences her likelihood of becoming a business owner and her expansion of the firm.[5]

Potential entrepreneurs who lack wealth or assets that can be used as collateral are unable to signal the potentially high returns of an entrepreneurial project to third parties by investing and/or collateralizing their own assets or, if necessary, to finance the entire project until further equity can be obtained through generated profits. In many cases, firm assets mainly consist of immaterial capital (patents, trademarks, copyrights, routines, trade secrets) and the competence of its personnel; however, the latter can resign and start a competing firm—which is not unusual in entrepreneurial industries and

---

5 See, for instance, Nykvist (2008) and Parker (2009).

     © THE AUTHORS AND STUDENTLITTERATUR

regions. In such cases, banks cannot protect themselves against credit losses and poor outcomes by using the firm's assets as collateral. Therefore, a lack of sufficient personal resources explains why many promising entrepreneurial projects do not take off.

However, obtaining loans from financial institutions is by no means a universal right. Not every project should receive funding. A person's inability to obtain a bank loan does not in itself constitute sufficient proof of a market failure or of a malfunctioning capital market. The credit market functions as an initial filter that weeds out the most unrealistic and overly optimistic projects. Banks and their credit officers have far more experience with regard to evaluating the viability of a project than a potential entrepreneur who applies for financing of her first project. On the other hand, the true viability of many projects can only be evaluated by testing the finished product in the marketplace. For many groundbreaking projects, determining *a priori* whether the likelihood of success is high or low is impossible. A failed project is not necessarily a waste of resources; it may have resulted in important new knowledge that contributes positively to the evolutionary process of the economy.

THE IMPORTANCE OF THE FORM OF SAVING

The availability of equity financing is a critical factor for both start-ups and the expansion of existing firms. As indicated in chapter 6, investments from venture capital firms have been shown to be of crucial importance for many rapidly growing firms. Venture capital funding is often superior to conventional bank financing because venture capitalists also contribute complementary skills and networks. Many entrepreneurial firms are initially too small to be eligible for formal venture capital financing. In these cases, the informal market for external equity financing in the form of business angels is very important.

Strong incentives and opportunities for personal savings ensure potential entrepreneurs better access to capital. Here, taxes on savings play a major role. The level of taxation on labor and the overall taxation on the return on savings are important in relation to how easily personal savings that can potentially be channeled into the entrepreneurial sector can be accumulated. In mature welfare states, a sizable share of the precautionary need for household savings disappears, as the state and the mandatory social security system can fulfill some of the needs that would otherwise require individual savings. The typical individual thus rarely has access to substantial savings to start or become a (co-)owner of a firm. In most rich countries, an increasing part of savings is channeled into large funds managed by financial institutions, which is particularly true for the largest savings in terms of volume: pension savings. In the mid-1970s, Peter Drucker noted a dilemma: An increasing share of individual savings was being channeled into large funds. Drucker argued that even the United States risked ending up with "pension fund socialism" rather than as an entrepreneurial economy.[6]

Therefore, strong driving forces for private savings are insufficient; savings must also be accumulated in forms that make it available to finance entrepreneurial companies. As such, an important part of a beneficial entrepreneurship policy involves not encouraging the channeling of savings into large funds. This is especially true if the channeling of savings is governed by collective agreements and legislation with long lock-in periods and at the expense of other forms of savings that are more likely to channel them into entrepreneurial companies. Some kind of tax deduction scheme for private individuals who make equity investments in entrepreneurial firms is a possible measure.

Starting a firm does not necessarily require a great deal of capital, and liquidity constraints do not always have to be binding for newly founded firms.[7] Developments in ICT have also helped reduce capital requirements in many industries.[8] However, to expand firms, particularly rapidly growing firms, limited access to capital is often a binding constraint. Many new companies wither away prematurely due to lack of capital for R&D and expansion. Therefore, an efficient venture capital sector is an important component for the creation of a dynamic entrepreneurial sector.

---

6 Drucker (1976).

7 Hurst and Lusardi (2004) and Shane (2008, p. 79).

8 Baumol, Litan and Schramm (2007, p. 236).

   © THE AUTHORS AND STUDENTLITTERATUR

THE PUBLIC SECTOR AND VENTURE CAPITAL

The public sector may support the venture capital sector both directly and indirectly. The state can use some of its tax revenues to directly provide the market with venture capital, either through its institutions or together with private actors. Arguments in favor of providing government risk capital directly to firms are most convincing with regard to seed financing—that is, financing during phases that are so early that venture capital is unavailable.

However, this type of support presents some cause for concern. All types of support require a selection procedure, which is based on more or less formalized criteria. The selection of the "right" projects among all the projects that one can potentially support is never perfect. The evaluation procedure used by the venture capital industry is both complex and sophisticated, but it is also largely qualitative because it is based on tacit knowledge.

Although venture capital firms specialize in finding the future "winners" among all of the high risk projects that they evaluate, they frequently fail to do so. Therefore, major difficulties are clearly involved. Unlike public sector actors, venture capital firms have strong private incentives to identify the most promising projects.[9] Becoming successful also often requires tight control of firms' management and at times brutal corrections when something has gone wrong. In the real world, these types of actions are impossible to undertake as a public financier. Only a small part of Swedish governmental support—definitely less than 20 percent—is channeled to the earliest stages, although market failures may justify public sector investments during these phases.[10]

Nothing, neither in theory nor in practice, suggests that government agencies will be better able than venture capitalists or business angels to evaluate the future success of a particular firm or a specific project. Many indications suggest that public agencies will not base their decisions on strict business criteria and will instead weigh political aspects and overemphasize formal aspects. Finding publicly controlled organizations or agencies that have performed better than their private counterparts is practically

9 Gompers and Lerner (2004) and Gompers, Lerner and Kovner (2009).
10 Svensson (2011).

impossible.[11] To alleviate this problem, one could require that government support only be given to firms that also receive private financing. However, this solution contradicts the fundamental reason that public funds are needed in the first place—namely, because of a market failure, no private financiers exist, although the project expects a high social return.

The government may also support the venture capital industry indirectly through an appropriately designed tax policy, which we will return to in the next chapter. However, other alternatives exist. For example, public agencies can provide soft loans to improve the supply of risk capital in the market. Soft loans are loans that do not require collateral or personal guarantees and that, under some circumstances, can be waived—for example, after an approved project reporting and cost accounting or the project's discontinuation for reasons beyond the borrower's control. The effects of such soft loans are generally disappointing,[12] partly because politicians may be tempted to establish, for political reasons, a number of agencies that are authorized to offer loans that target specific regions and/or industries. A complex maze of terms and conditions, often lacking consistency and encouraging strategic and short-term behavior, thus result.[13]

The most successful governmental support programs can be found in Israel, where a government agency provides loans to a number of "certified incubators," with clear rules regarding the amortization of the granted loans and the ways in which government involvement should be phased out. To be eligible for support, the newly established firm must have a stock option program that covers management and other key employees.

New research based on European data casts doubt on the idea that channeling more government funds into venture capital markets automatically stimulates a successful venture capital industry. A venture capital industry is more likely to be stimulated if the expected returns of innovative projects are higher because of, for instance, decreased corporate

---

11 Baumol, Litan and Schramm (2007, p. 220). See also Lerner (2009, chapter 9) for a discussion of why public investments often fail. For a more optimistic view on the role of the state, see Mazzucato (2013). However, she makes a different point, namely, that the most successful private innovations often require state-funded basic research.

12 See Lerner (2009) for a summary of the international research. For a Swedish overview, see Svensson (2011).

13 See IVA (2011) for the situation in Sweden.

        © THE AUTHORS AND STUDENTLITTERATUR

or capital gains taxes. The existence of exit opportunities also energizes the venture capital industry.[14] Although the problem of information asymmetries cannot be solved through tax policy, an appropriate tax policy can trigger informal and formal venture capital to alleviate these problems.

However, one should not focus exclusively on the venture capital industry. A well-developed financial sector offers a variety of other financial sources, ranging from readily available, highly liquid savings to long-term institutionalized pension-saving schemes that severely restrict the owner's control of the assets. Most importantly, the design of the regulatory framework should not exclude large parts of savings from the risk capital sector.

Hence, the composition of savings—not just the volume—influences potential entrepreneurship activity in the economy. For this reason, any arrangement that channels savings and asset control to large institutional investors will likely limit the supply of financial capital to potential entrepreneurs. In 1978, the United States began to allow pension funds to invest a portion of their assets in high-risk projects, which contributed to a significant expansion of the venture capital industry that subsequently boosted entrepreneurial activity.[15]

13.4 Regulation of Product Markets

Product market regulations come in a variety of forms. An extreme form of product market regulation involves granting a monopoly in a market to a particular firm—something that used to be common in the telecom industry and in radio and TV. Other examples include requirements for state licensing, detailed requirements regarding product design and rules that stipulate which production methods to use. To encourage entrepreneurship, the markets for goods and services must be subject to a regulatory framework that facilitates the search for information and knowledge to discover and create new entrepreneurial opportunities.

For product markets to incentivize actors to experiment, market-leading incumbent firms cannot be allowed to unduly exploit their dominant market positions. Drafting appropriately balanced regulations is easier said than

---

14 Da Rin, Nicodano and Sembenelli (2006).
15 Hart (2003, p. 10).

done; examples of the regulatory framework falling short of its objectives, favoring a certain interest group or giving rise to large fixed costs that effectively bar smaller actors from entering the market are easily found. Technological change may also turn regulations into obsolete constraints that render the adaptation to changed conditions more difficult.

Research also highlights the risk that regulations weaken competition by making it more difficult to create new firms and enter the market. Weak competitive pressure undermines the firms' motivation to exploit innovations and adopt new technologies. Hindering the adaptation of production and distribution to new information and communications technologies is particularly problematic, having major negative effects on productivity growth.

Regulations that reduce competitive pressures also implicitly reduce motivations to move capital and labor from low-productivity firms to firms with higher productivity. For instance, such lock-in may result from public procurement rules that lock in government institutions and agencies to a certain supplier for a long time. Because considerable productivity differences exist between firms in a particular industry at a given time, high productivity growth cannot be achieved unless resources can be transferred across firms relatively smoothly. Depending on the composition of the industry and the skills of the workforce, these effects may vary.[16]

During the 1980s and 1990s, a wave of deregulation occurred in product markets all over the world, which opened up a number of markets to entrepreneurship and new firm entry. This development serves as an important explanation of the increased entrepreneurial activity relative to the early decades of the post-war period. *Figure 13.1* presents the extent of product market regulation in leading countries in 1998, 2003 and 2008. Sweden fared very well compared with similar countries at the start of the new millennium, but many countries have since then matched and even surpassed Sweden.[17]

---

16 Arnold, Nicoletti and Scarpetta (2011).
17 Arnold, Nicoletti and Scarpetta (2011).

   © THE AUTHORS AND STUDENTLITTERATUR

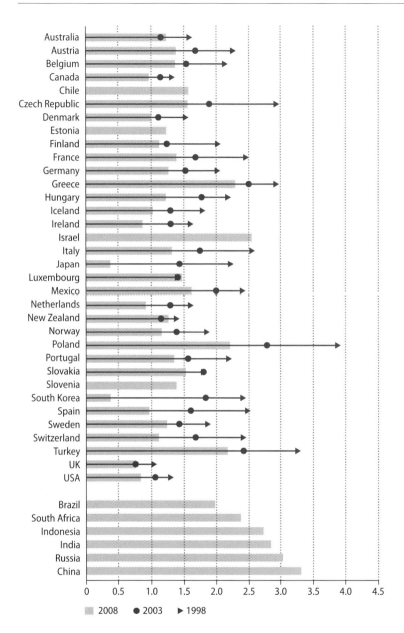

Figure 13.1 Product market regulations in a number of leading countries
(Index: 0 to 6). Source: Arnold, Nicoletti and Scarpetta (2011).

SOCIAL WELFARE SERVICES

The degree of transparency with regard to both the production and financing of large parts of the service sector—particularly central welfare services such as health care, education and the care of children, the elderly and the disabled—still varies considerably. In many cases, the large-scale production in the manufacturing sector has come to serve as a model for the production of welfare services. In this case, the public sector, rather than the large corporations, has started producing the services, which has led to the exclusion of private entrepreneurs from a large and rapidly expanding sector of the economy. These services are also characterized by a high degree of income elasticity, i.e., when real income increases by a certain percentage, the demand for these services rises even more.

The behavior of the public sector in these areas is of crucial importance with regard to how much these arenas have opened up for talented and ambitious entrepreneurs. If a country chooses to primarily produce health care, education and care for children, the elderly and the disabled in the public sector, then private entrepreneurs are excluded from a large and growing part of the economy. The opening up of tax-financed service production for competition in Sweden, which began in the early 1990s, has created a new arena for productive entrepreneurship pursued by profit-making firms. The private share of the production of many social services has increased rapidly. This particular effect can be seen in the free school reform enacted in the early 1990s, which has resulted in a large and rapidly growing share of pupils in primary and secondary education who attend private schools. Already in the early 1990s, there were some attempts to introduce contestability in health care, childcare, and the care of the elderly and the disabled. This development gained further momentum via the System of Freedom of Choice Act (LOV 2008:962), which went into effect in 2009. In 2014, slightly more than 12,000 private care-giving firms of all sizes and modes of operation employed almost 170,000 employees.[18]

On the one hand, the assertion that freedom of choice and competition benefit consumers in normal markets with private financing and production is hardly controversial. On the other hand, this positive effect on consumers

---

18 https://www.vardforetagarna.se.

  © THE AUTHORS AND STUDENTLITTERATUR

does not necessarily apply in markets with private production and tax financing. Manipulation and waste arise more easily when an anonymous and absent third party (the taxpayers) acts as an intermediary and finances transactions between the producer and the consumer. Today's welfare services are also supplied and consumed in so-called quasi-markets that are characterized by a series of problems that must be addressed:[19] the services in question are complex and difficult to procure; formalized procurement processes favor large actors and curb competition; producers cannot charge extra for quality improvements; costly excess capacity may arise; a lack of information makes rational decision making difficult for users; evaluations and compliance control are skill- and resource-intensive; segregating forces exist; and individual users do not consider how society is affected.

The most salient problems with quasi-markets involve credence goods. These goods are characterized by the producer knowing more than the consumer regarding her needs. The consumer finds assessing whether she needs a specific service, for example, a certain type of medical treatment, difficult. Ascertaining the utility impact of a credence good is difficult or impossible for the consumer. The utility gain or loss of credence goods is even difficult to measure after consumption. The seller of the good knows the utility impact of the good, creating a situation of asymmetric information.

Quasi-market: A public sector institutional structure that allows private firms to produce tax-financed services. This institutional structure is designed to reap the supposed efficiency gains of free markets without losing the equity benefits of traditional systems of public administration and financing. Although production is (almost) entirely financed by taxes, production is exposed to competition from private organizations. Private producers may be both for-profit and non-profit organizations, which creates freedom of choice for users, as they can choose which supplier they want to use, regardless of whether this supplier is private or public. The introduction of contestability intends to create a mechanism to raise quality given a stipulated cost. For a quasi-market to function properly, all parties must have access to accurate information regarding costs and quality.

---

19 Le Grand and Bartlett (1993) present a theoretical analysis of quasi-markets.

To some extent, consumers can rely on the producers' reputation, but reliable information can only be disseminated by consumers who understand and are able to evaluate the service in question. Empirical studies of public sector procurements confirm that credence goods have the worst outcomes.[20] How these problems are handled is crucial in relation to how well quasi-markets work.

IMPACT ASSESSMENT

Most sectors have plenty of detailed regulations, such as industry standards, safety regulations, rules regarding working hours, and certification requirements. Regulatory changes and tougher rules should always be preceded by thorough impact assessments, in which the risk of the new regulations having stifling effects on competition and innovation is evaluated.[21] A strategy that can sometimes be used involves randomized experiments; in other words, a certain policy measure could first be tried in a number of counties and/or municipalities and then be compared with the places where the policy was not implemented. All new proposals could also have a "sunset clause"—that is, new regulations should be reviewed regularly; otherwise, they ought to be phased out automatically after a pre-specified number of years. Politicians who underestimate or ignore the important experimentation and selection process required in a successful market economy are also likely to underestimate the costs of regulations and underestimate the benefits of deregulation.

Differences in contestability and competitive pressure may explain a significant part of the differences in productivity between the United States and Europe. The greater competition in the United States has resulted in its companies adapting their production and distribution more quickly to new information and communications technologies, which is particularly noticeable in the service sector.[22] Many studies show that regulations that reduce competition by restricting new actors' entry into the market lead to a

---

20 Andersson and Jordahl (2011).
21 See Eklund (2011).
22 Poschke (2010).

     © THE AUTHORS AND STUDENTLITTERATUR

lower productivity growth rate.[23] The explanation is straightforward: these regulations protect old and inefficient firms.

Social welfare services pose a particularly difficult challenge. The demand for these services tends to increase faster than real income. According to studies in the United States, the income elasticity for health care and education is approximately 1.6.[24] In other words, an increase of real income by 10 percent implies that Americans want to spend 16 percent more on health care and education. However, in Sweden no more than approximately 22 percent of GDP goes to publicly funded health care, education, childcare, and care for the elderly and the disabled. Furthermore, this share has not increased since the beginning of the 1980s despite considerable real income growth.

These services are almost entirely financed by taxes, which is problematic. The public sector has committed itself to tax-finance the services whose demand grows the most when people experience real income growth. Moreover, globalization makes upholding a high tax ratio relative to GDP increasingly difficult. As a result, what could have been growth industries in a regular market tend to become "cost problems" in tax-financed quasi-markets, thus making entry less attractive for ambitious and talented entrepreneurs.

A more realistic discussion has begun. For example, in a much-discussed ESO report, Per Borg noted that production of welfare services must be allowed to grow at least as rapidly as the aggregate economy.[25] However, this is only possible if additional private funding is allowed and if the boundaries for the public sector obligation in key areas are defined.

Since the turn of the millennium, more or less serious proposals on so-called "economic free zones" have been introduced.[26] These zones are specific, regionally or locally, demarcated areas excluded from (some) regulations and taxes or where companies and R&D activities are subsidized or otherwise supported by political means. The hope is that entrepreneurship and innovation will be stimulated in these areas and that spillover effects will have a positive impact on the surrounding areas. Little hard evidence suggests

---

23 Inklaar, Timmer and van Ark (2008) and Andersson, Johansson and Lööf (2012).
24 Murray (2003) and Fogel (1999).
25 Borg (2009) and Borg et al. (2010).
26 See the contributions in Bergh (2012).

that such measures have a positive social rate of return in rich countries today, except perhaps in terms of increasing employment in particularly vulnerable areas in which large groups are marginalized.

13.5 Regulation of Financial Markets

The basic functions of financial markets are to offer financing, risk management and payment services. For these services to be completed in a satisfactory manner, the financial system must gain the confidence of both savers and investors, which, in turn, requires a well-balanced regulatory framework. Overarching regulations that help maintain confidence in the financial markets—market-conforming regulations—should be safeguarded, while other regulations that impede the functioning of financial markets should be avoided. In reality, this is a difficult balancing act. Rules regarding government guarantees or requirements for government charter permits may not only help maintain confidence in the markets but also hamper innovation and economic development if they are too extensive or restrictive.[27]

If no financial intermediaries existed, all investors and savers would have to evaluate companies, business leaders and projects themselves. The efficiency of this essential component of the selection process is greatly improved by the intermediaries who make up the financial system. As we have already established in section 13.3, under the heading "Savings and Capital Formation," entrepreneurs are unable to fully leverage their efforts unless they have good access to financing. Well-functioning financial markets lower the inevitable information and transaction costs that arise in the relationship between lenders and borrowers. These markets then help more entrepreneurs receive financing and improve the allocation of capital— that is, financial resources are channeled more often to firms with the greatest expected potential. These factors are particularly important for entrepreneurs with low incomes, little personal wealth and/or few collateralizable assets.[28]

A more efficient financial system makes it easier for agents other than the established large corporations to obtain external financing, which contributes to greater efficiency and economic growth in the long run.

---

27 SOU 2000:11.
28 Greenwood and Jovanovic (1990).

   © THE AUTHORS AND STUDENTLITTERATUR

Regulatory frameworks that make buying and mortgaging one's home easier constitute one channel through which potential entrepreneurs can possibly increase their access to financing.[29] In other words, well-functioning financial markets are fundamental for economic development, which is supported by a large body of research.[30] The highly sophisticated financial system in the United States is often suggested as a major explanation of its innovative and entrepreneurial economy.[31]

Regulations that hamper competition among financial intermediaries and lenders reduce the supply of capital to potential entrepreneurs and thereby contribute to a decreasing number of entrepreneurs in the economy. Conversely, deregulation in the banking sector and increased credit market competition promote entrepreneurial activities.[32] In less developed countries, scholars have found that the perceived obstacles that keep companies from obtaining financing are greater in countries with a high degree of concentration in the banking sector. The negative relationship is stronger:[33]

- when more regulations exist,
- when the government meddles more in the granting of credit, and
- when the government owns a larger share of the banking sector.

During the 1970s, the liberal market economy experienced a renaissance in the major industrialized countries. Somewhat belatedly, Sweden also embarked on a similar reform path. First, capital markets were reformed. The most important steps in this process are summarized in *Table 13.1*. Without going into detail, we note that domestic credit markets were fully deregulated in 1986 and that the deregulation of the currency and capital markets, including the removal of the restrictions on foreign ownership, was finalized in 1993.

---

29 Henley (2005).
30 See Levine (2005) for a summary.
31 Kauffman Foundation (2007).
32 Gehrig and Stenbacka (2007), Cetorelli and Strahan (2006).
33 Beck, Demirgüc-Kunt and Maksimovic (2004).

Table 13.1 The major steps in the deregulation of Swedish capital markets.

Corporations and municipalities allowed to borrow abroad	1974
Deregulation of banks' deposit rates	1978
Deregulation of interest rates on corporate bonds	1980
Deregulation of lending rates by insurance companies	1980
Banks granted permission to issue CDs	1980
Liquidity ratios for banks are abolished	1983
Deregulation of banks' lending rates	1985
Loan ceiling on bank lending lifted	1985
Marginal placement ratios for banks and insurance companies abolished	1986
Relaxation of foreign exchange controls on stock market transactions	1986–88
Remaining foreign exchange controls lifted	1989
Removal or annulment of:	
Regulation on establishment of branches of foreign banks	1990
Regulation on foreign acquisition of shares in Swedish commercial banks, broker firms and finance companies	1990
Regulation on establishment of financial institutions other than banks	1991
The act on foreign acquisitions of Swedish companies	1992
Trade permit requirement for foreigners	1992
Restrictions in the articles of associations regarding the right of foreigners to acquire shares in Swedish companies	1993
The payment services act	1993

Source: Reiter (2003) and Jonung (1994).

13.6 Regulation of Labor Markets

The labor market is a fundamental factor market. In every country, the labor market is characterized by many rules that control matters such as the degree of employment protection, the ways in which employees should be notified in case of redundancy, types of conflict resolution methods between employers and employees, procedures for contractual and wage-

© THE AUTHORS AND STUDENTLITTERATUR

setting negotiations, strike and lockout rules, and the powers of elected trade union representatives.[34] To analyze the effects of its regulatory framework and institutional structure on the conditions for entrepreneurship, we must first explain how the labor market works. The labor market's inner workings are determined by a complex interplay between wage formation institutions, labor market legislation, regulations agreed upon by trade unions and employer organizations, and insurance and social safety nets that the public sector provides.

THE FUNCTION OF THE LABOR MARKET

A massive restructuring of job openings and employees is constantly occurring in a dynamic market economy. Companies hire and fire; young people enter, and retirees exit; and people leave for and return from parental leave, sickness, and further education. Technological changes and the ensuing changes in the market structure continually force companies to adapt their operations, including alterations in how they organize and remunerate their employees. The constant process of experimentation and selection in the market means firms enter and exit, expand and contract, which translates into sizable adjustments in the structure of employment and sometimes even into major drops in aggregate employment. For instance, during the major structural and cost crisis in Sweden in the early 1990s, more than 14 percent of all jobs were lost from 1990 to 1993, i.e., aggregate employment fell by 600,000 people.

A major restructuring in the labor market is an inevitable part of a modern economy and is thus something that characterizes every country in the OECD. Entrepreneurs establish new firms to commercialize new combinations. If successful, they expand; if unsuccessful, they exit. Similarly, existing firms are continuously challenged by—and are continuously challenging—new and existing competitors. If successful, they expand; if not, they contract and eventually exit. This dynamic process of creative destruction—channeled via firm entry, expansion, contraction and exit—brings about a structural transformation. The economy changes form in the perennial struggle between new and old structures. A successful economy exhibits disproportionate growth of high-productivity firms relative to other firms.

---

34 Nycander (2008) provides a comprehensive description.

The churning of firms and jobs is a ubiquitous feature of modern economies. The extent of this dynamism is illustrated in *Table 13.2*, which uses establishment-level data for the American economy that is averaged over almost three decades. The number of new jobs per year is as high as 18 percent of the total number of jobs. One-third of these new jobs are created in new establishments, and two-thirds are created through the expansion of existing establishments. At the same time, 16 percent of all jobs are lost through the closure and contraction of some establishments, resulting in an annual net job growth rate of 2 percent.

Thus, a gross job reallocation rate of 34 (18 + 16) percent is necessary to achieve a net gain of a mere two percent. The excess job reallocation rate—the number of jobs over and above the minimum required to accommodate the net employment change—equals 32 percent. In other words, to create one net job, you must create nine gross jobs.

Reallocation rates vary greatly between the various OECD countries. In the early 21st century, the average gross job reallocation rate in the OECD was 22 percent. However, rates varied considerably; for example, the rates in the United States and the United Kingdom were almost twice as high as those in Sweden and Germany. The reallocation rate for workers is also greater than that for jobs; workers may voluntarily quit/start new jobs without the job itself disappearing. The average gross reallocation rate for workers was 33 percent (i.e., 50 percent higher than the rate for jobs).[35]

Table 13.2 Annual averages for job creation and destruction at the establishment level in the United States, 1977–2005.

Job creation by entry	6%	Job destruction by exit	6%
Job creation by expansion	12%	Job destruction by contraction	10%
Gross job creation	18%	Gross job destruction	16%
Gross job reallocation rate (gross job creation + gross job destruction) = 18 + 16			34%
Net job growth (gross job creation – gross job destruction) = 18 – 16			2%
Excess job reallocation rate (gross job reallocation rate – net job growth) = 34 – 2			32%

Source: Davis, Haltiwanger and Jarmin (2008).

---

35 Martin and Scarpetta (2012).

    © THE AUTHORS AND STUDENTLITTERATUR

The gross flows of labor also tend to be larger in newer, smaller and heavily specialized firms and in firms that experience rapid growth in productivity and employment.[36] The gross reallocation of the work force is higher in new establishments because of the greater uncertainty, greater experimentation and greater variation in the quality of the products being produced. The share of jobs that are created and destroyed will decrease as the firm grows, matures and becomes more capital intensive.

LABOR MARKET REGULATIONS

As the gross flows of labor tend to be larger in newer, smaller, heavily specialized and rapidly growing firms, regulations, such as strict first-in-last-out rules in cases of redundancies, become a greater burden for these firms. Such firms have a greater need to modify the workforce than do larger, mature companies or companies without growth ambitions.[37] For potential gazelles to be able to grow quickly, flexibility is sorely needed to allow firms to quickly increase their number of employees when they experience an increased demand and, likewise, to rapidly reduce their activities when demand is lower than expected.[38] Compared with small firms, large firms have far greater scope to relocate individuals who are ultimately less suitable than expected for the position for which they were hired.

Labor market regulations thus tend to have a different impact on small and large firms. Smaller firms have a greater need to modify and change their knowledge bases—sometimes rapidly and comprehensively—while large firms are likely to benefit from a more rigid labor market in which their key employees are more easily retained.[39] Therefore, strict regulations favor relatively mature companies, while they negatively affect young and rapidly growing firms.

Labor market regulations, especially strict first-in-last-out rules in cases of redundancy and high firing costs, primarily affect entrepreneurial activity in two ways. First, strict employment regulations reduce the entrepreneur's room to maneuver with regard to adjusting the workforce to fluctuations

---

36 Reynolds (1999) and Bjuggren (2015).
37 Kanniainen and Vesala (2005).
38 Bornhäll, Daunfeldt and Rudholm (2014).
39 Braunerhjelm (2011).

© THE AUTHORS AND STUDENTLITTERATUR

in demand, which implies that innovative entrepreneurship becomes more risky.[40] Second, the relative advantage of being tenured at the current employer becomes more important for labor security than individual skills and productivity, which increases an employee's opportunity cost in changing employers or in leaving a secure salaried position to start a new firm. The opportunity cost grows over time, which makes luring people with key competencies away from their current positions even more difficult for new firms. A high degree of employment protection thus increases the opportunity cost both for changing jobs and for becoming self-employed, thereby both reducing an individual's willingness to start a high-growth firm and impeding the ability of these companies to recruit the people who they need to realize their potential.

Figure 13.2 presents the relationship between the strictness of employment protection and the rate of high-growth expectation early-stage entrepreneurship, i.e., new firms and firm owners with a willingness and potential for high growth (as measured by the GEM; see chapter 5). The figure clearly shows that stricter employment protection is associated with a lower share of this form of entrepreneurship. Studies have also shown that labor market regulations affect the start-up rate more than regulations that are linked directly to the start-up. The rate of entrepreneurship tends to be higher in countries in which changing the size of the workforce— that is, hiring and laying off staff—is easier and less costly.[41]

Scholars have also shown that the threshold for having the chance to try a new job is higher in more regulated labor markets. For jobs in which determining an individual's suitability in advance is difficult, the probability of matching the right position with the right employee decreases.[42] Greater mobility in the labor market covaries positively with productivity and the ability to pay wages. The matching process thus becomes more efficient. Likewise, greater mobility may be expected to stimulate innovation. The likelihood of the creation of valuable innovations increases when individuals find themselves in an environment in which their knowledge can be combined with that of others in the best way possible.

---

40 Audretsch et al. (2002).
41 van Stel et al. (2007).
42 Pries and Rogerson (2005).

 © THE AUTHORS AND STUDENTLITTERATUR

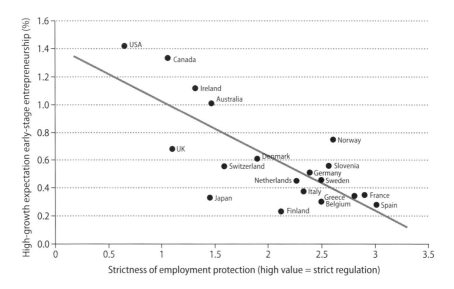

Figure 13.2 The strictness of employment protection and high-growth expectation early-stage entrepreneurship.

Note: Employment protection refers to the 2004 OECD index (version 2); high-growth expectation early-stage entrepreneurship is the average over the 2004–2009 period, according to the Global Entrepreneurship Monitor (GEM). R^2 = 0.57. Source: Bosma and Levie (2010).

The extent of labor market regulation differs greatly between different countries.[43] Liberalizations can and have stimulated entrepreneurial activity in many OECD countries.[44] The strict employment protection in Europe has probably contributed to its relative lack of new and fast-growing companies.[45] However, companies in many countries, such as Sweden and Spain, can increase flexibility by resorting to temporary employment contracts. Nevertheless, this strategy presents clear disadvantages. Employees on temporary contracts are less motivated to invest in firm-specific knowledge than are tenured employees, which makes attracting employees who possess—or are prepared to develop—highly valued skills difficult.

---

43 OECD (1994, 2004, 2013) and Skedinger (2010).
44 OECD (1998, 2000b).
45 Baumol, Litan and Schramm (2007, p. 210, 222).

© THE AUTHORS AND STUDENTLITTERATUR

WAGE-SETTING INSTITUTIONS

In markets in which wage setting is deregulated and individualized, wages tend to be lower in new firms than in older and larger firms, particularly in knowledge-intensive industries.[46] However, wages tend to quickly increase in entrepreneurial firms that survive and grow.[47] The option of paying low wages in start-ups is thus a mechanism that compensates for the lower productivity at the beginning of the firm's lifecycle. Therefore, institutions that impede or make it harder for entrepreneurs to offer wages that are initially lower than those in mature incumbents serve as obstacles to entrepreneurship and new venture creation. The differences in productivity—and thus in the capacity to pay wages—between firms are especially pronounced in not only new and small but also rapidly growing sectors and firms.[48] In these sectors and firms, considering the specific situation is important when employees are compensated for their work. Therefore, smaller companies often prefer a higher degree of flexibility and individualization with regard to wage setting.[49]

The farther away from the workplace wages are set and the less the idiosyncratic circumstances of individual cases are considered, the more difficult establishing the type of efficient competence structure that innovative entrepreneurial firms require to realize their full potential becomes. The more centralized and standardized the wage setting, the more it tends to disfavor small and entrepreneurial firms, particularly in service industries, where growing rapidly based on a high-quality business idea is otherwise usually easier.[50]

In conclusion, the road to success—from small to large—generally includes a few twists and turns, as new companies operate under genuine uncertainty. If the institutional conditions make quickly adjusting the competence structure and the size of the workforce difficult, we should expect a generally decreased willingness to expand and fewer firms that grow large in a short period of time. Therefore, regulations in the labor market and wage-

---

46 Brown and Medoff (1989).
47 Korobow (2002).
48 Caballero (2007) and Haltiwanger (2011).
49 Blau and Kahn (1996).
50 Henrekson and Johansson (2010).

   © THE AUTHORS AND STUDENTLITTERATUR

setting institutions are important for high-growth firms. As these firms play a key role in innovation and job growth in the economy, these conditions are also very important for development at the aggregate level.

13.7 The Design of the Social Insurance System

The social insurance system and its effects on entrepreneurial activity in the economy are closely linked to the design of the labor market's regulatory framework. The introduction of a public social insurance system, combined with extensive labor market regulations, tends to have a negative effect on individuals who want to become entrepreneurs because of the relative advantage of being employed.[51] Many insurances and benefits, such as unemployment insurance and sick leave compensation, are directly linked to employment. Therefore, the opportunity cost for leaving a tenured employment position increases, which weakens the incentives for entrepreneurship.[52] The generosity of the benefits in the social insurance system also plays a role. A generous unemployment insurance—in terms of its retention rate and duration—decreases unemployed individuals' willingness to become entrepreneurs or to seek employment in risky entrepreneurial firms. In countries with a generous unemployment insurance, new ventures are created less often.[53]

Health insurance may also be problematic. In the United States and in many other countries, the employer often supplies health insurance as part of a benefits package. Therefore, many employees and potential entrepreneurs may "get stuck" as employees in large firms that offer comprehensive health insurance benefits for their employees (and perhaps for their families). Generous retirement plans have similar effects. An important component of a policy that makes society more innovative and entrepreneurial involves making the individual's social insurances—public insurance as well as insurance paid by the individual herself and per agreement between employer and union—fully portable when changing jobs and moving between salaried employment and self-employment.

---

51 See, for instance, Ilmakunnas and Kanniainen (2001).
52 Audretsch et al. (2002).
53 Nickell (1997) and Koellinger and Minniti (2009).

© THE AUTHORS AND STUDENTLITTERATUR

By providing insurance against adverse outcomes, the public sector can also help alleviate the risk for individuals who engage in entrepreneurial firms that are characterized by great uncertainty. However, the public system needs to be sufficiently generous to be relevant to income earners with above-average salaries, and the security should not be linked to seniority at the current employer. A Danish flexicurity type system, which combines weaker employment protection with a more generous public income insurance, arguably makes it easier for firms to recruit and grow rapidly.[54] One component of this system is a relatively generous unemployment insurance, with an obligation to move, accept jobs and be willing to retrain and acquire new and more productive skills.

Sick leave and unemployment insurance should be designed to strongly incentivize rehabilitation, readjustment and/or retraining to push people back into productive activity as quickly as possible. By no means should these systems be considered an alternative to regular employment as a long-term source of personal income. Pension systems should be fully actuarial. For example, someone who switches to a lower-paying job late in her career should not lose economically compared to being granted pre-retirement from her more highly paid job.

Even if designing a social insurance system that applies to everyone and is portable were possible, entrepreneurs would not be able to make use of many benefits, such as parental leave insurance and paid leave for staying home with sick children. No matter what, being an entrepreneur means exposing oneself to higher risks and having less income protection. Therefore, a comprehensive social insurance system is likely to reduce one's willingness to become an entrepreneur, although some entrepreneurs are overly optimistic and thus do not appreciate a comprehensive and portable safety net.

13.8 Insolvency Regulation and Bankruptcy Law

A dynamic economy is characterized by the entry of new firms and the phasing out of other firms. This entry and exit of firms is a key constituent of the process of creative destruction and a prerequisite for dynamism and economic growth. An efficient process calls for a well-designed and effective

---

54 Klindt (2010).

© THE AUTHORS AND STUDENTLITTERATUR

insolvency regulation. A firm is insolvent when the value of its assets is less than its debt and when the firm is unable to repay its outstanding debt.

Insolvency regulation seeks to minimize the time and costs to society in phasing out unprofitable and inefficient firms, such that resources can be reallocated to more efficient uses. In addition, the damages for other parties involved, such as creditors, customers, suppliers, employees and the government, should be as small and as fairly distributed as possible. If the business idea is not competitive, then the invested capital will create more value if applied elsewhere. In such cases, closing down operations is the best option, and the firm files for bankruptcy; its assets are sold, and the proceeds are distributed to the creditors. However, not all insolvent firms should be closed down. A firm may experience temporary financial difficulties. If so, the best solution for both the firm and its creditors is normally firm restructuring and debt reduction ("haircut") through negotiations with the firm's creditors.

The design of the economic and legal framework for managing insolvency is thus not only an instrument for a liquidator but also a fundamental institution for preventing the unnecessary destruction of capital by facilitating debt restructuring.[55] However, unsuccessful and closed down firms should be regarded as a necessary part of an entrepreneurial market economy rather than a waste of resources. As long as it remains in operation, a firm that does not survive the competition contributes to the economy by pressuring its rivals to become more cost efficient and to produce more highly valued products. This positive effect persists among surviving firms after the failed firm is closed down. A firm failure also produces valuable information for other entrepreneurs by telling them what does not work. Because failed entrepreneurs do not consider that this information has a positive externality, i.e., that it benefits others in society, having relatively generous insolvency legislation makes sense.

From the entrepreneur's perspective, stringent insolvency legislation is a deterrent, as it increases the costs associated with creating and expanding a firm. Overly stringent insolvency legislation provides little room for the debt restructuring of fundamentally sound firms that experience temporary difficulties. Furthermore, after filing for bankruptcy, the previous owner

---

55 See Englund et al. (2015, chapter 3).

faces difficulties in getting personal debt that originates from the bankruptcy written off. The risk of failure is always present, even if the entrepreneur considers it unlikely. In several reports, the OECD has established that insolvency and bankruptcy legislation can directly affect new venture creation and entrepreneurial activity.[56]

Bankruptcy tends to lead to problems beyond ruining the private economy of the owner(s). For instance, the psychological costs of failure and bankruptcy are problematic. In many societies, business owners who fail are shunned, sometimes verging on ostracism. For instance, a study showed that 47 percent of Europeans were reluctant to order goods from a company whose owner had previously filed for bankruptcy. Such attitudes make it difficult for entrepreneurs who have failed in the past to launch new projects—let alone succeed in future projects.[57] These attitudes may also keep potential entrepreneurs from testing their ideas, even if they have a good chance of success and of thus contributing to the development of the economy. The United States tends to be highlighted as an economy in which people have more positive attitudes toward individuals who have tried—but failed—as entrepreneurs. Japan is known to fall on the other end of the spectrum from the United States; the personal cost of bankruptcy is very high in Japan. When Japanese bankruptcy legislation was reformed to decrease the economic cost of bankruptcy, people became more inclined to start firms. This effect was also most pronounced among the most highly educated entrepreneurs (those with a degree from one of Japan's ten elite universities).[58]

A country's business culture must give failed entrepreneurs a "second chance" and allow them to attempt new entrepreneurial projects. Many successful entrepreneurs have one or several bankruptcies behind them, and a bankruptcy can be a valuable experience that increases the likelihood of succeeding in future projects. Empirical research has also shown that so-called serial entrepreneurs are more successful.[59] Many pioneering projects originate from people who initially failed and then started all over again.

---

56 OECD (2005, 2007b).
57 EU (2008) and OECD (1998).
58 See Audretsch et al. (2002) regarding attitudes toward failure in the United States. Regarding Japan, see Eberhart, Eesley and Eisenhardt (2013).
59 See Ucbasaran et al. (2008) for a survey of the research on serial entrepreneurs.

          © THE AUTHORS AND STUDENTLITTERATUR

On the one hand, insolvency legislation should not make starting new business projects indefinitely difficult or impossible for those involved. The legislation must make failing possible within the framework of the law. On the other hand, the legislation must not be overly toothless and thus exploitable by dishonest entrepreneurs and business owners. Poorly designed bankruptcy and insolvency legislation negatively affects serious firms, while unproductive or destructive entrepreneurship is stimulated if the legislation can be used for devious and unwarranted debt restructuring, serial bankruptcies or pre-planned fraudulent bankruptcies.

13.9 Research, Education and the Diffusion of Knowledge

The entrepreneurial exploitation of inventions and the diffusion of economically valuable knowledge are crucial for economic development. The entrepreneur plays a crucial role in this process. Entrepreneurship policy is largely about facilitating and supporting this role.

All politicians, regardless of ideology, who are eager to demonstrate that they keep up with the latest economic insights claim that they are in favor of the "knowledge society" and that they, in different ways, want to encourage its growth and development. More resources for R&D tend to be the suggested solution. Forming a political majority in favor of public support for R&D is usually possible, and such support exists in some form in most developed countries. However, as we explained in chapter 8, more R&D does not automatically translate into more innovations, more start-ups or faster firm growth.

In the worst-case scenario, the quantitative targets for R&D investments may result in wasted resources because they focus on an "asset" that may not be exploited at all or may be exploited in other countries.[60] However, R&D expenditure is a production input and thus a cost, not a welfare-enhancing end product. R&D expenditure does not have intrinsic value. R&D may be necessary, but it cannot be a driver of economic development on its own. Causation may actually run in the opposite direction. In an economic system that encourages productive entrepreneurship, a great deal of R&D will be carried out because a demand exists for new knowledge that can

---

60 See, for instance, Svensson (2013) and Daunfeldt and Wallen (2013, chapter 5).

© THE AUTHORS AND STUDENTLITTERATUR

only be obtained through R&D. The transformation of R&D into valuable and attractively priced goods and services will not occur unless new and growing firms exist, which requires favorable conditions for innovative entrepreneurship.[61] For example, in one study, researchers examine how the level of innovation (measured as high-tech venture capital investments) is affected by public R&D investments in 14 countries between 1988 and 2001. They find no effect.[62] Thus, policymakers cannot simply focus on the quantity of R&D; they also must ensure that the R&D activities are conducted within an institutional setup that is conducive to productive entrepreneurship.

The effects of different forms of R&D support are not particularly impressive either. A number of reviews and evaluations of R&D support are now available, including a Swedish analysis.[63] The general conclusion is that state support to firms' R&D may induce firms to spend more on R&D but that the effects on innovation and growth vary. In addition, some firms act strategically vis-à-vis the support scheme: they increase the level of R&D just enough to qualify for maximum support. Regarding the choice of which type of support to use, the evidence indicates that tax deductions are less expensive and more efficient than direct subsidies to firms.[64]

Knowledge spillovers are an important mechanism for the diffusion and exploitation of valuable knowledge. Knowledge spillovers are facilitated by geographical proximity. Policy measures that facilitate the diffusion of knowledge between organizations and firms are thus recommended. One example is the support for the growth of clusters and science parks. A Swedish study found that technology-based firms located in research clusters fare somewhat better (for instance, in terms of sales and employment growth).[65] However, the most successful clusters have emerged spontaneously over an extended period.

Successful clusters normally emerge in response to opportunities—they cannot be planned with elaborate political support measures. A chance factor is usually also a component of successful clusters. The emergence of

---

61 Holcombe (2007).
62 Da Rin, Nicodano and Sembenelli (2006).
63 Bager-Sjögren (2011, 2012).
64 Guellec and van Pottelsberghe (2003) and OECD (2010).
65 Lindelöf and Löfsten (2003).

© THE AUTHORS AND STUDENTLITTERATUR

successful clusters is a result of creative and tenacious entrepreneurs, and policy should primarily support and amplify the effect of clusters that have emerged spontaneously.[66]

Economic policy may also support development in other ways that are linked to academia. Google and Netscape are two interesting examples of innovations that originated in the world of academia. Stimulating academic entrepreneurship and facilitating the commercialization of innovations that have emerged in this sector may be a way that politicians can stimulate entrepreneurship. For such a strategy to succeed, university management must encourage entrepreneurial initiatives. Furthermore, the incentives for spin-offs from universities cannot be weak. Some universities have special in-house organizations that facilitate and support the commercialization of inventions and new knowledge, so-called Technology Transfer Offices (TTOs). However, TTOs may also hamper entrepreneurial exploitation of university research through increased bureaucracy or the prioritization of a narrow university interest rather than social welfare.[67]

13.10 Attitudes and Cultural Perceptions

Of course, entrepreneurs and other actors are not entirely governed by economic incentives. Cultural and psychological factors also play an important role. For example, an entrepreneur may be driven by the desire to realize a certain business idea or a project. She may dream about proving to herself—and to others—that she is able to realize an idea and be successful. A society that rewards and encourages the pursuit of such dreams becomes more creative and more entrepreneurial than a society that rewards uniformity.

Entrepreneurs may thus be encouraged and rewarded in other non-monetary ways. Social appreciation, media attention, and awards of various kinds are among the many types of driving forces. Joseph Schumpeter highlights these non-pecuniary motives as the most important, as well as the desire to found a "private kingdom," which may give the entrepreneur a

---

66 Carlsson (2009).

67 Although many researchers find a positive effect, several studies find no effect or a negative effect (Kaufmann Foundation 2008; OECD 2007a). See Henrekson and Rosenberg (2001) for a further analysis of incentives for academic entrepreneurship.

high level of social esteem, influence and independence. William Baumol also believes that the entrepreneur's driving forces are multifaceted. According to him, most entrepreneurs are motivated by a desire for wealth, power and prestige.[68] However, even if profit seeking does not have to be a goal in itself, it still serves as an indicator of success and ability. Expected and/or realized economic profit is also a prerequisite for obtaining resources for innovation and expansion. If an entrepreneur needs co-financiers at some point, then she is normally obligated to contribute part of the financing herself. Hence, even if profit seeking is not a goal in itself, profit is a necessary means for those who want to realize their entrepreneurial vision in the form of a successful firm. Revenue in excess of costs must ultimately be generated to obtain the financial resources that are required to operate and expand the business.

In a broader sense, societal attitudes have a significant influence over the opportunities and career paths that an individual may consider or even perceive. To realize a successful entrepreneurial economy, room for curiosity, experimentation and testing is essential, and success must be rewarded and perhaps even revered. However, such concrete policy measures are unlikely to be implemented unless the prevailing norms and values embrace these traits. Therefore, positive attitudes regarding entrepreneurship are a necessary condition for maintaining a high level of entrepreneurial activity or for bringing about an increased rate of owner-managed businesses.

Many of our attitudes and perceptions are formed at an early age in our families, at school and in our close social circles. Much can be done to stimulate entrepreneurship, for example, training and encouraging creativity and entrepreneurship in childhood and adolescence. Entrepreneurs commonly have family members, often a parent, who are or have been entrepreneurs.[69]

Many of the attitudes vis-à-vis entrepreneurship also reflect the institutional setup and reward structures. For many individuals, embarking on a career as an entrepreneur does not seem sufficiently attractive. The expected compensation in the event of success is not considered proportionate to the risks that one faces and the uncertainty under which one must operate.

---

68 Schumpeter (2004 [1934]) and Baumol (2002b).

69 Reynolds, Hay and Camp (1999) find a positive relationship between respect for entrepreneurs and the rate of entrepreneurship. See Freytag (2007) for a comprehensive discussion on culture, attitudes and entrepreneurship.

© THE AUTHORS AND STUDENTLITTERATUR

Therefore, negative attitudes toward entrepreneurship may be based on fundamental factors and deep-seated values. The social structure of payoffs is largely a codification of current attitudes, norms and standards. For instance, from the late 1960s until 1990, the Swedish tax code was extremely unfavorable for running and owning firms unless the owner was a juridical person and the firm was large and very capital-intensive. However, these tax rules were fully compatible with the leading political vision that the desirable state of affairs was a well-functioning market economy—without individually successful and wealthy capitalists.[70]

The interaction between informal institutions—the socially shared rules that dictate people's behavioral patterns—and formal institutions is complex and difficult to change. If existing institutions facilitate and encourage value-creating activities that lead to higher welfare for most people, people are more likely to prefer institutions that lead to increased predictability and rule of law, stronger protection of individual property rights and high returns on productive entrepreneurship.[71] However, changing the rules of the game and the social structure of payoffs often requires changing attitudes. Therefore, a policy that aims to nurture a more entrepreneurial society includes both technical and practical measures with regard to tax rates and regulatory systems and sustained advocacy to change attitudes toward entrepreneurship. One important mechanism for creating a successful entrepreneurial ecosystem involves increasing the strength of cultural norms that facilitate entrepreneurship, such as positive views on freedom and risk taking.[72]

William Baumol argues that we should downplay the role of cultural factors because they are more difficult for politicians to influence and because they contribute to politicians' adoption of negative attitudes toward attempts to influence the extent of entrepreneurial activity.[73] However, claiming that differences in cultural backgrounds and attitudes contribute considerably to cross-country differences in entrepreneurial activity and that they block change to the institutional framework would be an exaggeration. To illustrate this point, the respective evolution of the East and West German

---

70 Henrekson and Jakobsson (2001).
71 Khalil (1995)
72 Coyne (2014).
73 Baumol (2010).

© THE AUTHORS AND STUDENTLITTERATUR

economies before reunification may be considered. The inhabitants of these two countries had the same cultural background, but they had completely different institutional setups that led to extremely dissimilar paths of development.[74] The extreme differences between the development paths in North and South Korea offer another case in point.

13.11 Institutional Conditions—Final Reflections

An innovation's successful commercialization, production and industrial distribution require a gamut of complementary competencies. The process is both complex and lengthy. Obstacles regarding financing and recruitment must be overcome. The entrepreneur plays the key role in this process. Many new, initially fast-growing, firms fail. However, those that succeed make major contributions to growth, development and job creation.

Linking the specific skill sets of various agents requires well-designed institutions and policies. Combined with an efficient judicial system, the regulatory framework should efficiently prevent destructive entrepreneurship and fraudulent business practices, preferably without incurring unnecessary costs for firms—costs that become entry barriers for new firms. The legal system must be characterized by transparency, consistency, equal treatment and swiftness with regard to handling legal disputes both between different private parties and between the government and individual firms.

In this chapter, we have highlighted a number of important areas in which policy can make a substantial difference and pave the way for entrepreneurial firms. The tax system will be discussed separately in the chapter 14.

13.12 Chapter Summary

In this chapter, we have learned the following:

- Direct measures in the form of subsidies and targeted support for firms is a double-edged sword that should be avoided as much as possible.

---

74 Saute (2008).

   © THE AUTHORS AND STUDENTLITTERATUR

- A number of key components must be in place to support the growth of an entrepreneurial economy:
  - The regulatory framework regarding savings and capital formation must encourage private savings, and saving in forms that make one's savings readily available for the financing of entrepreneurial firms should be encouraged.
  - The product markets should be sufficiently competitive to challenge dominant firms from below.
  - The regulatory framework for financial markets should be designed in such a way that new and potential high-growth firms can readily gain access to external capital.
  - The labor market must be sufficiently flexible and encourage mobility to ensure that the workforce can be reallocated from declining establishments, firms and industries to those with higher productivity and greater growth potential quickly and at low cost
  - Social safety nets—whether governmental or based on contractual agreements between employers and unions/individual employees—should encourage individuals to switch from less to more productive jobs and firms.
  - Insolvency and bankruptcy legislation should be designed to ensure that those who fail get a second chance. In addition, it should minimize costs for society and the time required to phase out unprofitable and inefficient firms, such that resources can be transferred and be more efficiently utilized. Legislation must also protect fundamentally sound firms to ensure that temporary financial distress does not lead to bankruptcy and closure.
  - Promoting entrepreneurship activities by supporting research, education and the dissemination of knowledge is a difficult task for the government. Focusing on narrow issues, such as R&D and seed funding, is insufficient.
  - Attitudes and cultural norms play a part with regard to the willingness to exercise entrepreneurship. The interaction between informal institutions—the unwritten attitudes and norms that influence behavioral patterns—and the formal institutional setup is complex and difficult to change.

© THE AUTHORS AND STUDENTLITTERATUR

Entrepreneurship and Economic Policy—Taxes

The design of the tax system has a major impact on entrepreneurial activity—in terms of both the total volume of entrepreneurship and the ways in which it is channeled. Tax rules and tax rates affect the net return both to potential entrepreneurs and to other actors in the competence structure, as outlined in chapter 6. Extensive research has analyzed the effects of taxes, both theoretically and empirically. In this chapter, we will discuss the main insights gleaned from these studies from a perspective of innovation and entrepreneurship.

14.1 Basic Points of Departure

Taxation affects innovation, entrepreneurship and the creation of firms in a variety of ways. The journey from an idea to a full-scale industrial company is often an arduous, time-consuming and costly process that consists of several phases. Taxation affects all phases of this process (as analyzed in chapters 6 and 7). However, as each phase is unique, understanding the effects of taxes requires detailed analysis.[1] Taxes affect the incentives to discover and create entrepreneurial opportunities and the desire to exploit these opportunities.

Taxes affect incentives by directly reducing the net financial compensation for entrepreneurial effort. As we have noted, other factors are also important for entrepreneurs, but the financial effect of taxes cannot be neglected. However, the relationship between taxes and entrepreneurship is complex, and the theory of taxation seldom offers clear-cut answers. Taxes affect

---

1 See Johansson et al. (2014) and Henrekson and Johansson (2009) for an in-depth discussion.

entrepreneurial activity through three fundamental mechanisms, which give rise to three distinct effects of taxes:

- an incentive effect,
- a tax evasion effect, and
- an insurance effect.

THE INCENTIVE EFFECT

The incentive effect refers to how the taxation of an entrepreneur's income flows reduces his net compensation, which directly dampens the economic incentives for exerting entrepreneurial effort. The incentive effect can be both absolute and relative. A tax hike results in an absolute decline in the expected after-tax compensation for starting or expanding a firm. Moreover, fewer financial resources will be available for reinvestment to expand the firm, and both the liquidity and the solvency of the entrepreneur and/or the firm will be weaker, which reduces a person's willingness to exercise entrepreneurship.[2]

The rate of taxation on entrepreneurship relative to alternative activities also plays a role. If the effective rate of taxation differs between activities and types of income, the activity that is, relatively speaking, taxed at the lowest rate is stimulated. Entrepreneurship is thus encouraged if it is taxed at a lower rate than the income from regular employment and/or the return on passively invested capital, and vice versa.[3]

From the analysis in chapters 10 and 11, we have learned that the expected compensation—the entrepreneurial rent—must be sufficiently high to make potential entrepreneurs willing to exercise and develop their entrepreneurial ability in the first place. What is considered attractive depends on the perceived risk and the individual's opportunity cost. The opportunity cost is mainly determined by the compensation and other rights and privileges that are linked to employment (when possible) and the ways in which they are taxed, along with the taxation of proceeds from passive capital investment.

---

2 See, for instance, the discussion in OECD (1998).
3 Harper (2003).

© THE AUTHORS AND STUDENTLITTERATUR

THE TAX EVASION EFFECT

A tax evasion effect exists if entrepreneurs find avoiding tax payments—legally or illegally—easier. For instance, self-employed individuals may find underreporting taxable income (by not registering part of firm revenue) or exaggerating costs (by registering expenses for private consumption as tax-deductible business costs) easier. One study found that Swedish self-employed individuals underreported their incomes by 30 percent.[4] Therefore, self-employment may be stimulated by high taxes.[5]

The tax rate could thus have a counter-intuitive impact on entrepreneurship. However, this type of entrepreneurship should be considered a type of non-productive entrepreneurship, which generally does not lead to entrepreneurship but to non-entrepreneurial self-employment of the kind discussed in chapter 4. It also creates a competitive advantage for firms and industries with lower productivity but with greater scope for evading taxes. Even if high taxes stimulate a specific type of entrepreneurship, they will not have a positive effect on the aggregate economy.

THE INSURANCE EFFECT

Finally, taxation may have an insurance effect. Taxation (combined with unlimited deductions for losses if profits are negative) may serve as an insurance mechanism that stimulates risk taking.[6] Applied to entrepreneurship, an increased tax on returns combined with unlimited tax deductions for losses will result in a reduced after-tax variance in the rate of return—and thus reduce the risk. If potential entrepreneurs are risk averse, this risk reduction may have a positive effect on entrepreneurial activity. The government may be considered a "sleeping partner" in the firm, sharing profits and losses with the entrepreneur.[7] For these theoretical conclusions to be empirically valid, the government must reimburse the taxpayer-entrepreneur if profits are negative. Few, if any, existing tax systems have this feature. If the tax code does not allow unlimited deductions of losses—i.e.,

---

4 Engström and Holmlund (2009).
5 OECD (2000b), Cullen and Gordon (2007) and Gordon (1998).
6 This mechanism was first proposed by Domar and Musgrave (1944).
7 See, for instance, Cullen and Gordon (2007) for an analysis.

Risk aversion: The reluctance of a person to accept a bargain with an uncertain payoff instead of another bargain with a lower, but more certain, expected payoff. For example, a risk-averse investor might choose to invest his money in a low-interest bank account rather than investing in the stock market, where expected returns are higher but loss of value is also possible.

if the government shares the profits but not the losses—then the effect can instead be reversed; in other words, the incentives for entrepreneurial efforts can be weakened.[8]

However, Richard Rumelt argues that increased risk can actually increase entrepreneurial activity. Rumelt notes that the downside for an entrepreneur is limited (bankruptcy), while the upside is unlimited. Therefore, greater risk and variance in the expected return increase the expected return, which may stimulate entrepreneurship.[9] Here, a comparison can be made with the price of a stock option, which, all else equal, increases in the event of increased variance in the price of the underlying asset.

OTHER POINTS OF DEPARTURE

The effective rate of taxation of entrepreneurial income is affected by the degree of tax progressivity. Even if average annual income is the same for a wage earner and an entrepreneur, total tax payments are likely to be higher for the entrepreneur if the tax schedule is progressive, as taxable incomes for entrepreneurs usually vary more than wage incomes do.[10] High marginal tax rates on entrepreneurial incomes (for high incomes) also greatly affect owners of successful gazelles and high-growth firms, thus functioning as a surtax on growth.[11]

Although total aggregate taxation likely affects the extent of entrepreneurial activity, the tax structure—what is taxed and how much—is also important. The complexity of the tax system may also constitute an obstacle

8 Atkinson and Stiglitz (2015).
9 Rumelt (2005, p. 22).
10 Gentry and Hubbard (2000).
11 Audretsch et al. (2002).

  © THE AUTHORS AND STUDENTLITTERATUR

and weaken incentives for productive entrepreneurial activity. Large cross-firm differences exist with regard to their ability to navigate a complex tax system. The European Commission has noted that the relative cost for small and medium-sized firms to comply with every tax regulation is a hundred times greater than it is for large firms.[12] Therefore, a few simple and easy-to-understand rules should be a goal in itself.

Identifying both the positive and negative effects of taxes on entrepreneurship *a priori* is thus possible. However, the positive effects are largely based on the absence of a distinction between productive entrepreneurship, on the one hand, and unproductive entrepreneurship and non-entrepreneurial business activity, on the other hand.

14.2 Taxation and Entrepreneurship: Overall Empirical Results

The empirical literature is extensive, but the results are not clear-cut, as positive, negative and zero effects have been found.[13] The OECD notes that establishing an unambiguous relationship between taxes and entrepreneurship is impossible.[14] The complexity of the OECD countries' tax systems also makes the effects of their incentives difficult to interpret. A systematic review of the literature seemingly indicates that a higher average tax rate has a positive effect on entrepreneurship but that a higher marginal tax rate and increased progressivity have a negative effect.[15]

---

12 European Commission (2004).

13 Parker (1996) and Schuetze (2000) find a positive relationship between taxes and entrepreneurship, whereas Moore (2004) finds a negative relationship. See Schuetze and Bruce (2004) for a survey and evaluation of the research on this topic through 2003, and Henrekson and Sanandaji (2016) for recent results.

14 OECD (2007a).

15 See, for instance, Robson and Wren (1999) or Parker and Robson (2004). Robson and Wren (1999) argue that the tax evasion effect is largely driven by the average effective tax rate, which may explain why a positive effect is found. In a study of Sweden during the post-war period, Stenkula (2012) finds that increased social security contributions decrease the self-employment rate (in the form of sole proprietorships), but he cannot find any other effects of taxes on the self-employment rate. Regarding the negative effects of progressive taxes, see Gentry and Hubbard (2000) and Baliamoune-Lutz and Garello (2015). However, the results are not clear-cut; Bacher and Brühlhart (2013) find the reverse effect.

Can we thus conclude that those who want to see more entrepreneurial activity in their country should advocate a high average tax rate and as little progressivity as possible? The answer is no. These results are driven by the effect of using self-employment (or similar metrics) as a measure of the rate of entrepreneurship in an economy. This measure is easily accessible and highly comparable across countries and over time.[16] However, as we have already noted, using the self-employment rate as a proxy for entrepreneurship is directly misleading. If the self-employed can avoid or evade high taxes more easily, we can expect that a high average tax rate will lead to more self-employment. Considering what we know about entrepreneurship, a more reasonable hypothesis is that if a high average tax rate leads to more self-employment, then it also leads to reduced entrepreneurship.

Many of the studies that examine the relationship between taxes and entrepreneurship explore the effect of a specific tax, for example, the tax on earned income, or they estimate the effect of an aggregate indicator, such as total tax revenue as a share of GDP. Instead, the effect of either a specific tax or all taxes combined on entrepreneurship should be analyzed. However, no specific tax on income from entrepreneurship exists. In the tax code, no tax category for "income from entrepreneurship" exists, which means that the compensation for entrepreneurial efforts, depending on the circumstances, can be taxed as corporate income (corporate tax), capital income (current or capital gains) or as income from employment/earned income.[17]

These taxes may affect entrepreneurial activity in various ways. Therefore, how income from entrepreneurship is classified and to what extent entrepreneurs are able to act strategically to ensure that their income is classified in the most favorable tax category matters. Such a strategic approach may also partly determine what entrepreneurs decide to do and how they run their firms. An accurate analysis of the effects of taxes on entrepreneurship must be able to distinguish between these effects.

---

16 See Bjuggren, Johansson and Stenkula (2012) for a discussion of potential measurement problems with regard to self-employment.

17 See the discussion in OECD (1998), Rosen (2005) and Henrekson and Sanandaji (2016).

© THE AUTHORS AND STUDENTLITTERATUR

14.3 Taxation of Entrepreneurial Rents

If we assume that a factor of production must be categorized as either labor or capital, then the characterization of the tax system becomes relatively unambiguous, at least in theory. Compensation for work should be taxed as labor income, and compensation distributed to suppliers of capital should be taxed as capital income. However, how should suppliers of capital who simultaneously fulfil an entrepreneurial role in the firm be taxed?

One can easily forget that the intellectual foundation of the idea that income must come either from capital or from labor is a highly simplified model of reality. Because the model only includes capital and labor, total income must necessarily be split between those two factors. The more sophisticated the economy, the more this conceptual simplification departs from reality.

A firm's capital consists of assets that its owner chooses not to consume in the current period; instead, this capital is used as an input for future production. Whether the capital assets are created through labor is irrelevant; future returns are regarded as compensation for postponing consumption and for taking risks. In the early stages of the lifecycle of their firms, entrepreneurs combine their labor with previously invested financial capital to create additional capital. Such capital may be technological, intellectual, or organizational. Such entrepreneurial venturing may result in a successful firm with an economic value that is many times larger than the financial resources invested. Skype and Facebook are recent examples of this phenomenon.

When examining entrepreneurship, distinguishing the return on labor from the return on capital is impossible because the value created is a result of the input of the inseparable combination of entrepreneurial talent, work effort, human capital and financial capital.

To determine the proportion of the return that comes from work or capital, we may ask ourselves what the rate of return would have been if the entrepreneur had not worked at the firm in the first place. The answer may very well be close to zero (for example, if the value of the firm is closely linked to the individual entrepreneur's vision, human capital and continuous effort in the firm), meaning that all or almost all of the return comes from labor. An alternative question asks how large the return would have been had no capital existed in the firm from previous years. The answer to this question may also be close to zero, for instance, if previously created organizational capital is necessary to generate revenue, which implies that all or almost all of the return comes from capital investments. In other words, the questions regarding the origin of the return on entrepreneurship will not necessarily produce any consistent answers.

The theoretical separation between capital and labor is simply not suitable for analyzing entrepreneurship. When an important factor interacts positively with the other inputs, it is misleading to only ask the first question and thereby reach the conclusion that almost all returns derive from labor. An entrepreneurial firm in which the founder does not reinvest a very high proportion of the return in the firm will generally be unable to grow. It would not be possible to sell the firm without the labor put in by the founder; however, such a sale is also impossible if the founder does not annually increase the capital value of the firm by postponing his private consumption and/or refraining from diversifying his savings to reduce his financial risk. Entrepreneurship is largely a matter of building and expanding firms that can generate future returns, i.e., create capital with the help of the entrepreneur's labor and previously generated capital.

This question can be re-conceptualized by asking what the outcome would have been if Bill Gates and Ingvar Kamprad had not created companies and had instead—as employees—invested the same amount in other companies in the stock market as they actually invested in Microsoft and IKEA, respectively. The value of their entrepreneurial activity is thus the difference between the hypothetical wealth from their stock market investments and the wealth that they actually created by founding and developing their own companies.

Entrepreneurship combines a business idea, human capital, effort, and re-invested capital over the many years that are required for a firm to grow; it is thus part of an inseparable bundle of inputs that specific individuals supply. Dividing and taxing the return on this bundle of inputs in a way that clearly separates what should be attributable to capital and labor is difficult; so far, no one has succeeded in doing so.

As long as no specific tax rules apply to entrepreneurs, their tax obligations must be determined within the framework of existing legislation. In practice, the taxation of both labor and capital income will thus be relevant.

© THE AUTHORS AND STUDENTLITTERATUR

14.4 Taxation of Earned Income

First, business owners (regardless of whether they are entrepreneurs or simply run their firm to provide income) can often select the type of firm that they run and thus the form of taxation that applies to the type of firm in question. Taxable income from work and income from sole proprietorships and partnerships are often combined (referred to as earned income) and taxed together according to the same tax rate schedule.[18] As long as the tax rate on earned income is higher than the corporate tax rate (as is normally the case) and the new firm initially incurs losses that are deductible (as is normally the case), people who want to start a new firm will do so in the form of a sole proprietorship or a partnership. Once the firm becomes profitable, the business owner has incentives to transform the firm into an incorporated business. Because of these taxation differences, an increase in the tax on business income in relation to the corporate tax may stimulate the creation of new firms.[19] A high tax on business income results in the initial loss of the new firm being less burdensome, as the loss may be offset against highly taxed earned income or against future surpluses.

The self-employed can select not only the type of firm but also the formal nature of their engagement in the firm. For example, business owners who work in their incorporated business may choose to compensate themselves with dividends that are taxed as capital income or as capital gains and thereby avoid taxation on earned income.

However, the tax code may stipulate that entrepreneurial income be taxed as earned income more than the entrepreneur would like. First, the tax system may contain rules that limit the amount or share of income generated by a closely held corporation that can be taxed as capital income for owners who are employed in the firm. In Sweden, special legislation,

---

18 Even if active business owners do not operate within an incorporated business there are often special rules and relief measures that mitigate or postpone tax payments.
19 Kauffman Foundation (2007) and Cullen and Gordon (2007). There is strong empirical support for the hypothesis that the tax code influences the choice of organizational form (Johansson et al. 2014, p. 37; Gordon and Edmark 2013).

the so-called 3:12 rules, prevents active owners of closely held corporations from minimizing their total tax payments; these rules reduce the scope of compensation that can be received in the form of capital income, which is taxed at a lower rate.[20]

When these rules were introduced as part of the 1990–1991 tax reform, the return that could be paid as dividends was low compared to the commonly required rate of return. Returns above this level were taxed as labor income. A study in the United States found that the required after-tax rate of return varied between 8 and 30 percent in 200 large American companies and that the average return was 17 percent at a time when the nominal interest rate after tax was 4 percent and the real interest rate was close to zero.[21] Modern private equity firms usually assert that they demand a nominal rate of return before tax of approximately 25–30 percent per year. Smaller Swedish firms, such as those of local electricians or plumbers, are usually sold at a price that corresponds to four to six times their annual profit, which indicates a required rate of return in the range of 15–25 percent.

The maximum rate of return that can be paid out and taxed as dividend income was also extremely low compared to the rate of return generated by successful entrepreneurship. Since 1995, the 3:12 rules have been reformed several times and now (2016) heavily favor some actors. Today, the effective tax rate for closely held incorporated firms would generally increase if the 3:12 rules were abolished. However, the rules are complex, and understanding just how favorable the rules have become is difficult for those who do not manage their own firm. However, the rules are significantly less generous for partners in R&D-intensive firms with a small aggregate wage sum but

20 Closely held corporations are defined as incorporated businesses in which four or fewer partners own shares that represent more than half of the votes in the company. People who belong to the same circle of related individuals are treated as a single individual. People who—through their ownership of shares, per agreement or in similar ways—can be considered fully or partially entitled to make management decisions, and thereby able to dispose of the company's results, are also subject to the 3:12 rules.
21 Summers (1987).

 © THE AUTHORS AND STUDENTLITTERATUR

with a high market value. In this case, the partners will often largely be taxed according to the labor income schedule.[22]

A large part of entrepreneurial activity is carried out by employees who do not have an ownership share in the firm that employs them. For these intrapreneurs, the tax on labor income always applies. For this category, high tax rates on labor income will have negative effects on incentives, regardless of the presence of 3:12 rules or their specific design.

14.5 Firm-Level Taxation and Owner-Level Taxation

In theory, a project's value is a function of the present value of future dividends and the company's potential sales value. Therefore, taxes on corporate profits, dividends and capital gains have an impact on an entrepreneur's willingness to take on a project.[23] The taxation associated with the alternatives to such entrepreneurial projects will also play a role, such as the tax on interest income and the tax on returns from financial instruments.

CORPORATE VERSUS OWNER-LEVEL TAXES

In taxation theory, the corporate tax clearly affects the willingness to invest and thus the willingness to initiate and pursue entrepreneurial ventures. A high corporate tax also benefits debt financing relative to equity financing. The required rate of return will be lower for projects that are debt financed. To the extent that debt financing is more advantageous and more readily available to established and large firms, high corporate taxes, combined with fully deductible interest payments, will negatively affect new and small firms

---

22 For individuals who do not have any so-called "unused dividend allowance," which arises if they do not withdraw the maximum allowed annual dividends that are subject to capital income taxation and withdraw the maximum allowed dividends the same year as the company is sold, the capital gains below 100 income base amounts (SEK 5.7 million) will be taxed as labor income (capital gains above that level are taxed at 30 percent). Normally, this implies a tax rate corresponding to 57 percent on the successful sale of a company whose value consists of patents or other intangible assets.

23 If the owner receives (or is obligated to receive) part of his gains as labor income, the tax on labor income combined with the rate of mandatory social security contributions will also play a role.

© THE AUTHORS AND STUDENTLITTERATUR

and potential entrepreneurs. Corporate taxation also decreases the amount of retained earnings that can be used for investment purposes.

Far less consensus exists regarding the effects of owner-level taxes (dividend and capital gains taxation). In taxation theory, different schools or "views" exist. According to the traditional or "old" view, both the dividend tax and the capital gains tax affect the required rate of return and the willingness to invest. However, according to the "new" view, the dividend tax has no effect, as firms are assumed to use retained earnings to finance investments.[24]

These models assume a closed economy in which the interest rate is determined domestically and saving equal investment. If one instead assumes that firms operate in a small open economy with free capital movement, then the interest rate and the amount of investment will be determined by the international capital market, which, according to this so-called "open economy" view, implies that domestic owner-level taxes do not affect investments.

According to the so-called residence principle of taxation, owners are taxed where they live. If owner-level taxes increase in Sweden, foreign owners are not affected, whereas the willingness of those living in Sweden to save and invest may decrease if domestic owner-level taxes increase. However, according to the "open economy" view, firms can always offset the loss of capital supplied by domestic actors by issuing shares or debt instruments to the risk-adjusted interest rate that applies in the international capital market. Foreign ownership and foreign debt financing are simply assumed to replace domestic ownership and lending from domestic actors, while the volume of investment remains unchanged. The required rate of return will be unaffected by domestic owner-level taxes because it is determined in the international capital market.

The corporate tax is levied according to the so-called source principle of taxation—that is, according to the country in which the profits arise—and does not depend on the owners' country of residence. Therefore, the corporate tax will always be considered a cost for investors/owners and will invariably have a negative effect on investment, which also holds true in a small open economy in which financial markets are fully integrated. A lower corporate

---

24 Auerbach and Hassett (2003). For an in-depth discussion of the different views, see Henrekson and Sanandaji (2016).

© THE AUTHORS AND STUDENTLITTERATUR

tax rate reduces the required rate of return before tax for Swedish and foreign investors alike, and more investment projects will have an expected rate of return greater than or equal to the required rate.

However, reality is more complex than this simplified model suggests. Domestic and foreign capital are far from perfectly substitutable. International investors may be almost as inclined as Swedes to buy shares and bonds issued by well-known large public corporations, such as Volvo and Ericsson, but nothing suggests that they are just as interested in investing in new and small or medium-sized firms in peripheral countries such as Sweden. Many entrepreneurial investment projects will not be carried out unless they receive financing from Swedish investors.[25]

In addition, a Swedish entrepreneur does not regard a portfolio investment in a foreign stock exchange as a viable alternative to an equally large investment in his own firm. Entrepreneurs invest their personal commitment, time and capital in their firms. If high owner level taxes make investing in Sweden unprofitable compared with investing in foreign stock exchanges, the entrepreneur cannot divest in Sweden and instead invest the divested capital abroad.

Owner-level taxes are believed to be an important determinant of a country's rate of entrepreneurial activity for many reasons. High owner-level taxes may not prevent globally active large corporations from obtaining (passive) investment capital. By issuing stocks and corporate bonds, these global firms also have access to funding from tax-exempt institutions such as pension funds and government investment funds (so-called sovereign wealth funds). However, Swedish owner-level taxes will always affect Swedish entrepreneurs' commitment of time and personal effort and their willingness to invest in their ventures.[26]

Owner-level taxes also affect the investment *structure*—i.e., what we invest in. Dividend taxes confine capital in large, mature firms that have generated

---

25 See Henrekson and Sanandaji (2016) for a research survey.
26 Anyone who is skeptical of such an effect may consider why the most successful Swedish entrepreneurs left the country when Swedish owner-level taxes were at their peak, resulting in real negative rates of return after tax also for highly profitable firms before tax (Du Rietz, Johansson and Stenkula 2015). Lundgren et al. (2005, p. 134) maintain that economists agree that owner-level taxes have a negative effect on new companies that want to (or have an inherent potential to) expand. The different implications of the old and the new view mainly relate to how owner-level taxes affect the behavior of mature firms.

large profits historically, which has a negative effect on entrepreneurial activity. Old and large businesses may also be entrepreneurial, but a dividend tax essentially becomes a tax on the owner(s)' exercise of control. If the owner(s)' incentives for exercising active control and ensuring good governance are reduced, the risk that management will invest in projects that primarily contribute to its own status, consumption and career aspirations increases. Groundbreaking innovations also largely occur in new firms, and dynamics and renewal require that new entrepreneurial firms be created.

Therefore, mature firms should distribute large parts of their surplus to their owners. This surplus can then be channeled into new and promising firms. Dividend taxes build a "fence" between the assets in older firms and their owners, which leads to resources being confined in older and mature firms instead of being transferred to new firms with better investment opportunities and greater growth potential.[27]

THE CAPITAL GAINS TAX

A high capital gains tax may also hamper entrepreneurial activity. As we explained in chapter 6, a firm's development consists of a series of events—from the original innovation and the product's introduction in the market to the eventual realization of a large-scale operation. In each phase, the actors in the competence structure play a decisive role, and different owners may be more suitable for various successive stages in a firm's lifecycle. The capital gains tax becomes highly relevant with regard to the sale of firms. It then functions as a tax on the transfer of ownership, which may prevent more competent owners from stepping in and further developing the firm.

The bulk of the economic return from a high-growth firm—or other forms of value-creating entrepreneurship—will manifest itself as a sharp rise in the firm's value. The capital gains tax (paid on the profit from selling shares) will thus have a major impact on the incentives for ambitious and potentially successful entrepreneurs.[28]

---

27 Chetty and Saez (2005).

28 Henrekson and Johansson (2009). High corporate and capital gains taxes have also been shown to reduce investments by venture capital firms (Da Rin, Nicodano and Sembenelli 2006).

© THE AUTHORS AND STUDENTLITTERATUR

High capital gain taxes make selling the firm less profitable, which means that the original entrepreneur is more likely to continue running the firm on his own. If the firm is not growing quickly enough to reach the minimum efficient scale (MES) within a reasonable period, the company risks bankruptcy. In its comprehensive study of the determinants of entrepreneurship, the OECD argues that capital gains taxes are critical in stimulating entrepreneurial activity.[29]

Therefore, a high capital gains tax not only would make starting firms less profitable but also would weaken the incentives to create value in existing entrepreneurial firms and to completely or partially sell firms to others. A high capital gains tax increases the value of control at the expense of growth, which results in fewer firms being interested in raising capital and obtaining necessary skills by broadening the circle of ownership in the secondary market. Studies also show that Swedish business owners in the 1990s valued control highly and were reluctant to prioritize growth if it implied reduced control.[30] In a study from 2013, 90 percent of the business owners stated that control and independence were important and that they preferred to finance expansion via internally generated funds and personal savings rather than by raising external risk capital. Business owners were also reluctant to sell their firms even if they were offered a high price. Even if the price tag on a share in the company exceeded the estimated market value by 70–100 percent, a quarter of the business owners said that they were not prepared to sell all or part of the company.[31]

OTHER FORMS OF TAXATION

Successful entrepreneurship may also be affected by property tax, inheritance tax, gift tax and wealth tax.[32] Some assets are exempted from taxation in many countries, such as shares in certain firms or pension savings, and arbitrary flat-rate taxation is sometimes used for these (or other) assets. These types of rules may affect entrepreneurial investment both positively or negatively. For

---

29 OECD (2005).
30 Wiklund, Davidsson and Delmar (2003).
31 Johansson, Palmberg and Bornhäll (2013).
32 See Rosen (2005) for a survey.

example, an exemption of shares in unlisted firms, as opposed to alternative assets, from wealth tax can have a positive effect. By contrast, an exemption of pension savings from wealth tax can have a negative effect, since such funds cannot be readily channeled into entrepreneurial projects.

To make an overall assessment of the effects of taxes on investment and firm management, one must consider the total tax position at both the firm and owner levels. Therefore, one must consider the corporate tax (including the sometimes extensive deduction possibilities that exist to lower the effective corporate tax) combined with the taxes on interest, capital gains and dividends. The total tax position will also largely depend on the choice of financing and the type of owner.[33]

In developed countries, the tax systems are hardly ever neutral with respect to a firm's owner(s) and the share of equity financing. Historically, the tax systems in the rich countries have tended to favor debt financing and institutional ownership, where the latter tends not to be taxed at all. However, entrepreneurial firms have frequently been subject to double taxation, and the effective capital gains tax has been higher. The various tax reforms implemented in many countries since the mid-1980s have greatly reduced the differences between various categories of ownership and sources of financing.[34]

The differences that still exist tend to favor institutional ownership over personal ownership and debt financing over equity financing.[35] If individual ownership is at a disadvantage relative to institutional ownership and the latter owner category is less inclined to invest in small, new or entrepreneurial projects, then entrepreneurial activity will be hampered.

14.6 Taxation of Stock Options

Stock options can be used to encourage and reward individuals who contribute key skills to entrepreneurial firms or, more generally, to incentivize employees to become more entrepreneurial. To become and

---

33 Researchers have developed a useful and widely used method to calculating the effective marginal tax rate on capital income (King and Fullerton 1984). See Du Rietz, Johansson and Stenkula (2015) and Södersten (1984) for Sweden.

34 Jorgenson and Landau (1993).

35 Rydqvist et al. (2014).

© THE AUTHORS AND STUDENTLITTERATUR

remain innovative, firms must have either a strong cash flow or a strong equity position.[36] However, entrepreneurial firms often have a weak cash flow during the early stages of their lifecycle. Stock options are the equivalent of promises of future ownership stakes in the firm if a number of premises or milestones are fulfilled. In essence, the future ownership stakes will be realized if the firm develops according to plan and manages to achieve the prescribed objectives for value creation. The granting of stock options is also an important mechanism through which future ownership stakes can be substituted for high wages to moderate costs at the beginning of the lifecycle.

Many entrepreneurs are unwilling to accept new owners and co-financiers—although accepting such actors may be necessary to expand their firms—because they are unwilling to cede the control rights over their firms. Stock option agreements may help remedy this problem. The use of stock options may induce the original owner to remain with the firm; these options can be used to also give the original owner the opportunity to regain control if the firm becomes successful in the future. Correctly designed, this instrument can cause employees and former owners to act as though they own the firm. Thus, stock options alleviate the principal-agent problems that exist in many industries.

The efficiency of stock options also depends on how they are taxed. Stock options may generally be taxed on three occasions:

- when they are received,
- when they are converted into shares or redeemed as shares, and
- when the underlying asset (the share) is sold.

Taxation may also vary depending on whether the options in question are so-called employee stock options or warrants. Synthetic stock options also exist; when the grantee converts this type of stock option, he receives monetary compensation rather than future equity/shares in the firm.[37]

---

36 Martinsson and Lööf (2010).

37 Synthetic options can be used if the issuer wants to get the stock option holder to behave as if he were a shareholder (up until conversion) without the former being forced to actually give up equity (in the future).

> **Employee stock options**: Call options granted by the company to an employee (normally without any cash outlay from the employee) as part of the employee's remuneration package. Such options have conditions tied to employment or the task of the individual who holds the stock option. For example, they expire if the person leaves the firm; they are not transferable; and/or they can only be used after a certain vesting period.

If profits from stock options are taxed fully or partially as labor income, then most of the incentive effect is lost, especially when the marginal tax rate on labor income is high and when the firm is obliged to pay social security contributions on the profit, which is the case in Sweden.[38] Unless the use of stock options is practicable, founders and other key employees do not have any incentive to work at a lower salary in exchange for future equity stakes.

If the founder stays with the firm after the entry of external investors, he normally wants to retain control over the firm until it goes public or until it is sold to another firm in a trade sale. If the tax code makes using stock options as an instrument impossible, then external owners cannot simultaneously take control of the firm and retain the founder and other key employees as long as it is beneficial for the development of the firm.

The situation is reversed if the employee is able to defer all taxation until the underlying shares are eventually sold. If obtaining or exercising stock options has no tax consequences and if the employee faces a low capital gains tax, then stock options can be used to create strong incentives for entrepreneurial effort. The key employees who drive the innovation and entrepreneurship in the firm can then receive a substantial part of the capital value created, even though they do not invest financially. In the United States,

---

38 In Sweden, the value of employee stock options is taxed as labor income when they are converted (with the employer paying the associated social security contributions). When sold, the capital gain is then taxed as capital income (but if the employee is subject to the 3:12 rules, the labor income tax schedule may still apply). If instead ordinary options (warrants) are issued below market price, the difference is taxed directly as labor income. If employees purchase ordinary options at market price, there is no taxable labor income. When converted into shares, there is no taxation, and any future profit is only subject to capital gains tax when the shares acquired in the conversion are sold. (However, the 3:12 rules may apply, and in that case capital gains may still be taxed at the much higher labor income tax rate.) See Henrekson and Sanandaji (2014b) for further details.

© THE AUTHORS AND STUDENTLITTERATUR

the tax code was changed along these lines in the early 1980s, which paved way for the emergence of the modern venture capital industry and the wave of entrepreneurial ventures in Silicon Valley and elsewhere.[39]

The Swedish tax rules for stock options hinder the drafting of effective agreements between founders and key individuals, on the one hand, and external investors, on the other hand. The Swedish venture capital market is extremely small relative to the buyout market (see Box 5.2). Together with the United Kingdom, Sweden has the largest buyout sector in Europe. The considerable difference between the growth and profitability between buyout and venture capital firms is in line with what should be expected in light of the unfavorable taxation of stock options, which makes offering efficient incentive contracts to founders and other key employees virtually impossible for external investors in newly formed innovative firms.[40]

14.7 Taxation and Entrepreneurship in the Service Sector

Taxes affect entrepreneurial activity in other ways. High taxes on consumption and labor (including social security contributions) shift tasks from the formal sector toward unpaid do-it-yourself production and the informal sector (the black market sector), which reduces regular employment and distorts production decisions.[41] Large areas—all the services for which unpaid household production is a realistic alternative—are thus inaccessible for commercial exploitation and entrepreneurial business development. Given that almost half of all the work performed in countries such as Sweden consists of unpaid household work or undeclared work, a very large proportion of all tasks is ultimately carried out outside the formal economy.[42] However, when services are provided professionally, entrepreneurs are, among other things, incentivized to invest in new knowledge and capital equipment, to develop new technologies, to design improved types of contracts, and to

---

39 Gompers and Lerner (2001), Henrekson and Rosenberg (2001) and Kortum and Lerner (2000). See Tåg (2012) for a comparison between Europe and the United States.
40 Söderblom (2011) compares growth and rates of return in the venture capital and buyout sectors in Sweden. Henrekson and Sanandaji (2014b, chapter 6) show that Swedish tax rules are highly favorable for the buyout sector.
41 Rogerson (2006), Davis and Henrekson (2005) and Freeman and Schettkat (2005).
42 SOU 1997:17.

create more flexible organizational structures. In short, a higher taxation on labor services obstructs the production of goods and services in the market that are close substitutes for household production, thus reducing the scope for entrepreneurial expansion into new arenas in which a large part of the value relates to saving the customers' time.

From a static perspective, many effective market exchanges will not occur if labor is highly taxed. Even more important is the dynamic effect of the lower momentum for renewal and product development in the production of services. Lower taxes on labor thus generally stimulate the emergence of an efficient service sector that competes with unpaid household work. The arena for entrepreneurship and business development simply grows larger.

14.8 Effects of Taxation—Final Reflections

The societal benefits of productive entrepreneurship tend to be far greater than the entrepreneur's private utility/income. After all, William Nordhaus found that more than 95 percent of the value accrues to consumers in the form of better products and lower prices.[43] The positive externalities are considerable, which is a compelling reason to have a tax system that stimulates productive entrepreneurship.

Entrepreneurs seem to behave differently than employees, which is another reason to regard entrepreneurship as a separate factor of production.[44] In particular, the former are more sensitive than the latter to economic incentives. In some cases, the efforts of entrepreneurs should arguably be taxed differently than, for example, employees and retirees.

However, entrepreneurship should not necessarily be subsidized; instead, having a favorable—relative to others—tax structure that encourages productive entrepreneurial activity may be justified. Moreover, a tax structure that taxes successful entrepreneurship more harshly should be avoided. Likewise, one should refrain from policies that encourage non-entrepreneurial firms instead of productive entrepreneurship. In the worst-

---

43 Nordhaus (2005).
44 See, for instance, Baumol (2010), Chetty et al. (2011) and Carroll, Holtz-Eakin and Rosen (2000).

© THE AUTHORS AND STUDENTLITTERATUR

case scenario, such policies encourage self-employment at the expense of entrepreneurship.[45]

The design of the tax system is fundamentally important in relation to the rate of productive entrepreneurship. If the tax code does not encourage entrepreneurship and active ownership, it becomes cumbersome and costly to use other measures to fully compensate for this shortcoming. For example, first launching a tax system that inhibits the market supply of risk capital and then remedying this deficiency with a public support system for start-up firms or firms that are targeted based on bureaucratically determined criteria is highly inefficient.

Potentially successful entrepreneurs are few in number, and they are not easy to replace. Those with the greatest potential already tend to have well-paying, secure positions in existing firms. The rewards must be sufficiently attractive to inspire the few who succeed to abandon attractive positions, expose themselves to the risks of failure and bear a high degree of uncertainty for a long period. If taxes devour most of the return, potential entrepreneurs are not incentivized to take such risks. Because the exercise of entrepreneurship entails supplying an inseparable bundle of effort, human capital, and financial capital, neatly dividing the return on entrepreneurship between capital and labor income is extraordinarily difficult. Hence, the taxation on both labor and capital income will play a role. Furthermore, not only the tax on income from entrepreneurship but also the tax on alternative options—gainful employment and passive investments in financial markets—play a role.[46]

At the individual level, entrepreneurial activity does not merely entail how much work the entrepreneur supplies. It also concerns whether a potential entrepreneur will attempt to start a new firm in the first place. Individuals will be more interested in becoming entrepreneurs if the discovered or created opportunities are expected to be more profitable and if more opportunities that are expected to be profitable exist. A higher tax rate on entrepreneurial rents reduces the number of attractive business opportunities. Therefore, viewing the compensation to entrepreneurs as "manna from heaven"—i.e.,

---

45 Inci (2013).
46 Johansson et al. (2014).

© THE AUTHORS AND STUDENTLITTERATUR

as a windfall gain that can be taxed harshly without affecting entrepreneurs' willingness to supply effort—is simply wrong.

One should also consider the risk of potentially productive entrepreneurs being drawn, fully or partially, into areas that provide a better return on—and appreciation for—their skills but that present no, or less, social value. The channeling of entrepreneurship will largely depend on the *relative* return on productive entrepreneurship relative to non-productive/destructive entrepreneurship. A high tax on entrepreneurship may result in entrepreneurs engaging in the "wrong" activities, which destroy rather than create value.

With regard to taxes, it may be worthwhile to stress that, even if the motivation of potential entrepreneurs were unaffected by very high taxes, their opportunities would still be impeded. The capital values created through successful entrepreneurship can provide the basis for expanding existing ventures and/or starting new entrepreneurial projects. A low tax on entrepreneurial rents implies that successful entrepreneurs have more resources for future projects, which makes obtaining more mileage from their entrepreneurial effort possible. Many successful entrepreneurs also pursue new entrepreneurial projects that are financed with earnings from previous projects. Furthermore, for small and medium-sized firms, internally generated funds are the most important source of financing for investment and expansion.[47]

A high rate of return provides successful entrepreneurs with an incentive to embark on new entrepreneurial projects. A high level of taxation can then be considered a penalty for a skill set that is highly valuable from a socio-economic perspective. Financial resources are taken from those with proven entrepreneurial ability and transferred to others who almost certainly have a lower level of entrepreneurial ability. Because entrepreneurial talent is a scarce resource with a high social value if channeled appropriately, such redistribution is likely to be very costly.

Finally, we would like to emphasize the importance of viewing the tax system and the tax structure from a holistic perspective. Taxation has several purposes, such as financing public goods, redistributing income and stabilizing aggregate demand. A tax system should be efficient, transparent

---

47 See, for instance, Olofsson and Berggren (1998).

© THE AUTHORS AND STUDENTLITTERATUR

and fair. Policymakers must consider all of these factors when designing the tax system. Therefore, understanding and considering the effects of taxes on entrepreneurship is important when designing and reforming the tax system in a country.

14.9 Chapter Summary and Overall Lessons from Part III

In this chapter, we have learned the following:

- The relationship between taxes and entrepreneurship is complex, and economic theory seldom provides clear and unambiguous guidance.
- In general, taxes can affect entrepreneurs through an incentive effect, a tax evasion effect and an insurance effect.
- The tax code does not contain specific tax rules for entrepreneurs or for the taxation of entrepreneurial rents. In reality, the specific rules determining whether and to what extent entrepreneurial rents will be taxed as labor or capital income will influence the behavior of entrepreneurs.
- The design of the tax system is of fundamental importance for the degree of productive entrepreneurship. A high effective tax rate on entrepreneurial rents reduces the number of attractive entrepreneurial opportunities, regardless of whether the taxation of entrepreneurial rents occurs at the firm level or at the ownership level and whether entrepreneurial rents are taxed as earned income, current capital income or capital gains.

In chapters 12–14, which address how economic policy can stimulate productive entrepreneurship, we have learned the following:

- Productive entrepreneurial efforts are crucial for renewal, economic growth and job creation. However, the entrepreneur does not automatically aspire to these noble ends.
- An entrepreneurial and wealth-creating growth process can only be initiated and sustained when the institutional framework conditions ("the reward structure") encourage the right form of entrepreneurship.

- Political decisions in a number of areas determine the framework conditions. For promising ideas to become the foundation of growing firms, the conditions for productive entrepreneurship simply need to be sufficiently favorable.
- Those who wish for strong economic development in the future cannot simply hope that a number of forceful entrepreneurs will step forward and provide jobs and good incomes to the rest of the population. However, if the conditions for productive entrepreneurship are improved along a number of margins and the opportunities and payoffs for destructive entrepreneurship are resolutely curtailed, great prospects exist for economic development and increased prosperity.

© THE AUTHORS AND STUDENTLITTERATUR

CHAPTER 15

Summary and Conclusions

In this book, we have analyzed what entrepreneurship is. We have shown that the extent and orientation of entrepreneurial activity is of crucial importance for economic development, and we have discussed how such activity is affected by social reward structures.

Entrepreneurship is multifaceted and difficult to define; it is a function rather than a clearly defined profession or position. In addition, entrepreneurship is not synonymous with starting or managing a firm. Therefore, several different research traditions have emerged that emphasize vastly different aspects of entrepreneurship. Classical definitions stress the entrepreneur as an innovator (Joseph Schumpeter), an arbitrageur/creator of equilibrium (Israel Kirzner), a bearer of uncertainty (Frank Knight) and/or a coordinator (Jean-Baptiste Say). Entrepreneurship is fundamentally about judgmental decision making under uncertainty. Thus, entrepreneurs are not in the business of calculated risk taking or the pursuit of commercial ventures in hopes of getting rich through pure luck.

All of these aspects are important. In this book, we have defined entrepreneurship as the ability and the willingness of individuals

- to discover and create new economic opportunities;
- to introduce their ideas in the market under uncertainty, making decisions regarding the localization, product design, use of resources and reward systems; and
- to create value, which often, though not always, means that the entrepreneur aims to expand the firm to its full potential.

According to this definition, entrepreneurship is a function, but that function is always linked to identifiable individuals. Entrepreneurship is also vital for economic development, as it serves an unquestionably necessary function, namely, identifying (or generating) and commercializing new economic opportunities in the market. The result can then be observed in the growth and employment statistics. A selection takes place in the market. The market process ensures efficiency with respect to the use of resources, accelerates structural change, increases the inclination to innovate, creates greater variety in the market, which is necessary for maintaining competitiveness and innovativeness in the economic system. Therefore, the entrepreneur plays a key role through her renewal function. In reality, the entry of new entrepreneurial firms is necessary, as genuine renewal often occurs in such firms. New firms also challenge incumbent firms, which puts pressure on the latter to innovate and increase efficiency.

However, not all types of entrepreneurship have positive effects on the economy. Entrepreneurship can also be unproductive and destructive. The long-term development of the economy will depend on the quality and the channeling of entrepreneurship and on the efficiency of the selection process. The Industrial Revolution was the starting point for the first sustained growth process in human history, which continues to this day. Entrepreneurs certainly existed before the Industrial Revolution, but their efforts were almost exclusively channeled toward purposes other than creating and developing firms; for example, they might have focused more on warfare, looting, and legal activities that aimed to redistribute, rather than create, wealth.

The views on what drives economic development and growth that have been developed in this book differ in several respects from the standard mainstream theories. The latter focus primarily on the traditional factors of production, even if some models have been augmented in recent years. R&D and knowledge spillover effects have been highlighted as particularly important. Still, more recent theories tend to take firms, business ideas and innovations as givens. These models do not consider that someone has to discover, devise or create business ideas and firms. The theories also ignore that someone needs to successfully combine new or available factors of production—in other words, someone needs to start a profit-making firm and thereby create a supply and, in the long run, economic growth. This "someone" is usually the entrepreneur, who can be regarded as the agent

© THE AUTHORS AND STUDENTLITTERATUR

who transforms the new knowledge into business opportunities. This process benefits society to the extent that the firm manages to exploit the business opportunity by yielding valuable goods and services that are cost efficiently produced and distributed to customers.

In economic analyses, regarding entrepreneurship as a factor of production in its own right is frequently useful. We have seen that the level of entrepreneurial activity in the economy can be expected to depend on the following four factors: entrepreneurial ability (competence), exploitable opportunities, willingness (motivation) and access to capital in forms that are suitable for the specific context. The willingness to become an entrepreneur is crucial for whether entrepreneurship will actually be exercised. If the individual considers the cost of becoming an entrepreneur greater than the utility ("the profit"), then whether this person has the opportunity, the ability and a sufficiently large personal fortune is irrelevant.

Some economists have attempted to view entrepreneurship from a more traditional perspective of demand and supply. The supply of entrepreneurs consists of potential entrepreneurs who possess competence and capital, while the demand is linked to the presence of entrepreneurial opportunities. A form of equilibrium arises when supply equals demand. However, the same person often supplies *and* demands entrepreneurship, as is the case for entrepreneurial business owners who demand their own services as entrepreneurs.

The entrepreneurial rent is the compensation, exceeding the profit that corresponds to the risk-adjusted market rate of return, that an entrepreneurial firm may generate and benefit from. An entrepreneurial rent results from superior entrepreneurial competence, which originates from the entrepreneur actively discovering or creating opportunities and making decisions about how to combine factors of production and (re)allocate resources.

The search for entrepreneurial rents is a key characteristic of a market-based economic system and a necessary part of the process that results in economic development. Entrepreneurial rents act as signals to economic decision makers that reallocating and recombining resources to use them more efficiently is profitable. Likewise, entrepreneurs are strongly motivated to find or create entrepreneurial rents by combining factors of production in new and more value-creating ways. Without potential entrepreneurial rents, no one would want to take on the role of the entrepreneur and agent of change in the business sector. Entrepreneurs are needed for economic development, and entrepreneurial rents are a prerequisite for the emergence and exercise of entrepreneurship.

The exploitation of entrepreneurial opportunities that generate growth necessitates the use of other complementary inputs, which gives rise to a strong statistical correlation between economic growth and the amount of inputs used. At first glance, one may perceive that the increased use of inputs is what creates growth. However, such a conclusion is misleading. A spontaneous increase in the use of inputs is a response to a potentially exploitable opportunity or a potential demand. The increase in the use of inputs is not what creates opportunities. Instead, the change in inputs is a response to and a consequence of economic agents (entrepreneurs) who discover or create potential opportunities that they consider worth exploiting. Increasing inputs does not create opportunities. Therefore, development strategies that directly target inputs have generally failed.

Hence, the increase of or abundant access to inputs does not generate growth and create wealth. The basis for growth is innovative entrepreneurs who combine inputs in more value-creating ways. An economy can be filled to the brim with natural resources, financial capital and human capital, but someone must organize these inputs and take advantage of existing opportunities.

Somebody who seeks to understand why a particular country is rich and another one is poor, or why prosperity increases much faster in one country compared with another, should attempt to identify major differences in market institutions and reward systems. Focusing on differences in the inputs in the production process is likely to be misleading. These differences have evolved over time because of the differences in institutions and reward systems.

Policymakers who would like to improve the wealth-creating conditions in their countries should ask themselves the following two questions:

- What makes people save, invest and acquire economically valuable knowledge and abilities?
- What makes people look for, discover, create and exploit entrepreneurial opportunities within the framework of profit-making firms?

© THE AUTHORS AND STUDENTLITTERATUR

The good news is that economic policies may influence the level of entrepreneurship in a country or region. In short, favorable microeconomic conditions and an institutional framework that discourages rent seeking and encourages productive entrepreneurship are the prerequisites for a favorable entrepreneurial climate. Obviously, other factors also matter, notably macroeconomic stability, a world-class educational system and high-quality infrastructure.

Tax structures and tax levels, the design of the social insurance system, the extent and appropriateness of product market regulations, the design of bankruptcy legislation and the availability of risk capital are factors that politicians, in one way or another, can influence and that have an impact on the rate of entrepreneurial activity and the direction in which it is channeled.

Technological and structural changes in the world economy have also led to more intense institutional competition. Individual countries need to have competitive institutional framework conditions that encourage the creation of new firms, business expansion and risk taking. When firms can reasonably outsource some of their operations, business opportunities arise in the vicinity of outsourcing firms, which tend to be large and mature firms. If a country or a region suffers from a lack of potential entrepreneurs, it runs the risk of transferring activities abroad through international outsourcing or offshoring that could have otherwise served as the basis for new domestic firms.

Internationally competitive framework conditions for innovation and entrepreneurship primarily concern institutional structures, not least tax rules, which encourage a spontaneous bottom-up growth of suitable incentive structures for all actors involved. Such a policy package encourages the growth of voluntary profit-sharing arrangements among universities, researchers, departments, venture capitalists, entrepreneurs and other actors with competencies that are needed to transform knowledge and innovation into growth and prosperity.

The policy areas that we have discussed in this book are summarized in *Table 15.1*. For each policy area, we list the conditions that pave the way for an entrepreneurial economy and a non-entrepreneurial or "managed" economy. Measures may reinforce or offset one another. The overall mix of the policy package and the rules of the game that apply ultimately determine the extent to which people's inherent entrepreneurial abilities are utilized and channeled into wealth-creating activities.

Economic growth is always high on policymakers' agendas. To identify the most efficient measures, political leaders and their advisors often turn to the leading growth models for guidance. We have seen that the entrepreneurial function, which is crucial in terms of how a market economy works, is rarely included in these models. Instead, growth is driven by increased inputs, including human capital and new knowledge/technology. Therefore, growth policy unsurprisingly tends to focus directly on these inputs; for example, increased labor supply, more people attending universities, and increased investment and R&D expenditure as a share of GDP.

Still, such policy measures sidestep the most crucial questions: How do policies and institutions create an ecosystem that encourages the emergence of innovations that lead to qualitative changes in what is produced and how efficiently it is produced? Such innovations and their utilization and diffusion require productive entrepreneurship.

Productive entrepreneurship, not investments in R&D, human capital or physical capital, is the source of economic development. In an innovative and entrepreneurial economy, people are properly incentivized to invest in new knowledge, make capital investments, develop new technologies and use existing technologies in value-creating ways. This does not imply that capital investments, education and R&D are not important or that the public sector is not needed. In addition to providing and maintaining good institutions, the public sector is also important because it provides a range of services that the market is partially or entirely unable to provide, such as a high-quality educational system, an efficient and disinterested judicial system and world-class infrastructure.

Only under certain conditions are entrepreneurs incentivized to discover new resources, to find better and cheaper substitutes for existing resources, to exploit and continuously develop their own comparative advantages through trade and to discover and develop new products and production methods. Unless propitious institutional conditions are in place, increased investments and extensive support systems for technological development will not translate into economic growth and increased social welfare. Therefore, economic policy should focus on creating and maintaining an institutional setup that favors productive entrepreneurship as much as possible.

© THE AUTHORS AND STUDENTLITTERATUR

In addition, entrepreneurship is not an exhaustible resource. In an entrepreneurial economy, new opportunities tend to be continuously generated. In turn, other actors in the competence structure adapt to exploit the opportunities and to use their respective competencies in this ever-changing setting: banks and other financiers develop their skills with respect to financing entrepreneurial firms; specialist actors, such as venture capitalists, business angels and lawyers, emerge and assist with important support functions; and customers and the population at large learn to embrace innovation and renewal. Entrepreneurship becomes an integral part of the culture and the way of life. Entrepreneurship begets more entrepreneurship because every innovation creates new entrepreneurial opportunities that can be exploited by someone else.

Table 15.1 Public policy that supports an entrepreneurial economy vs. a managed economy.

Public policy	Managed economy	Entrepreneurial economy
Regulatory entry and growth barriers		
– Entry barriers	High	Low
– Production of welfare services/merit goods	Government production	Sizeable private production, contestability
– Financing of welfare services/merit goods	Tax financing only	Government ensures basic high-quality supply, then private financing
– Profit-driven organizations	Partly *de facto* prohibited in key areas facing income-elastic demand	Fully allowed within the framework of well-designed regulations
Liquidity and capital constraints		
– Wealth formation	High levels of income redistribution and wealth tax	Support private wealth formation
– Venture capital	Direct support	Indirect support
Labor market		
– Labor security mandates	Tied to years of tenure	Portable tenure rights
– Wage-setting arrangements	Centralized and closely tied to formal criteria	Decentralized and individualized

cont.

© THE AUTHORS AND STUDENTLITTERATUR

283

Social security		
– Design	Tied to employment	Portable tenure rights
– Unemployment insurance	Mandated rights	Flexicurity
R&D, commercialization and knowledge spillover		
– Focus	Quantitative input goals (spending on R&D)	No quantitative goals, indirect support, enabling and general
Targeted support	Yes	No
Property rights		
– General	Weak	Stable and secure
– Intellectual property rights	Very strong, easily obtained	Balance interests of inventors against need for knowledge diffusion
Taxation		
– Earned income tax rate	High and progressive	Low or moderate
– Capital income tax rate	High	Low
– Capital gains tax rate	High	Low
– Tax on stock options	High	Low
– Degree of tax neutrality across owner categories	Favors institutional owners over individuals	Neutrality
– Degree of neutrality across sources of finance	Favors debt over equity	Neutrality
– Personal taxation on asset holdings	Yes	No, or exemption for equity holdings
– Corporate tax rate	High statutory rate, low effective rate	Low or moderate statutory rate, effective rate equal to statutory rate and neutral across types of firms and industries
Bankruptcy laws	Onerous and lengthy	Relatively generous and allow for a "second chance"
Trade and regulation	Protection of national and incumbent firms	Openness

Source: Henrekson and Stenkula (2010).

© THE AUTHORS AND STUDENTLITTERATUR

REFERENCES

Acemoglu, Daron, Philippe Aghion and Fabrizio Zilibotti (2006). "Distance to Frontier, Selection and Growth." *Journal of the European Economic Association* 4(1), 37–74.

Acemoglu, Daron, Simon Johnson and James A. Robinson (2005). "The Rise of Europe: Atlantic Trade, Institutional Change and Economic Growth." *American Economic Review* 95(3), 546–579.

Acs, Zoltan J. (1984). *The Changing Structure of the U.S. Economy.* New York: Praeger.

Acs, Zoltan J. (2008). "Foundations of High Impact Entrepreneurship." *Foundations and Trends in Entrepreneurship* 4(6), 1–86.

Acs, Zoltan J. and Catherine Armington (2004). "Employment Growth and Entrepreneurial Activity in Cities." *Regional Studies* 38(8), 911–927.

Acs, Zoltan J. and David B. Audretsch (1987). "Innovation in Large and Small Firms." *Economics Letters* 23(1), 109–112.

Acs, Zoltan J. and David B. Audretsch (1990). *Innovation and Small Firms.* Cambridge, MA: MIT Press.

Acs, Zoltan J., David B. Audretsch, Pontus Braunerhjelm and Bo Carlsson (2009). "The Knowledge Spillover Theory of Entrepreneurship." *Small Business Economics* 32(1), 15–30.

Acs, Zoltan J. and Pamela Mueller (2008). "Employment Effects of Business Dynamics: Mice, Gazelles and Elephants." *Small Business Economics* 30(1), 85–100.

Acs, Zoltan J. and László Szerb (2007). "Entrepreneurship, Economic Growth and Public Policy." *Small Business Economics* 28(2–3), 109–122.

Acs, Zoltan J., László Szerb and Erkko Autio (2014). *Global Entrepreneurship and Development Index 2014.* Washington, D.C.: Global Entrepreneurship and Development Institute.

Aghion, Philippe, Richard Blundell, Rachel Griffith, Peter Howitt and Susanne Prantl (2006). "The Effects of Entry on Incumbent Innovation and Productivity." NBER Working Paper No. 12027. Cambridge, MA: National Bureau of Economic Resarch.

Aghion, Philippe, Robin Burgess, Stephen Redding and Fabrizio Zillibotti (2004). "Entry and Productivity Growth: Evidence from Microlevel Panel Data." *Journal of the European Economic Association* 2(1), 265–276.

Aghion, Philippe and Rachel Griffith (2005). *Competition and Growth: Reconciling Theory and Evidence.* Cambridge, MA: MIT Press.

Aghion, Philippe and Peter Howitt (1992). "A Model of Growth through Creative Destruction." *Econometrica* 60(2), 323–351.

Almus, Matthias and Eric A. Nerlinger (2000). "Testing 'Gibrat's Law' for Young Firms—Empirical Results for West Germany." *Small Business Economics* 15(1), 1–12.

Alvarez, Sharon A. (2005). "Theories of Entrepreneurship: Alternative Assumptions and the Study of Entrepreneurial Action." *Foundations and Trends in Entrepreneurship* 1(3), 105–148.

Andersson, Fredrik and Henrik Jordahl (2011). "Outsourcing Public Services: Ownership, Competition, Quality and Contracting." IFN Working Paper No. 874. Stockholm: Research Institute of Industrial Economics (IFN).

Andersson, Martin and Magnus Henrekson (2015). "Local Competiveness Fostered through Local Institutions for Entrepreneurship." In David B. Audretsch, Albert N. Link and Mary Walshok, eds., *Oxford Handbook of Local Competitiveness.* Oxford: Oxford University Press.

Andersson, Martin, Börje Johansson and Hans Lööf, eds. (2012). *Innovation and Growth: From R&D Strategies of Innovating Firms to Economy-wide Technological Change.* Oxford: Oxford University Press.

Andersson, Martin and Steven Klepper (2013). "Characteristics and Performance of New Firms and Spinoffs in Sweden." *Industrial and Corporate Change* 22(1), 245–280.

Andersson, Martin and Jing Xiao (2014). "Acquisitions of Start-ups by Incumbent Businesses: A Market Selection Process of 'High-Quality' Entrants?" Working Paper No. 2014/19. CIRCLE, Lund University.

Andersson, Thomas, Pontus Braunerhjelm and Ulf Jakobsson (2006). *Det svenska miraklet i repris? Om den tredje industriella revolutionen, globaliseringen och tillväxten.* Stockholm: SNS Förlag.

Arnold, Jens, Giuseppe Nicoletti and Stefano Scarpetta (2011). "Regulation, Resource Reallocation and Productivity Growth." In Hubert Strauss, ed., *Productivity and Growth in Europe: Long-Term Trends, Current Challenges and the Role of Economic Dynamism.* EIB Papers, vol. 11, No. 1, 90–115. Luxemburg: European Investment Bank.

Arrow, Kenneth J. (1962). "Economic Welfare and the Allocation of Resources for Invention." In Richard R. Nelson, ed., *The Rate and Direction of Inventive Activity: Economic and Social Factors.* National Bureau of Economic Research Book Series. Princeton, NJ: Princeton University Press.

Åstebro, Thomas (2003). "The Return to Independent Invention: Evidence of Unrealistic Optimism, Risk Seeking or Skewness Loving." *Economic Journal* 113(484), 226–239.

© THE AUTHORS AND STUDENTLITTERATUR

Atkinson, Anthony B. and Joseph E. Stiglitz (2015). *Lectures on Public Economics.* Updated edition. Princeton, NJ: Princeton University Press.

Audretsch, David B. (1995). *Innovation and Industry Evolution.* Cambridge, MA: MIT Press.

Audretsch, David B. (2002). "The Dynamic Role of Small Firms: Evidence from the US." *Small Business Economics* 18(1–3), 13–40.

Audretsch, David B., William J. Baumol and Andrew E. Burke (2001). "Competition Policy in Dynamic Markets." *International Journal of Industrial Organization* 19(5), 613–634.

Audretsch, David B., Martin A. Carree, André van Stel and A. Roy Thurik (2002). "Impeded Industrial Restructuring: The Growth Penalty." *Kyklos* 55(1), 81–97.

Audretsch, David B. and Michael Fritsch (1994). "The Geography of Firm Births in Germany." *Regional Studies* 28(4), 359–365.

Audretsch, David B. and Michael Fritsch (2002). "Growth Regimes over Time and Space." *Regional Studies* 36(2), 137–150.

Audretsch, David B. and Max Keilbach (2004). "Entrepreneurship Capital and Economic Performance." *Regional Studies* 38(8), 949–959.

Audretsch, David B. and A. Roy Thurik (2000). "Capitalism and Democracy in the 21st Century: From the Managed to the Entrepreneurial Economy." *Journal of Evolutionary Economics* 10(1), 17–34.

Audretsch, David B. and A. Roy Thurik (2004). "A Model of the Entrepreneurial Economy." *International Journal of Entrepreneurship Education* 2(2), 143–166.

Auerbach, Alan J. and Kevin A. Hassett (2003). "On the Marginal Source of Investment Funds." *Journal of Public Economics* 87(1), 205–232.

Autio, Erkko, Mathias Kronlund and Anne Kovalainen (2007). *High-Growth SME Support Initiatives in Nine Countries: Analysis, Categorization, and Recommendations.* Helsinki: Ministry of Trade and Industry.

Axelsson, Sten (2006). "Entreprenören från sekelskifte till sekelskifte – kan företag växa i Sverige?" In Dan Johansson and Nils Karlson, eds., *Svensk utvecklingskraft.* Stockholm: Ratio.

Bacher, Hans Ulrich and Marius Brühlhart (2013). "Progressive Taxes and Firm Births." *International Tax and Public Finance* 20(1), 129–168.

Bager-Sjögren, Lars (2011). "Svenska uppfinnare – nytt datamaterial och ny inblick i innovationsprocessen." Growth Analysis Working Paper PM 2011:14. Östersund: Tillväxtanalys.

Bager-Sjögren, Lars (2012). "Översikt av några länders användande av skatte-incitament för FoU. Underlag till Företagsskattekommittén." Dnr: 2011/307. Stockholm and Östersund: Tillväxtanalys.

Baldwin, John R. and Joanne Johnson (1999). "Entry, Innovation and Firm Growth." In Zoltan J. Acs, ed., *Are Small Firms Important? Their Role and Impact.* Dordrecht: Kluwer.

Baliamoune-Lutz, Mina and Pierre Garello (2015). "The Effect of Tax Progressivity on the Quality of Entrepreneurship." IREF Working Paper No. 201501. Paris: Institute for Research in Economic and Fiscal Issues.

Bandiera, Olivier (2003). "Land Reform, the Market for Protection, and the Origins of the Sicilian Mafia: Theory and Evidence." *Journal of Law, Economics and Organization* 19(1), 218–244.

Barba Navaretti, Giorgio and Anthony J. Venables (2004). *Multinational Firms in the World Economy*. Princeton, NJ: Princeton University Press.

Barreto, Humberto (1989). *The Entrepreneur in Micro-Economic Theory: Disappearance and Explanation*. London: Routledge.

Basker, Emek (2007). "The Causes and Consequences of Wal-Mart's Growth." *Journal of Economic Perspectives* 21(3), 177–198.

Baumol, William J. (1968). "Entrepreneurship in Economic Theory." *American Economic Review* 56(2), 64–71.

Baumol, William J. (1990). "Entrepreneurship: Productive, Unproductive, and Destructive." *Journal of Political Economy* 98(5), 893–921.

Baumol, William J. (1993). *Entrepreneurship, Management and the Structure of Payoffs*. Cambridge, MA: MIT Press.

Baumol, William J. (2002a). "Entrepreneurship, Innovation and Growth: The David-Goliath Symbiosis." *Journal of Entrepreneurial Finance and Business Ventures* 7(2), 1–10.

Baumol, William J. (2002b). *The Free-Market Innovation Machine: Analyzing the Growth Miracle of Capitalism*. Princeton, NJ: Princeton University Press.

Baumol, William J. (2004). "Entrepreneurial Enterprises, Large Established Firms and Other Components of the Free-Market Growth Machine." *Small Business Economics* 23(1), 9–21.

Baumol, William J. (2010). *The Microtheory of Innovative Entrepreneurship*. Princeton, NJ: Princeton University Press.

Baumol, William J., Robert E. Litan and Carl J. Schramm (2007). *Good Capitalism, Bad Capitalism and the Economics of Growth and Prosperity*. New Haven, CT and London: Yale University Press.

Beck, Thorsten, Asli Demirgüç-Kunt and Ross Levine (2005). "SMEs, Growth, and Poverty: Cross-Country Evidence." NBER Working Paper No. 11224. Cambridge, MA: National Bureau of Economic Research.

Beck, Thorsten, Asli Demirgüc-Kunt and Vojislav Maksimovic (2004). "Bank Competition and Access to Finance: International Evidence." *Journal of Money, Credit and Banking* 36(3), 627–648.

Bergh, Andreas, ed. (2012). *Från utsatt till utmärkt område – bortom ekonomiska frizoner*. Stockholm: FORES.

Berglund, Henrik (2007). "Opportunities as Existing and Created: A Study of Entrepreneurs in the Swedish Mobile Internet Industry." *Journal of Enterprising Culture* 15(3), 243–273.

© THE AUTHORS AND STUDENTLITTERATUR

Berglund, Henrik (2011). "Early Stage Venture Capital Investing: Comparing California and Scandinavia." *Venture Capital* 13(2), 119–145.

Berglund, Henrik, Tomas Hellström and Sören Sjölander (2007). "Entrepreneurial Learning and the Role of Venture Capitalists." *Venture Capital* 9(3), 165–181.

Bergman, Karin (2012). *The Organization of R&D – Sourcing Strategy, Financing and Relation to Trade*. Doctoral Dissertation. Lund: Department of Economics, Lund University.

Besanko, David, David Dranove and Mark Shanley (1996). *Economics of Strategy*. New York: John Wiley & Sons.

Besley, Timothy and Maitreesh Ghatak (2010). "Property Rights and Economic Development." In Dani Rodrik and Mark R. Rosenzweig, eds., *Handbook of Development Economics*, vol. 5. Amsterdam: North-Holland.

Bianchi, Milo and Magnus Henrekson (2005). "Is Neoclassical Economics still Entrepreneurless?" *Kyklos* 58(3), 353–377.

Birch, David L. (1979). *The Job Generation Process*. Cambridge, MA: MIT.

Birch, David L., Anne Haggerty and William Parsons (1995). *Who's Creating Jobs?* Boston: Cognetics Inc.

Birch, David L. and James Medoff (1994). "Gazelles." In Lewis C. Solmon and Alec R. Levenson, eds., *Labor Markets, Employment Policy and Job Creation*. Boulder and London: Westview Press.

Bjuggren, Carl Magnus (2015). "The Effect of Employment Protection on Labor Productivity." IFN Working Paper No. 1061. Stockholm: Research Institute of Industrial Economics (IFN).

Bjuggren, Carl Magnus, Dan Johansson and Mikael Stenkula (2012). "Using Self-Employment as Proxy for Entrepreneurship: Some Empirical Caveats." *International Journal of Entrepreneurship and Small Business* 17(3), 290–303.

Blanchflower, David G. (2000). "Self-Employment in OECD Countries." NBER Working Paper No. 7648. Cambridge, MA: National Bureau of Economic Research.

Blau, Francine D. and Lawrence M. Kahn (1996). "International Differences in Male Wage Inequality: Institutions versus Market Forces." *Journal of Political Economy* 104(4), 791–837.

Block, Joern H., A. Roy Thurik and Haibo Zhou (2013). "What Turns Knowledge into Innovative Products? The Role of Entrepreneurship and Knowledge Spillovers." *Journal of Evolutionary Economics* 23(4), 693–718.

Boettke, Peter J. and Christopher J. Coyne (2003). "Entrepreneurship and Development: Cause or Consequence?" In Roger Koppl, Jack Birner and Peter Kurrild-Klitgaard, eds., *Advances in Austrian Economics*, Vol. 6, 67–87. Amsterdam: JAI Press.

Boettke, Peter J. and Christopher J. Coyne (2009). "Context Matters: Institutions and Entrepreneurship." *Foundations and Trends in Entrepreneurship* 5(3), 135–209.

Bornhäll, Anders, Sven-Olov Daunfeldt and Niklas Rudholm (2014). "Employment Protection Legislation and Firm Growth: Evidence from a Natural Experiment." HUI Working Paper No. 102. Stockholm: HUI Research.

Borg, Per (2009). *Den långsiktiga finansieringen – välfärdspolitikens klimatfråga*, Expertgruppen för Studier i Offentlig Ekonomi (ESO). Stockholm: Ministry of Finance.

Borg, Per, Eva Fernvall, Jens Magnusson, Niklas Nordström, Berit Rollén, Lars Tobisson and Monica Werenfels Röttorp (2010). *Vi har råd med framtiden – men då krävs en långsiktig och sammanhållen politik för välfärdens finansiering.* Report to the Commission on the Furure Financing of Social Welfare Services. Stockholm: Arena Idé and Timbro.

Bosma, Niels S. and Jonathan Levie, eds. (2010). *Global Entrepreneurship Monitor 2009 Executive Report.* Babson College, Universidad del Desarrollo, Reykjavík University and London Business School.

Bottazzi, Laura, Marco Da Rin and Thomas Hellmann (2004). "The Changing Face of the European Venture Capital Industry: Facts and Analysis." *Journal of Private Equity* 7(2), 26–53.

Braunerhjelm, Pontus (2006). "Svensk strukturomvandling från ett sysselsättnings-perspektiv – myten om ett kunskapslyft." In Dan Johansson and Nils Karlson, eds., *Svensk utvecklingskraft.* Stockholm: Ratio.

Braunerhjelm, Pontus (2008). "Entrepreneurship, Knowledge and Growth." *Foundations and Trends in Entrepreneurship* 4(5), 451–533.

Braunerhjelm, Pontus, ed. (2011). *Ett innovationspolitiskt ramverk – ett steg vidare.* Swedish Economic Forum Report 2011. Stockholm: Swedish Entrepreneurship Forum.

Braunerhjelm, Pontus (2012). "Innovation and Growth." In Martin Andersson, Börje Johansson and Hans Lööf, eds., *Innovation and Growth: From R&D Strategies of Innovating Firms to Economy-Wide Technological Change.* Oxford: Oxford University Press.

Braunerhjelm, Pontus, Zoltan J. Acs, David B. Audretsch and Bo Carlsson (2010). "The Missing Link: Knowledge Diffusion and Entrepreneurship in Endogenous Growth." *Small Business Economics* 34(2), 105–125.

Braunerhjelm, Pontus and Johan E. Eklund (2014). "Taxes, Tax Administrative Burdens and New Firm Formation." *Kyklos* 67(1), 1–11.

Braunerhjelm, Pontus, Klas Eklund and Magnus Henrekson (2012). *Ett ramverk för innovationspolitiken – Hur göra Sverige mer entreprenöriellt?* Stockholm: Samhällsförlaget.

Braunerhjelm, Pontus, Carin Holmquist, Maria Adenfelt, Per Thulin and Mikael Jorstig (2014). *Entreprenörskap i Sverige – Nationell rapport 2014.* Stockholm: Swedish Entrepreneurship Forum.

Braunerhjelm, Pontus and Johan Wiklund (2006). *Entreprenörskap och tillväxt. Kunskap, kommersialisering och ekonomisk politik.* Örebro: FSF.

© THE AUTHORS AND STUDENTLITTERATUR

Brooke, Geoffrey T. F. (2010). "Uncertainty, Profit and Entrepreneurial Action: Frank Knight's Contribution Reconsidered." *Journal of the History of Economic Thought* 32(2), 221–235.

Brown, Charles and James Medoff (1989). "The Employer Size Wage Effect." *Journal of Political Economy* 97(5), 1027–1059.

Brynjolfsson, Erik and Andrew McAfee (2014). *The Second Machine Age: Work, Progress and Prosperity in a Time of Brilliant Technologies*. New York: W.W. Norton & Company.

Buchanan, James M. (1980). "Rent Seeking and Profit Seeking." In James M. Buchanan, Gordon Tullock and Roger Tollison, eds., *Toward a Theory of the Rent-Seeking Society*. College Station: Texas A&M University Press.

Caballero, Ricardo J. (2007). *Specificity and the Macroeconomics of Restructuring*. Cambridge, MA: MIT Press.

Caliendo, Marco and Alexander S. Kritikos (2008). "Is Entrepreneurial Success Predictable? An Ex-Ante Analysis of the Character-Based Approach." *Kyklos* 61(2), 189–214.

Cantillon, Richard (1755). *Essai sur la Nature du Commerce en Général*. Paris.

Carlson, Benny and Mats Lundahl (2014). *Ett forskningsinstitut växer fram – IUI från grundandet till 1950*. Stockholm: Ekerlids.

Carlsson, Bo (1999). "Small Business, Entrepreneurship, and Industrial Dynamics." In Zoltan J. Acs, ed., *Are Small Firms Important? Their Role and Impact*. Dordrecht: Kluwer.

Carlsson, Bo (2009). "Entrepreneurship and Public Policy in Emerging Clusters." SNEE Working Paper, May 2009.

Carlsson, Bo and Ann-Charlotte Fridh (2002). "Technology Transfer in United States Universities." *Journal of Evolutionary Economics* 12(1), 199–232.

Carree, Martin A. (2002). "Does Unemployment Affect the Number of Establishments? A Regional Analysis for U.S. States." *Regional Studies* 36(4), 389–398.

Carree, Martin A., André van Stel, A. Roy Thurik and Sander Wennekers (2002). "Economic Development and Business Ownership: An Analysis Using Data of 23 OECD Countries in the Period 1976–1996." *Small Business Economics* 19(3), 271–290.

Carree, Martin A. and A. Roy Thurik (1999). "Industrial Structure and Economic Growth." In David B. Audretsch and A. Roy Thurik, eds., *Innovation, Industry Evolution, and Employment*. Cambridge: Cambridge University Press.

Carree, Martin A. and A. Roy Thurik (2006). "Understanding the Role of Entrepreneurship for Economic Growth." In Martin A. Carree and A. Roy Thurik, eds., *Entrepreneurship and Economic Growth*. Cheltenham, UK and Northampton, MA: Edward Elgar.

Carree, Martin A. and A. Roy Thurik (2008). "The Lag Structure of the Impact of Business Ownership on Economic Performance in OECD Countries." *Small Business Economics* 30(1), 101–110.

Carree, Martin A. and A. Roy Thurik (2010). "The Impact of Entrepreneurship on Economic Growth." In Zoltan J. Acs and David B. Audretsch, eds., *Handbook of Entrepreneurship Research*. New York: Springer.

Carroll, Robert, Douglas Holtz-Eakin and Harvey S. Rosen (2000). "Entrepreneurs, Income Taxes and Investment." In Joel Slemrod, ed., *Does Atlas Shrug? The Economic Consequences of Taxing the Rich*. New York: Russel Sage.

Casson, Mark C. (2003). *The Entrepreneur: An Economic Theory*. Second edition. Cheltenham, UK and Northampton, MA: Edward Elgar.

Cetorelli, Nicola and Philip E. Strahan (2006). "Finance as a Barrier to Entry: Bank Competition and Industry Structure in Local US Markets." *Journal of Finance* 61(1), 437–461.

Cheng, Leonard and Elias Dinopoulos (1992). "Schumpeterian Growth and International Business Cycles." *American Economic Review* 82(2), 409–414.

Chesbrough, Henry and Richard S. Rosenbloom (2002). "The Role of the Business Model in Capturing Value from Innovation: Evidence from Xerox Corporation's Technology Spin-Off Companies." *Industrial and Corporate Change* 11(3), 529–555.

Chetty, Raj, John Friedman, Tore Olsen and Luigi Pistaferri (2011). "Adjustment Costs, Firm Responses, and Micro vs. Macro Labor Supply Elasticities: Evidence from Danish Tax Records." *Quarterly Journal of Economics* 126(2), 749–804.

Chetty, Raj and Emmanuel Saez (2005). "Dividend Taxes and Corporate Behavior: Evidence from the 2003 Dividend Tax Cut." *Quarterly Journal of Economics* 120(3), 791–833.

Chilosi, Alberto (2001). "Entrepreneurship and Transition." *MOCT-MOST: Economic Policy in Transitional Economies* 11(4), 327–357.

Christensen, Clayton M. and Michael E. Raynor (2003). *The Innovator's Solution: Creating and Sustaining Successful Growth*. Boston, MA: Harvard Business School Press.

Coad, Alex, Sven-Olov Daunfeldt, Werner Hölzl, Dan Johansson and Paul Nightingale (2014). "High-Growth Firms: Introduction to the Special Section." *Industrial and Corporate Change* 23(1), 91–112.

Coase, Ronald (1937). "The Nature of the Firm." *Economica* 4(16), 386–405.

Cohen, Wesley M. and Steven Klepper (1992). "The Trade-Off between Firm Size and Diversity in the Pursuit of Technological Progress." *Small Business Economics* 4(1), 1–14.

Coyne, Christopher J. and Peter T. Leeson (2004). "The Plight of Underdeveloped Countries." *Cato Journal* 24(3), 235–249.

Coyne, Rachel L. (2014). "Economic Freedom, Entrepreneurship and Growth." In Robert F. Salvino, Jr., Michael T. Tasto and Gregory M. Randolph, eds., *Entrepreneurial Action, Public Policy, and Economic Outcomes*. Cheltenham, UK and Northampton, MA: Edward Elgar.

Crawford, G. Christopher, Herman Aguinis, Benyamin Lichtenstein, Per Davidsson and Bill McKelvey (2015). "Power Law Distributions in Entrepreneurship:

© THE AUTHORS AND STUDENTLITTERATUR

Implications for Theory and Research." *Journal of Business Venturing* 30(5), 696–713.

Cullen, Julie Berry and Roger H. Gordon (2006). "Hur påverkar skatternas utformning företagande, risktagande och innovationer? En jämförelse mellan USA och Sverige." In Pontus Braunerhjelm and Johan Wiklund, eds., *Entreprenörskap och tillväxt*. Örebro: FSF.

Cullen, Julie Berry and Roger H. Gordon (2007). "Taxes and Entrepreneurial Risk-Taking: Theory and Evidence for the U.S." *Journal of Public Economics* 91(7), 1479– 1505.

Cumming, Douglas, ed. (2012). *The Oxford Handbook of Venture Capital*. Oxford and New York: Oxford University Press.

Dahmén, Erik (1970). *Entrepreneurial Activity and the Development of Swedish Industry 1919–1939*. Homewood, IL: Richard D. Irwin.

Danish Government Platform (2005). *New Goals, Government Platform 2005*. Danish Prime Minister's Office, http://www.stm.dk/publikationer/UK_reggrund05/index.htm.

Da Rin, Marco, Giovanna Nicodano and Alessandro Sembenelli (2006). "Public Policy and the Creation of Active Venture Capital Markets." *Journal of Public Economics* 90(8–9), 1699–1723.

Daunfeldt, Sven-Olov, Niklas Elert and Dan Johansson (2014). "The Economic Contribution of High-Growth Firms: Do Policy Implications Depend on the Choice of Growth Indicator?" *Journal of Industry, Competition and Trade* 14(3), 337–365.

Daunfeldt, Sven Olov, Niklas Elert and Åsa Lang (2012). "Does Gibrat's Law Hold for Retailing? Evidence from Sweden." *Journal of Retailing and Consumer Services* 19(5), 464–469.

Daunfeldt, Sven-Olov and Daniel Halvarsson (2015). "Are High-Growth Firms One-Hit Wonders? Evidence from Sweden." *Small Business Economics* 44(2), 361–383.

Daunfeldt, Sven-Olov and Fabian Wallen (2013). *Svenska citroner – åtta fräscha idéer som lämnade en sur eftersmak*. Stockholm: Kalla Kulor Förlag.

Davidsson, Per and Frédéric Delmar (2002). "Tillväxt i små och nya – och något större och mognare – företag." In Dan Johansson and Nils Karlson, eds., *Den svenska tillväxtskolan*, Stockholm: Ratio.

Davidsson, Per and Frédéric Delmar (2003). "Hunting for New Employment: The Role of High Growth Firms." In David A. Kirby and Anna Watson, eds., *Small Firms and Economic Development in Developed and Transition Economies*. Hampshire: Ashgate Publishing.

Davidsson, Per, Leif Lindmark and Christer Olofsson (1996). *Näringslivsdynamik under 90-talet*. Stockholm: NUTEK.

Davidsson, Per, Leif Lindmark and Christer Olofsson (1998). "The Extent of Overestimation of Small Firm Job Creation – An Empirical Examination of the Regression Bias." *Small Business Economics* 11(1), 87–100.

Davidsson, Per and Marcello Tonelli (2013). "Killing our Darling: Why we Need to Let Go of the Entrepreneurial Opportunity Construct." In Per Davidsson, ed., *Conference Proceedings: Australia Centre for Entrepreneurship (ACE) Research Exchange Conference 2013*. Brisbane: Australia Centre for Entrepreneurship, Queensland University of Technology.

Davis, Steven J., John Haltiwanger and Ron Jarmin (2008). "Young Businesses, Economic Churning, and Productivity Gains." Kaufman Foundation Research Series: Turmoil and Growth. Kansas City, MO: Ewing Marion Kauffman Foundation.

Davis, Steven J., John Haltiwanger and Scott Schuh (1996). "Small Business and Job Creation: Dissecting the Myth and Reassessing the Facts." *Small Business Economics* 8(4), 297–315.

Davis, Steven J. and Magnus Henrekson (2005). "Tax Effects on Work Activity, Industry Mix and Shadow Economy Size: Evidence from Rich Country Comparisons." In Ramón Gómez-Salvador et al., eds., *Labour Supply and Incentives to Work in Europe*. Cheltenham, UK and Northampton, MA: Edward Elgar.

Davis, Steven J. and Kevin M. Murphy (2000). "A Competitive Perspective on Internet Explorer." *American Economic Review* 90(2), 184–187.

de Soto, Hernando (2000). *The Mystery of Capital: Why Capitalism Triumphs in the West but Fails Everywhere Else*. New York: Basic Books.

Diehl, Richard A. and Margaret D. Mandeville (1987). "Tula and Wheeled Animal Effigies in Mesoamerica." *Antiquity* 61(232), 239–246.

Domar, Evsey and Richard Musgrave (1944). "Proportional Income Taxation and Risk Sharing." *Quarterly Journal of Economics* 58(3), 388–422.

Drucker, Peter F. (1976). *The Unseen Revolution: How Pension Fund Socialism Came to America*. London: Heinemann.

Drucker, Peter F. (1998). "The Discipline of Innovation." *Harvard Business Review* 76(6), 149–157.

Du Rietz, Anita (2013). *Kvinnors entreprenörskap under 400 år*. Stockholm: Dialogos.

Du Rietz, Gunnar, Dan Johansson and Mikael Stenkula (2015). "Swedish Capital Income Taxation (1862–2013)." In Magnus Henrekson and Mikael Stenkula, eds., *Swedish Taxation: Developments since 1862*. New York: Palgrave Macmillan.

Eberhart, Robert N., Charles E. Eesley and Kathleen M. Eisenhardt (2013). "Failure is an Option: Failure Barriers and New Firm Performance." Working Paper. Department of Management Science and Engineering, Stanford University.

Edquist, Charles and Maureen McKelvey (1998). "High R&D Intensity without High-Tech Products: A Swedish Paradox?" In Klaus Nielsen and Björn Johnson, eds., *Institutions and Economic Change: New Perspectives on Markets, Firms and Technology*. Cheltenham, UK and Northampton, MA: Edward Elgar.

Ejermo, Olof, Astrid Kander and Martin Henning (2011). "The R&D-Growth Paradox Arises in Fast-Growing Sectors." *Research Policy* 40(5), 664–672.

© THE AUTHORS AND STUDENTLITTERATUR

Ekholm, Karolina and Katariina Hakkala (2006). "Hur påverkar handel och utflyttning av produktion den svenska arbetsmarknaden?" *Ekonomisk Debatt* 34(4), 7–21.

Eklund, Johan E. (2011). "Effektiva regleringar för en konkurrenskraftig ekonomi." In Pontus Braunerhjelm, ed., *Ett innovationspolitiskt ramverk – ett steg vidare.* Stockholm: Swedish Entrepreneurship Forum.

Elert, Niklas, Fredrik W. Andersson and Karl Wennberg (2015). "The Impact of Entrepreneurship Education in High School on Long-Term Entrepreneurial Performance." *Journal of Economic Behavior & Organization* 111, 209–223.

Elert, Niklas and Magnus Henrekson (2015). "Evasive Entrepreneurship and Institutional Change." IFN Working Paper No. 1044. Stockholm: Research Institute of Industrial Economics (IFN).

Eliasson, Gunnar (1996). *Firm Objectives, Controls and Organization. The Use of Information and the Transfer of Knowledge within the Firm.* Dodrecht: Kluwer.

Englund, Peter, Bo Becker, Torbjörn Becker, Marieke Bos and Pehr Wissén (2015). *Den svenska skulden. Konjunkturrådets rapport 2015.* Stockholm: SNS.

Engström, Per and Bertil Holmlund (2009). "Tax Evasion and Self-Employment in a High-Tax Country: Evidence from Sweden." *Applied Economics* 41(19), 2419–2430.

EU (2007). "Models to Reduce the Disproportionate Regulatory Burden on SMEs." Enterprise and Industry Directorate-General. Report of the Expert Group. Brussels: European Commission.

EU (2008). "Think Small First. A Small Business Act for Europe." DG Enterprise. Brussels: European Commission.

European Commission (2004). "European Tax Survey." Taxation Papers Working Paper No. 3/2004. Luxembourg: Office for Official Publications of the European Communities.

Evans, David. S. and Linda S. Leighton (1990). "Small Business Formation by Unemployed and Employed Workers." *Small Business Economics* 2(4), 319–330.

Feldman, Maryann P. and David B. Audretsch (1999). "Innovation in Cities: Science-Based Diversity, Specialization and Localized Monopoly." *European Economic Review* 43(2), 409–429.

Foss, Kirsten, Nicolai Juul Foss, Peter G. Klein and Sandra K. Klein (2006). "The Entrepreneurial Organization of Heterogeneous Capital." *Journal of Management Studies* 44(7), 1165–1186.

Foss, Nicolai Juul and Peter G. Klein (2010a). "Entrepreneurial Alertness and Opportunity Discovery: Origins, Attributes, Critique." In Hans Landström and Franz Lohrke, eds., *The Historical Foundation of Entrepreneurship Research.* Cheltenham, UK and Northampton, MA: Edward Elgar.

Foss, Nicolai Juul and Peter G. Klein (2010b). "Alertness, Action, and the Antecedents of Entrepreneurship." *Journal of Private Enterprise* 25(2), 145–164.

Foss, Nicolai Juul and Peter G. Klein (2012). *Organizing Entrepreneurial Judgment. A New Approach to the Firm.* Cambridge: Cambridge University Press.

Freeman, Richard B. and Ronald Schettkat (2005). "Marketization of Production and the US-Europe Employment Gap." *Economic Policy* 20(41), 6–50.

Freytag, Andreas and A. Roy Thurik (2007). "Entrepreneurship and Its Determinants in a Cross-Country Setting." *Journal of Evolutionary Economics* 17(2), 117–131.

Fritsch, Michael (2011). "The Effect of New Business Formation on Regional Development – Empirical Evidence, Interpretation, and Avenues for Further Research." In Michael Fritsch, ed., *Elgar Handbook of Research on Entrepreneurship and Regional Development* (pp. 58–106). Cheltenham, UK and Northampton, MA: Edward Elgar.

Fritsch, Michael and Oliver Falck (2002). "New Firm Formation by Industry over Space and Time: A Multi-Level Analysis." Working Paper 2002/11, Faculty of Economics and Business Administration, Technical University of Freiberg.

Fritsch, Michael and Pamela Mueller (2004). "Effects of New Business Formation on Regional Development over Time." *Regional Studies* 38(8), 961–975.

Fritsch, Michael and Florian Noseleit (2013). "Investigating the Anatomy of the Employment Effect of New Business Formation." *Cambridge Journal of Economics* 37(6), 349–377.

Galbraith, John Kenneth (1956). *American Capitalism: The Concept of Countervailing Power*. Boston, MA: Houghton Mifflin.

Galindo, Miguel-Angel, Maria Teresa Méndez Picazo and José Luis Alfaro Navarro, (2010). "Entrepreneurship, Income Distribution and Economic Growth." *International Entrepreneurship and Management Journal* 6(2), 131–141.

Gans, Joshua S., David H. Hsu and Scott Stern (2002). "When Does Start-Up Innovation Spur the Gale of Creative Destruction?" *RAND Journal of Economics* 33(4), 571–586.

Gans, Joshua S. and Scott Stern (2003). "The Product Market and the Market for 'Ideas': Commercialization Strategies for Technology Entrepreneurs." *Research Policy* 32(2), 333–350

Gartner, William B. (1988). "Who is an Entrepreneur? is the Wrong Question." *American Journal of Small Business* 12(4), 11–32.

Gehrig, Thomas and Rune Stenbacka (2007). "Information Sharing and Lending Market Competition with Switching Costs and Poaching." *European Economic Review* 51(1), 77–99.

Gentry, William M. and R. Glenn Hubbard (2000). "Entrepreneurship and Household Saving." NBER Working Paper No. 7894. Cambridge, MA: National Bureau of Economic Research.

Geroski, Paul (1995). "What Do We Know about Entry?" *International Journal of Industrial Organization* 13(4), 421–440.

Ghio, Niccolo, Massimiliano Guerini, Erik E. Lehmann, Cristina Rossi-Lamastra (2015). "The Emergence of the Knowledge Spillover Theory of Entrepreneurship." *Small Business Economics* 44(1), 1–18.

© THE AUTHORS AND STUDENTLITTERATUR

Glaeser, Edward L. (2012). *Stadens triumf – hur vår största uppfinning gör oss rikare, smartare, grönare, friskare och lyckligare.* Stockholm: SNS Förlag.

Glaeser, Edward L., Heidi D. Kallal, Jose A. Scheinkman, and Andrei Shleifer (1992). "Growth in Cities." *Journal of Political Economy* 100(6), 1126–1152.

Glancey, Keith S. and Ronald W. McQuaid (2000). *Entrepreneurial Economics.* New York: Palgrave.

Glete, Jan (1994). *Nätverk i näringslivet.* Stockholm: SNS Förlag.

Gompers, Paul A. and Josh Lerner (2001). *The Money of Invention: How Venture Capital Creates New Wealth.* Cambridge, MA: Harvard University Press.

Gompers, Paul A. and Josh Lerner (2004). *The Venture Capital Cycle.* Second edition. Cambridge, MA: MIT Press.

Gompers, Paul A., Josh Lerner and Anna Kovner (2009). "Specialization and Success: Evidence from Venture Capital." *Journal of Economics and Management Strategy* 18(3), 817–844.

Gordon, Roger H. (1998). "Can High Personal Tax Rates Encourage Entrepreneurial Activity?" *IMF Staff Papers* 45(1), 49–80.

Gordon, Roger H. and Karin Edmark (2013). "The Choice of Organizational Form by Closely Held Firms in Sweden: Tax versus Non-Tax Determinants." *Industrial and Corporate Change* 22(1), 219–243.

Granstrand, Ove and Sverker Alänge (1995). "The Evolution of Corporate Entrepreneurship in Swedish Industry – Was Schumpeter Wrong?" *Journal of Evolutionary Economics* 5(2), 133–156.

Greenwood, Jeremy and Boyan Jovanovic (1990). "Financial Development, Growth, and the Distribution of Income." *Journal of Political Economy* 98(5), 1076–1107.

Guellec, Dominique and Bruno van Pottelsberghe (2003). "The Impact of Public R&D Expenditure on Business R&D." *Economics of Innovation and New Technology* 12(3), 225–244.

Gunter, Frank R. (2012). "A Simple Model of Entrepreneurship for Priciples of Economics Courses." *Journal of Economic Education* 43(4), 386–396

Hall, Robert E. and Susan E. Woodward (2010). "The Burden of the Nondiversifiable Risk of Entrepreneurship." *American Economic Review* 100(3), 1163–1194.

Halldin, Torbjörn (2012). *Born Globals.* Globaliseringsforum Report No. 3. Stockholm: Swedish Entrepreneurship Forum.

Haltiwanger, John (2011). "Firm Dynamics and Productivity Growth." In Hubert Strauss, ed., *Productivity and Growth in Europe: Long-Term Trends, Current Challenges and the Role of Economic Dynamism.* EIB Papers, vol. 11, No. 1, 116–136. Luxembourg: European Investment Bank.

Haltiwanger, John, Ron S. Jarmin and Javier Miranda (2013). "Who Creates Jobs? Small versus Large versus Young." *Review of Economics and Statistics* 95(2), 347–361.

Hamilton, Barton H. (2000). "Does Entrepreneurship Pay? An Empirical Analysis of the Returns to Self-Employment." *Journal of Political Economy* 108(3), 604–631.

Harper, David A. (1996). *Entrepreneurship and the Market Process*. London: Routledge.

Harper, David A. (2003). *Foundations of Entrepreneurship and Economic Development*. London: Routledge.

Hart, David, ed. (2003). *The Emergence of Entrepreneurship Policy: Governance, Start-Ups, and Growth in the U.S. Knowledge Economy*. Cambridge, UK: Cambridge University Press.

Hart, Peter E. and Nicholas Oulton (1996). "Growth and Size of Firms." *Economic Journal* 106(3), 1242–1252.

Hartog, Chantal, André van Stel and Chantal Hartog (2000). "Institutions and Entrepreneurship: The Role of the Rule of Law." *EIM Research Reports*. Zoetermeer: EIM.

Hausman, Jerry and Ephraim Leibtag (2009). "CPI Bias from Supercenters: Does the BLS Know that Wal-Mart Exists?" In W. Erwin Diewert, John S. Greenlees and Charles R. Hulten, eds., *Price Index Concepts and Measurement*. NBER Book Series Studies in Income and Wealth. Chicago: University of Chicago Press.

Hayek, Friedrich A. (1945). "The Use of Knowledge in Society." *American Economic Review* 35(4), 519–530.

Hayek, Friedrich A. (1989). *The Fatal Conceit: The Errors of Socialism*. Chicago: University of Chicago Press.

Hébert, Robert F. and Albert N. Link (1989). "In Search of the Meaning of Entrepreneurship." *Small Business Economics* 1(1), 39–49.

Hébert, Robert F. and Albert N. Link (2006). "Historical Perspectives on the Entrepreneur." *Foundations and Trends in Entrepreneurship* 2(4), 261–408.

Hellmann, Thomas and Manju Puri (2002). "Venture Capital and the Professionalization of Start-Up Firms: Empirical Evidence." *Journal of Finance* 57(1), 169–197.

Helpman, Elhanan (1992). "Endogenous Macroeconomic Growth Theory." *European Economic Review* 36(2–3), 237–267.

Henley, Andrew (2005). "Job Creation by the Self-Employed. The Roles of Entrepreneurial and Financial Capital." *Small Business Economics* 25(2), 175–196.

Henrekson, Magnus (1998). "Spelregler för entreprenörskapet." *Ekonomiska Samfundets Tidskrift* 51(2), 99–111.

Henrekson, Magnus (2007). "Entrepreneurship and Institutions." *Comparative Labor Law & Policy Journal* 28(4), 717–742.

Henrekson, Magnus (2015). "Kapitalägare då och nu – förmögenheter, beskattning och samhällets syn." In Birgitta Swedenborg, ed., *Svensk ekonomisk politik – då, nu och i framtiden – vänbok till Hans Tson Söderström*. Stockholm: Dialogos Förlag.

Henrekson, Magnus and Dan Johansson (1999). "Institutional Effects on the Evolution of the Size Distribution of Firms." *Small Business Economics* 12(1), 11–23.

© THE AUTHORS AND STUDENTLITTERATUR

Henrekson, Magnus and Dan Johansson (2009). "Competencies and Institutions Fostering High-Growth Firms." *Foundations and Trends in Entrepreneurship* 5(1), 1–80.

Henrekson, Magnus and Dan Johansson (2010). "Gazelles as Job Creators: A Survey and Interpretation of the Evidence." *Small Business Economics* 35(2), 227–244.

Henrekson, Magnus, Dan Johansson and Mikael Stenkula (2012), "Den svenska företagsstrukturen – utvecklingen i de medelstora företagen efter 1990-talskrisen." *Ekonomisk Debatt* 40(2), 27–38.

Henrekson, Magnus and Nathan Rosenberg (2001). "Designing Efficient Institutions for Science-Based Entrepreneurship: Lessons from the US and Sweden." *Journal of Technology Transfer* 26(3), 207–231.

Henrekson, Magnus and Tino Sanandaji (2011). "The Interaction of Entrepreneurship and Institutions." *Journal of Institutional Economics* 7(1), 47–75.

Henrekson, Magnus and Tino Sanandaji, eds. (2012). *Institutional Entrepreneurship.* The International Library of Entrepreneurship Series, vol. 24. Cheltenham, UK and Northampton, MA: Edward Elgar.

Henrekson, Magnus and Tino Sanandaji (2014a). "Small Business Activity Does not Measure Entrepreneurship." *Proceedings of the National Academy of Sciences of the United States of America* (*PNAS*) 111(5), 1760–1765.

Henrekson, Magnus and Tino Sanandaji (2014b). *Företagandets förutsättningar – en ESO-rapport om den svenska ägarbeskattningen.* Report to Expertgruppen för studier i offentlig ekonomi (ESO) 2014:3. Stockholm: Ministry of Finance and Fritzes.

Henrekson, Magnus and Tino Sanandaji (2015). "Superentrepreneurship and Global Imbalances: Closing Europe's Gap to Other Industrialized Regions." In Antonina Bakardjieva Engelbrekt, Lars Oxelheim and Thomas Persson, eds., *The EU's Role in Fighting Global Imbalances.* Cheltenham, UK and Northampton, MA: Edward Elgar.

Henrekson, Magnus and Tino Sanandaji (2016). "Owner-Level Taxes and Business Activity." *Foundations and Trends in Entrepreneurship* 12(1), 1–94.

Henrekson, Magnus and Mikael Stenkula (2010). "Entrepreneurship and Public Policy." In Zoltan J. Acs and David B. Audretsch, eds., *Handbook of Entrepreneurship Research.* New York: Springer.

Heyman, Fredrik, Pehr-Johan Norbäck and Lars Persson (2013). *Var skapas jobben? En ESO-rapport om dynamiken i svenskt näringsliv 1990 till 2009.* Report to Expertgruppen för studier i offentlig ekonomi (ESO) 2013:3. Stockholm: Fritzes.

Hoffmann, Anders N. (2007). "A Rough Guide to Entrepreneurship Policy." In David B. Audretsch, Isabel Grilo and A. Roy Thurik, eds., *Handbook of Research on Entrepreneurship Policy* (pp. 140–161). Cheltenham, UK and Northampton, MA: Edward Elgar.

Holcombe, Randall G. (1998). "Entrepreneurship and Economic Growth." *Quarterly Journal of Austrian Economics* 1(2), 45–62.

Holcombe, Randall G. (2003). "The Origins of Entrepreneurial Opportunities." *Review of Austrian Economics* 16(1), 25–43.

Holcombe, Randall G. (2007). *Entrepreneurship and Economic Progress*. New York: Routledge.

Holmes, Thomas J. and James A. Schmitz, Jr (1990). "A Theory of Entrepreneurship and Its Application to the Study of Business Transfers." *Journal of Political Economy* 98(2), 265–294

Holmström, Bengt (1989). "Agency Costs and Innovation." *Journal of Economic Behavior and Organization* 12(3), 305–327.

Holtz-Eakin, Douglas (2000). "Public Policy toward Entrepreneurship." *Small Business Economics* 15(4), 283–291.

Horowitz, Ben (2010). "Why We Prefer Founding CEOs." *Andreesen Horowitz Website*, 28 April, http://www.bhorowitz.com/why_we_prefer_founding_ceos/ (downloaded 10 May 2015).

Howitt, Peter (2007). "Innovation, Competition and Growth: A Schumpeterian Perspective on Canada's Economy." *C.D. Howe Institute Commentary*, issue 246. Toronto: C.D. Howe Institute.

Hurst, Erik and Annamaria Lusardi (2004). "Liquidity Constraints, Household Wealth, and Entrepreneurship." *Journal of Political Economy* 112(2), 319–347.

Ilmakunnas, Pekka and Vesa Kanniainen (2001). "Entrepreneurship, Economic Risks, and Risk Insurance in the Welfare State. Results with OECD Data 1978–93." *German Economic Review* 2(3), 195–218.

Inci, Eren (2013). "Occupational Choice and the Quality of Entrepreneurs." *Journal of Economic Behavior & Organization* 92(C), 1–21.

Inklaar, Robert, Marcel P. Timmer and Bart van Ark (2008). "Market Services Productivity across Europe and the US." *Economic Policy* 23(53), 139–194.

IVA (2011), *Innovationsplan Sverige – underlag till en svensk innovationsstrategi.* Final report in the project Innovation för tillväxt. Stockholm: Royal Academy of Engineering Sciences.

Jaffe, Adam B. and Josh Lerner (2004). *Invention and Its Discontents: How Our Broken Patent System Is Endangering Innovation and Progress, and What to Do About It.* Princeton, NJ: Princeton University Press.

Jensen, Richard and Marie Thursby (2001). "Proofs and Prototypes for Sale: The Tale of University Licensing." *American Economic Review* 91(1), 240–259.

Johannisson, Bengt (1984). "A Cultural Perspective on Small Business—Local Business Climate." *International Small Business Journal* 2(4), 32–43.

Johannisson, Bengt (2004). "Den heliga Gnosjöandan." In Eva Londos, ed., *I skuggan av Gnosjöandan.* Jönköping: Jönköpings läns museum.

Johansson, Dan (2004). "Economics without Entrepreneurship or Institutions: A Vocabulary Analysis of Graduate Textbooks." *Econ Journal Watch* 1(3), 515–538.

Johansson, Dan, Hans-Peter Larsson, Erik Norrman, Tino Sanandaji, Mikael Stenkula and Arvid Malm (2014). *Företagsskattekommittén och entreprenörskapet.*

   © THE AUTHORS AND STUDENTLITTERATUR

Näringspolitiskt Forum Report No. 10. Stockholm: Swedish Entrepreneurship Forum.

Johansson, Dan, Johanna Palmberg and Anders Bornhäll (2013). "Riskkapitalförsörjning till små och medelstora företag – utbud eller efterfrågan?" Repport No. 6 to the project Företagsamt ägande. Stockholm: Confederation of Swedish Enterprise.

Johnson, Anders (2006). *Tidernas entreprenörer i Sverige*. Malmö: Gleerups.

Johnson, Simon, John McMillan and Christopher Woodruff (2002). "Property Rights and Finance." *American Economic Review* 92(5), 1335–1356.

Jonung, Lars (1994). "The Rise and Fall of Credit Controls: The Case of Sweden, 1939–89." In Michael D. Bordo and Forest Capie, eds., *Monetary Regimes in Transition*. Cambridge, UK: Cambridge University Press.

Jorgenson, Dale W. and Ralph Landau, eds. (1993). *Tax Reform and the Cost of Capital: An International Comparison*. Washington, D.C.: Brookings.

Jörnmark, Jan (2007). *Övergivna platser*. Lund: Historiska Media.

Kander, Astrid and Olof Ejermo (2009). "The Swedish Paradox." In Charlie Karlsson, Börje Johansson and Roger R. Stough, eds., *Entrepreneurship and Innovation in Functional Regions*. Cheltenham, UK and Northampton, MA: Edward Elgar.

Kanniainen, Vesa and Timo Vesala (2005). "Entrepreneurship and Labor Market Institutions." *Economic Modelling* 22(5), 828–947.

Kasper, Wolfgang, Manfred E. Streit and Peter J. Boettke (2012). *Institutional Economics: Property, Competition, Policies*. Cheltenham, UK and Northampton, MA: Edward Elgar.

Kauffman Foundation (2007). "On the Road to an Entrepreneurial Economy: A Research and Policy Guide." Ewing Marion Kauffman Foundation Working Paper, July 2007.

Kauffman Foundation (2008). "Entrepreneurship summit. Executive summary." Ewing Marion Kauffman Foundation and the International Economic Development Council Working Paper, September.

Kerr, William R., Josh Lerner and Antoinette Schoar (2010). "The Consequences of Entrepreneurial Finance: Evidence from Angels Financings." *Review of Financial Studies* 27(1), 20–55.

Kerr, William R., Ramana Nanda and Matthew Rhodes-Kropf (2014). "Entrepreneurship as Experimentation." *Journal of Economic Perspectives* 28(3), 25–48.

Khalil, Elias L. (1995). "Organizations versus Institutions." *Journal of Institutional and Theoretical Economics* 151(3), 445–466.

Kihlstrom, Richard E. and Jean-Jacques Laffont (1979). "A General Equilibrium Entrepreneurial Theory of Firm Formation Based on Risk Aversion." *Journal of Political Economy* 87(4), 719–748.

King, Mervyn A. and Don Fullerton, eds. (1984). *The Taxation of Income from Capital: A Comparative Study of the United States, the United Kingdom, Sweden, and West Germany*. Chicago: University of Chicago Press.

Kirchoff, Bruce A. (1994). *Entrepreneurship and Dynamic Capitalism*. London: Praeger.

Kirzner, Israel M. (1973). *Competition and Entrepreneurship*. Chicago: University of Chicago Press.

Kirzner, Israel M. (1997). "Entrepreneurial Discovery and the Competitive Market Process: An Austrian Approach." *Journal of Economic Literature* 35(1), 60–85.

Kirzner, Israel M. (1999). "Creativity and/or Alertness: A Reconsideration of the Schumpeterian Entrepreneur." *Review of Austrian Economics* 11(1), 5–17.

Klapper, Leora, Raphael H. Amit and Mauro F. Guillén (2010). "Entrepreneurship and Firm Formation Across Countries." In Josh Lerner and Antoinette Schoar, eds., *International Differences in Entrepreneurship*. Chicago: University of Chicago Press.

Klein, Peter G. (2008). "Opportunity, Discovery, Entrepreneurial Action, and Economic Organization." *Strategic Entrepreneurship Journal* 2(3), 175–190.

Klepper, Steven (2001). "Employee Startups in High-Tech Industries." *Industrial and Corporate Change* 10(3), 639–674.

Klindt, Mads Peter (2010). *Barrierer og løftestænger for kortuddannedes opkvalificering*. Doctoral Dissertation. Aalborg, DK: Institut for Political Science, University of Aalborg.

Knight, Frank H. (1921). *Risk, Uncertainty and Profit*. Boston, MA: Houghton Mifflin Company.

Knudsen, Thorbjørn and Richard Swedberg (2009). "Capitalist Entrepreneurship: Making Profit through the Unmaking of Economic Orders." *Capitalism and Society* 4(2), 1–26.

Koellinger, Philipp and Maria Minniti (2009). "Unemployment Benefits Crowd Out Entrepreneurial Activity." *Economics Letters* 103(2), 96–98.

Korobow, Adam K. (2002). *Entrepreneurial Wage Dynamics in the Knowledge Economy*. Dordrecht: Kluwer.

Korsgaard, Steffen, Henrik Berglund, Claus Thrane and Per Blenker (2015). "A Tale of Two Kirzners: Time, Uncertainty, and the 'Nature' of Opportunities." *Entrepreneurship Theory and Practice*, forthcoming.

Kortum, Samuel and Josh Lerner (2000). "Assessing the Contribution of Venture Capital to Innovation." *RAND Journal of Economics* 31(4), 674–692.

Kuhn, Thomas S. (1962). *The Structure of Scientific Revolutions*. Chicago: University of Chicago Press.

Landström, Hans, ed. (2007). *Handbook of Research on Venture Capital*. Cheltenham, UK and Northampton, MA: Edward Elgar.

Larsson, Johan P. (2015). *Innovation utan entreprenörskap?* Näringspolitiskt Forum Report No. 10. Stockholm: Swedish Entrepreneurship Forum.

 © THE AUTHORS AND STUDENTLITTERATUR

Lawler, Ryan (2015). "a16z Hires Former Facebooker Ted Ullyot To Help Portfolio Companies Deal with Regulatory Issues." *TechCrunch Newsletter*, 16 april, http://techcrunch.com/2015/04/16/a16z-ted-ullyot-regulatory-policy-issues/ (downloaded 10 May 2015).

Lazear Edward P. (2005). "Entrepreneurship." *Journal of Labor Economics* 23(4), 649–680

Lazear Edward P. and Sherwin Rosen (1981). "Rank-Order Tournaments as Optimum Labor Contracts." *Journal of Political Economy* 89(5), 841–864.

Le Grand, Julian and Will Bartlett (1993). "The Theory of Quasi Markets." In Julian Le Grand and Will Bartlett, eds., *Quasi Markets and Social Policy*. London: Palgrave Macmillan.

Leibenstein, Harvey (1966). "Allocative Efficiency vs. X-Efficiency." *American Economic Review* 56(3), 392–415.

Leibenstein, Harvey (1968). "Entrepreneurship and Development." *American Economic Review* 58(2), 72–83.

Leonard-Barton, Dorothy (1992). "Core Capabilities and Core Rigidities: A Paradox in Managing New Product Development." *Strategic Management Journal* 13(1), 111–125.

Lerner, Josh (2009). *Boulevard of Broken Dreams: Why Public Efforts to Boost Entrepreneurship and Venture Capital Have Failed – and What to Do about It.* Princeton, NJ: Princeton University Press.

Levine, Ross (2005). "Finance and Growth: Theory and Evidence." In Philippe Aghion and Steven Durlauf, eds., *Handbook of Economic Growth, Volume 1A.* Amsterdam: North-Holland.

Levine, Ross and David Renelt (1992). "A Sensitivity Analysis of Cross-Country Growth Regressions." *American Economic Review* 82(4), 942–963.

Lewin, Peter and Steven E. Phelan (2002). "Rents and Resources: A Market Process Perspective." In Nicolai J. Foss and Peter G. Klein, eds., *Entrepreneurship and the Firm*. Cheltenham, UK and Northampton, MA: Edward Elgar.

Li, Young and Shaker Zahra (2012). "Formal Institutions, Culture, and Venture Capital Activity." *Journal of Business Venturing* 27(1), 95–111.

Lif, Anders (2015). *Direktörernas direktör Sigfrid Edström – ASEA-chef, SAF-bas och OS-pamp.* Stockholm: Atlantis.

Lindelöf, Peter and Hans Löfsten (2003). "Science Park Location and New Technology Based Firms in Sweden – Implications for Strategy and Performance." *Small Business Economics* 20(3), 245–258.

Lindgren, Gunnar (1953). "Shareholders and Shareholder Participation in the Larger Companies' Meetings in Sweden." *Weltwirtschaftliches Archiv* 71(2), 281–298.

Litan, Robert E. and Alice M. Rivlin (2002). *Bortom dot.com-bolagen.* Stockholm: SNS Förlag.

Loveman, Gary and Werner Sengenberger (1991). "The Reemergence of Small-Scale Production: An International Comparison." *Small Business Economics* 31(1), 1–37.

Lucas, Robert E. (1988). "On the Mechanics of Economic Development." *Journal of Monetary Economics* 22(1), 3–42.

Lundgren, Stefan (ed.), Peter Birch Sørensen, Ann-Sofie Kolm, Erik Norrman (2005). *Tid för en ny skattereform! Konjunkturrådets rapport 2005.* Stockholm: SNS Förlag.

Lundström, Anders and Lois Stevenson (2001). *Entrepreneurship Policy for the Future.* Stockholm: FSF.

Lundström, Anders and Lois Stevenson (2005). *Entrepreneurship Policy: Theory and Practices.* ISEN International Studies in Entrepreneurship. New York: Springer.

Malcolmson, James M. (1997). "Contracts, Hold-Up, and Labor Markets." *Journal of Economic Literature* 35(4), 1916–1957.

Mantzavinos, Chrysostomo (2001). *Individuals, Institutions and Markets.* Cambridge, UK: Cambridge University Press.

Marshall, Alfred (1961 [1890]). *Principles of Economics.* London: MacMillan.

Martin, John P. and Stefano Scarpetta (2012). "Setting It Right: Employment Protection, Labour Reallocation and Productivity." *De Economist* 160(2), 89–116.

Martinsson, Gustav and Hans Lööf (2010). "Innovationer, riskkapital och tillväxt." In Pontus Braunerhjelm, ed., *En innovationsstrategi för Sverige.* Stockholm: Swedish Entrepreneurship Forum.

Mazzucato, Mariana (2013). *The Entrepreneurial State: Debunking Public vs. Private Sector Myths.* London and New York: Anthem Press.McMillan.

John and Christoffer Woodruff (2002). "The Central Role of Entrepreneurs in Transition Economies." *Journal of Economic Perspectives* 16(3), 153–170.

Milhaupt, Curtis J. and Mark D. West (2000). "The Dark Side of Private Ordering: An Institutional and Empirical Analysis of Organized Crime." *University of Chicago Law Review* 67(1), 41–98.

Minniti, Maria, William D. Bygrave and Erkko Autio (2006). *Global Entrepreneurship Monitor: 2005 Executive Report*, Babson College and London Business School.

Mises, Ludwig von (1949). *Human Action.* New Haven, CT: Yale University Press.

Moen, Jarle (2005). "Is Mobility of Technical Personnel a Source of R&D Spillovers?" *Journal of Labor Economics* 23(1), 81–114.

Mokyr, Joel (1990). *The Lever of Riches. Technological Creativity and Economic Progress.* Oxford: Oxford University Press.

Moore, Kevin B. (2004). "The Effects of the 1986 and 1993 Tax Reforms on Self-Employment." FEDS Working Paper No. 2004-05. Washington, D.C.: Board of Governors of the Federal Reserve System.

Murphy, Kevin M., Andrei Shleifer and Robert W. Vishny (1991). "The Allocation of Talent: Implications for Growth." *Quarterly Journal of Economics* 106(2), 503–530.

Murray, Richard (2003). *Alternativ finansiering av offentliga tjänster,* Bilaga 7 till LU 2003, SOU 2003:57. Stockholm: Fritzes.

© THE AUTHORS AND STUDENTLITTERATUR

Nelson, Richard and Sidney Winter (1982). *An Evolutionary Theory of Economic Change*. Cambridge: Cambridge University Press.

Nevin, Séamus (2013). "Richard Cantillon – The Father of Economics." *History Ireland* 21(2), 20–23.

Nickell, Stephen J. (1997). "Unemployment and Labor Market Rigidities: Europe versus North America." *Journal of Economic Perspectives* 11(3), 55–74.

Norbäck, Pehr-Johan and Lars Persson (2009). "The Organization of the Innovation Industry: Entrepreneurs, Venture Capitalists, and Oligopolists." *Journal of the European Economic Association* 7(6), 1261–1290.

Nordhaus, William D. (2005). "Schumpeterian Profits and the Alchemist Fallacy." Yale Working Papers on Economic Applications and Policy No 6. New Haven, CT: Department of Economics, Yale University.

NUTEK (2005). *De bortglömda innovationerna*, Serie B 2005:4. Stockholm: NUTEK Förlag.

Nycander, Svante (2008). *Makten över arbetsmarknaden – ett perspektiv på Sveriges 1900-tal*. Stockholm: SNS Förlag.

Nygren, Bengt and Bengt Ericson (2005). *Mitt grönskande liv: Berättelsen om springpojken som blev Sveriges blomsterkung*. Stockholm: Fischer & Co.

Nykvist, Jenny (2008). "Entrepreneurship and Liquidity Constraints: Evidence from Sweden." *Scandinavian Journal of Economics* 110(1), 23–43.

OECD (1994). "Employment Protection Regulation and Labor Market Performance." In *OECD Employment Outlook*, June. Paris: OECD.

OECD (1998). *Fostering Entrepreneurship, the OECD Jobs Strategy*. Paris: OECD.

OECD (2000a). "Science, Technology and Innovation in the New Economy." OECD Policy Brief, September.

OECD (2000b). *OECD Employment Outlook*. Paris: OECD.

OECD (2002). *OECD Small and Medium Enterprise Outlook*. Paris: OECD.

OECD (2004). "Labor Standards and Economic Integration." In *OECD Employment Outlook*, July. Paris: OECD.

OECD (2005). *Micro-Policies for Growth and Productivity: Final Report*. Paris: OECD.

OECD (2007a). *OECD Framework for the Evaluation of SME and Entrepreneurship Policies and Programmes*. Paris: OECD.

OECD (2007b). *OECD Economic Surveys: Sweden*. Paris: OECD.

OECD (2010). *The OECD Innovation Strategy: Getting a Head Start on Tomorrow*. Paris: OECD.

OECD (2013). "Protecting Jobs, Enhancing Flexibility: A New Look at Employment Protection Legislation." In *OECD Employment Outlook*, July. Paris: OECD.

OECD (2014). *Entrepreneurship at a Glance*. Paris: OECD.

Olivecrona, Gustaf (1970). *De nya miljonärerna*. Stockholm: Wahlström & Widstrand.

Olofsson, Christer and Björn Berggren (1998). "De mindre företagens finansiella villkor – en replikstudie." CEF Working Report 1998:102, Uppsala.

Oreland, Carl (2012). "Snabbväxande företag i Sverige – en jobbskapande sprintstafett." *Ekonomisk Debatt* 40(8), 23–34.

Orsenigo, Luigi (2009). "Clusters and Clustering in Biotechnology: Stylised Facts, Issues and Theories." In Pontus Braunerhjelm and Maryann P. Feldman, eds., *Cluster Genesis*. Oxford: Oxford University Press.

Orszag, Mike and Dennis Snower (1998). "Anatomy of Policy Complementarities." *Swedish Economic Policy Review* 5, 303–343.

Ovaska, Tomi (2014). "Institutions, Entrepreneurship and Economic Growth." In Robert F. Salvino, Michael T. Tasto and Gregory M. Randolph, eds., *Entrepreneurial Action, Public Policy, and Economic Outcomes*. Cheltenham, UK and Northampton, MA: Edward Elgar.

Pagano, Patrizio and Fabiano Schivardi (2003). "Firm Size Distribution and Growth." *Scandinavian Journal of Economics* 105(2), 255–274.

Parker, Simon C. (1996). "A Time Series Model of Self-Employment under Uncertainty." *Economica* 63(251), 459–475.

Parker, Simon C. (2009). *The Economics of Entrepreneurship*. Cambridge: Cambridge University Press.

Parker, Simon C. and Martin T. Robson (2004). "Explaining International Variations in Self-Employment: Evidence from a Panel of OECD Countries." *Southern Economic Journal* 71(2), 287–301.

Phipps, Barbara J., Robert J. Strom and William J. Baumol (2012). "Principles of Economics without the Prince of Denmark." *Journal of Economic Education* 43(1), 58–71.

Piore, Michael J. and Charles F. Sabel (1984). *The Second Industrial Divide: Possibilities for Prosperity*. New York: Basic Books.

Polanyi, Michael (1967). *The Tacit Dimension*. Garden City, NY: Anchor Books.

Poschke, Markus (2010). "The Regulation of Entry and Aggregate Productivity." *Economic Journal* 120(549), 1175–1200.

Pries, Michael and Richard Rogerson (2005), "Hiring Policies, Labor Market Institutions, and Labor Market Flows." *Journal of Political Economy* 113(4), 811–839.

Rai, Arti, Stuart Graham and Mark Doms (2010). "Patent Reform Unleashing Innovation, Promoting Economic Growth and Producing High-Paying Jobs." White Paper from the U.S. Department of Commerce April 13. Washington, D.C.

Rauch, Andreas and Michael Frese (2000). "Psychological Approaches to Entrepreneurial Success: A General Model and an Overview of Findings." In Cary L. Cooper and Ivan T. Robertson, eds., *International Review of Industrial and Organizational Psychology*, Vol. 15. New York: Wiley.

Reiter, Joakim (2003). "Changing the Microfoundations of Corporatism: The Impact of Financial Globalisation on Swedish Corporate Ownership?" *New Political Economy* 8(1), 103–126.

 © THE AUTHORS AND STUDENTLITTERATUR

Reynolds, Paul D. (1994). "Autonomous Firm Dynamics and Economic Growth in the United States 1986–90." *Regional Studies* 28(4), 429–442.

Reynolds, Paul D. (1999). "Creative Destruction: Source or Symptom of Economic Growth?" In Zoltan J. Acs, Bo Carlsson and Charlie Karlsson, eds., *Entrepreneurship, Small and Medium-Sized Enterprises and the Macroeconomy.* Cambridge, UK: Cambridge University Press.

Reynolds, Paul D., William D. Bygrave, Erkko Autio and Michael Hay (2002). *Global Entrepreneurship Monitor Executive Report 2002.* Babson College and London Business School.

Reynolds, Paul D., Michael Hay and Michael Camp (1999). *Global Entrepreneurship Monitor: 1999 Executive Report.* Babson College and London Business School.

Ricketts, Martin (2002). *The Economics of Business Enterprise.* Cheltenham, UK and Northampton, MA: Edward Elgar.

Robson, Martin T. and Colin Wren (1999). "Marginal and Average Tax Rates and the Incentive for Self-Employment." *Southern Economic Journal* 65(4), 757–773.

Rodrik, Dani (2007). *One Economics, Many Recipes: Globalization, Institutions, and Economic Growth.* Princeton, NJ and Oxford: Princeton University Press.

Rogerson, Richard (2006). "Understanding Differences in Hours Worked." *Review of Economic Dynamics* 9(3), 365–409.

Romer, Paul M. (1986). "Increasing Returns and Economic Growth." *Journal of Political Economy* 94(5), 1002–1037.

Romer, Paul M. (1990). "Endogenous Technical Change." *Journal of Political Economy* 98(5), 71–102.

Rosen, Harvey S. (2005). "Entrepreneurship and Taxation: Empirical Evidence." In Vesa Kanniainen and Christian Keuschnigg, eds., *Venture Capital, Entrepreneurship and Public Policy.* CESifo Seminar Series. Cambridge, MA: MIT Press.

Rosendahl Huber, Laura, Randolph Sloof and Mirjam van Praag (2014). "The Effect of Early Entrepreneurship Education: Evidence from a Randomized Field Experiment." *European Economic Review* 72, 76–97.

Rothbard, Murray N. (1985). "Professor Hébert on Entrepreneurship." *Journal of Libertarian Studies* 7(2), 281–286.

Rumelt, Richard (2005). "Theory, Strategy and Entrepreneurship." In Sharon A. Alvarez, Rajshree Agarwal and Olav Sorenson, eds., *Handbook of Entrepreneurship Research.* New York: Springer.

Rydqvist, Kristian, Joshua Spizman and Ilya Strebulaev (2014), "Government Policy and Ownership of Equity Securities." *Journal of Financial Economics* 111(1), 70–85.

Sala-i-Martin, Xavier (2002). "15 Years of New Growth Economics: What Have We Learnt?" *Journal Economía Chilena (The Chilean Economy)* 5(2), 5–15.

Salgado-Banda, Hector (2007). "Entrepreneurship and Economic Growth: An Empirical Analysis." *Journal of Developmental Entrepreneurship* 12(1), 3–29.

Sandström, Christian (2010). *A Revised Perspective on Disruptive Innovation. Exploring Value, Networks and Business Models*. Doctoral Dissertation. Göteborg: Chalmers University of Technology.

Sandström, Christian (2014). *Var skapades Sveriges 100 främsta innovationer?* Stockholm: Reforminstitutet.

Sarasvathy, Saras D. (2001). "Causation and Effectuation: Toward a Theoretical Shift from Economic Inevitability to Entrepreneurial Contingency." *Academy of Management Review* 26(2), 243–263.

Sarasvathy, Saras D. (2009). *Effectuation: Elements of Entrepreneurial Expertise*. Cheltenham, UK and Northampton, MA: Edward Elgar.

Sautet, Frédéric (2008). "Entrepreneurship, Institutions and Economic Growth." Ways of Thinking about Economic Growth, Occasional Paper Series.

Say, Jean-Baptiste (1845). *A Treatise on Political Economy*. Philadelphia: Grigg & Elliot.

Schmitz, Jr., James A. (1989). "Imitation, Entrepreneurship and Long-Run Growth." *Journal of Political Economy* 97(3), 721–739.

Schuetze, Herbert (2000). "Taxes, Economic Conditions and Recent Trends in Male Self-Employment: A Canada-US Comparison." *Labour Economics* 7(5), 507–544.

Schuetze, Herbert J. and Donald Bruce (2004). "Tax Policy and Entrepreneurship." *Swedish Economic Policy Review* 11(2), 233–265.

Schultz, Theodore W. (1980). "Investment in Entrepreneurial Ability." *Scandinavian Journal of Economics* 82(4), 437–448.

Schumpeter, Joseph A. (2004 [1934]). *The Theory of Economic Development*. London: Transaction Publishers.

Schumpeter, Joseph A. (1942). *Capitalism, Socialism and Democracy*. New York: Harper & Row.

Segerstrom, Paul S. (1991). "Innovation, Imitation, and Economic Growth." *Journal of Political Economy* 99(4), 190–207.

Segerstrom, Paul S., T. C. A. Anant and Elias Dinopoulos (1990). "A Schumpeterian Model of the Product Life Cycle." *American Economic Review* 80(5), 1077–1091.

Shackle, George L. S. (1979). Imagination and the Nature of Choice. Edinburgh: Edinburgh University Press.

Shane, Scott A. (2003). *A General Theory of Entrepreneurship: The Individual-Opportunity Nexus*. Cheltenham, UK and Northampton, MA: Edward Elgar.

Shane, Scott A. (2008). *The Illusions of Entrepreneurship*. New Haven, CT and London: Yale University Press.

Shane, Scott A. and Sankaran Venkataraman (2000). "The Promise of Entrepreneurship as a Field of Research." *Academy of Management Review* 25(1), 217–226.

Singer, Slavica, José Ernesto Amorós and Daniel Moska (2014). *Global Entrepreneurship Monitor: 2014 Global Report*. Babson College, Universidad del

© THE AUTHORS AND STUDENTLITTERATUR

Desarrollo, Universiti Tun Abdul Razak, Technológico de Monterrey and London Business School.

Sjöö, Karolin, Josef Taalbi, Astrid Kander and Jonas Ljungberg (2014). *SWINNO: A Database of Swedish Innovations, 1970–2007.* Lund Papers in Economic History No. 133. CIRCLE, Lund University.

Skedinger, Per (2010). *Employment Protection Legislation: Evolution, Effects, Winners and Losers.* Cheltenham, UK and Northampton, MA: Edward Elgar.

Sloan, Alfred P. and John McDonald (1964). *My Years with General Motors.* Garden City, NY: Doubleday.

Solow, Robert M. (1956). "A Contribution to the Theory of Economic Growth." *Quarterly Journal of Economics* 70(1), 65–94.

Solow, Robert M. (1957). "Technical Change and the Aggregate Production Function." *Review of Economics and Statistics* 39(3), 312–320.

SOU 1997:17. *Skatter, tjänster och sysselsättning.* Slutbetänkande från Tjänstebeskattningsutredningen. Stockholm: Ministry of Finance.

SOU 2000:11. *Finanssektorns framtid.* Bilagor till Finansmarknadsutredningen. Volym A. Stockholm: Fritzes.

Stam, Erik, Niels Bosma, Arjen van Witteloostuijn, Jeroen de Jong, Sandy Bogaert, Nancy Edwards, Ferdinand Jaspers (2012). "Ambitious Entrepreneurship. A Review of the State of the Art." Brussels: Vlaamse Raad voor Wetenschap en Innovatie.

Stam, Erik, Kashifa Suddle, Jolanda Hessels and André van Stel (2009). "High-Growth Entrepreneurs, Public Policies, and Economic Growth." In João Leitão and Rui Baptista, eds., *Public Policies for Fostering Entrepreneurship: A European Perspective.* International Studies in Entrepreneurship 22. New York: Springer.

Stenkula, Mikael (2012). "Taxation and Entrepreneurship in a Welfare State." *Small Business Economics* 39(1), 77–97.

Stigler, George J. (1968). *The Organization of Industry.* Homewood, IL: Richard D. Irwin.

Storey, David J. (1991). "The Birth of New Firms – Does Unemployment Matter? A Review of the Evidence." *Small Business Economics* 3(3), 167–178.

Storey, David J. (1994). *Understanding the Small Business Sector.* London: Routledge.

Storey, David J. (2003). "Entrepreneurship, Small and Medium Sized Enterprises and Public Policies." *Handbook of Entrepreneurship Research* 1, 473–511.

Sull, Donald N. (2004). "Disciplined Entrepreneurship." *Sloan Management Review* 46(1), 71–77.

Summers, Lawrence H. (1987). "Investment Incentives and the Discounting of Depreciation Allowances." In Martin S. Feldstein, ed., *The Effects of Taxation on Capital Accumulation.* Chicago: University of Chicago Press.

Svensson, Roger (2011). *När är statligt stöd till innovativa företag och entreprenörer effektivt?* Stockholm: Confederation of Swedish Enterprise.

Svensson, Roger (2012). "Commercialization, Renewal and Quality of Patents." *Economics of Innovation and New Technology* 21(1–2), 175–201.

Svensson, Roger (2013). "Effekter av ökade offentliga satsningar på FoU." In Specialstudie nr 37, December. *Tillväxt- och sysselsättningseffekter av infrastrukturinvesteringar, FoU och utbildning – En litteraturöversikt.* Stockholm: National Institute of Economic Research.

Söderblom, Anna (2011). *Private Equity Fund Investing: Investment Strategies, Entry Order and Performance.* Doctoral Dissertation in Business Administration. Stockholm: Stockholm School of Economics.

Södersten, Jan (1984). "Sweden." In Mervyn A. King and Don Fullerton, eds., *The Taxation of Income from Capital: A Comparative Study of the United States, the United Kingdom, Sweden and West Germany.* Chicago: University of Chicago Press.

Tellis, Gerard J. and Rajesh K. Chandy (2000). "The Incumbent's Curse? Incumbency, Size and Radical Product Innovation." *Journal of Marketing* 64(1), 1–17.

Teruel, Mercedes and Gerrit de Wit (2011). "Determinants of High-Growth Firms. Why Have Some Countries More High-Growth Firms than Others?" EIM Research Report H201107. Zoetermeer, NL: EIM.

Thurik, A. Roy, Martin A. Carree, André van Stel and David B. Audretsch (2008). "Does Self-Employment Reduce Unemployment?" *Journal of Business Venturing* 23(6), 673–686.

Tåg, Joacim (2012). "The Real Effects of Private Equity Buyouts." In Douglas Cumming, ed., *The Oxford Handbook of Private Equity.* Oxford: Oxford University Press.

Ucbasaran, Deniz, Gry Agnete Alsos, Paul Westhead and Mike Wright (2008). "Habitual Entrepreneurs." *Foundations and Trends in Entrepreneurship* 4(4), 309–450.

Valliere, David and Rein Peterson (2009). "Entrepreneurship and Economic Growth: Evidence from Emerging and Development Countries." *Entrepreneurship and Regional Development* 21(5–6), 459–480.

van Praag, C. Mirjam (2009). "Who Values the Status of the Entrepreneur?" IZA Discussion Papers 4245. Bonn: Institute for the Study of Labor (IZA).

van Praag, C. Mirjam and Peter H. Versloot (2007). "What is the Value of Entrepreneurship? A Review of Recent Research." *Small Business Economics* 29(4), 351–382.

van Stel, André (2005). *Entrepreneurship and Economic Growth: Some Empirical Studies.* Doctoral Dissertation. Amsterdam: Tinbergen Institute Research Series 350.

van Stel, André and David J. Storey (2004). "The Link between Firm Birth and Job Creation: Is there a Upas Tree Effect?" *Regional Studies* 38(8), 893–909.

© THE AUTHORS AND STUDENTLITTERATUR

van Stel, André, David Storey and A. Roy Thurik (2007). "The Effect of Business Regulations on Nascent and Young Business Entrepreneurship." *Small Business Economics* 28(2–3), 171–186.

Venkataraman, Sankaran (1997). "The Distinctive Domain if Entrepreneurship Research." *Advances in Entrepreneurship, Firm Emergence and Growth* 3(1), 119–138.

Verheul, Ingrid, Sander Wennekers, David B. Audretsch and A. Roy Thurik (2001). "An Eclectic Theory of Entrepreneurship." Tinbergen Institute Discussion Paper 2001-030/3. Amsterdam.

von Hippel, Eric, Susumu Ogawa and Jeoron P. J. de Jong (2011). "The Age of the Consumer-Innovator." *MIT Sloan Management Review* 53(1), 27–35.

Waldenström, Daniel (2006). "Privat äganderätt och ekonomisk tillväxt." In Niclas Berggren and Nils Karlson, eds., *Äganderättens konsekvenser och grunder*. Stockholm: Ratio.

Watson, Tom (2013). "Out in the Streets: When Venture Capital Meets Networked Activism." *Forbes Magazine online*, 18 February, http://www.forbes.com/sites/tomwatson/2013/02/18/out-in-the-streets-when-venture-capital-meets-networked-activism (downloaded 10 May 2015).

Wennekers, Sander, André van Stel, A. Roy Thurik and Paul D. Reynolds, (2005). "Nascent Entrepreneurship and the Level of Economic Development." *Small Business Economics* 24(3), 293–309.

Wennekers, Sander and A. Roy Thurik (1999). "Linking Entrepreneurship and Economic Growth." *Small Business Economics* 13(1), 27–55.

Wiklund, Johan, Per Davidsson and Frédéric Delmar (2003). "What Do They Think and Feel about Growth? An Expectancy-Value Approach to Small Business Managers' Attitudes Toward Growth." *Entrepreneurship Theory and Practice* 27(3), 247–269.

Williamson, Oliver E. and Scott E. Masten, eds. (1999). *The Economics of Transaction Costs*. Cheltenham, UK and Northampton, MA: Edward Elgar.

Wong, Poh, Yuen Ho and Erkko Autio (2005). "Entrepreneurship, Innovation and Economic Growth: Evidence from GEM Data." *Small Business Economics* 24(3), 335–350.

Wu, Shih-Yen (1989). *Production and Entrepreneurship*. Oxford: Basil Blackwell.

Wulf, Julie (2012). "The Flattened Firm: Not as Advertised." *California Management Review* 55(1), 5–23.

Zacharakis, Andew L., William D. Bygrave and Dean A. Shepherd (2000). *Global Entrepreneurship Monitor. National Entrepreneurship Assessment, United States of America, 2000 Executive Report*. Babson Park, MA: Babson College.

Zingales, Luigi (2012). *A Capitalism for the People: Recapturing the Lost Genius of American Prosperity*. New York: Basic Books.

ABOUT THE AUTHORS

Magnus Henrekson is a professor and president of the Research Institute of Industrial Economics (IFN). Until 2009, he held the Jacob Wallenberg Research Chair in the Department of Economics at the Stockholm School of Economics. He received his PhD in 1990 at the Gothenburg School of Business, Economics and Law with his dissertation *An Economic Analysis of Swedish Government Expenditure.*

Throughout the 1990s, he conducted several projects that aimed to explain cross-country growth differences. Since the turn of the new millennium, his primary research focus has been entrepreneurship economics and the institutional determinants of the business climate. In this area, he has published more than 25 articles in scientific journals and has contributed four research surveys to *Handbooks* in the entrepreneurship field. He has edited (together with Robin Douhan and Tino Sanandaji, respectively) two volumes in Edward Elgar's *International Library of Entrepreneurship Series*, where the most central contributions have been selected in a given area (*The Political Economy of Entrepreneurship* and *Institutional Entrepreneurship*), and he is on the editorial board of two journals: *Small Business Economics* and *Foundations and Trends in Entrepreneurship.*

He has published several books in Swedish that address entrepreneurship and business operations, including *Sveriges tillväxtproblem* (*Sweden's Growth Problem*, SNS, 1992), *Företagandets villkor* (*Entrepreneurial and Business Conditions: Rules of the Game for Employment and Growth*, SNS, 1996), *Akademiskt entreprenörskap* (*Academic Entrepreneurship*; jointly with Nathan Rosenberg; SNS, 2000), *Ägarbeskattningen och företagandet* (*Ownership Taxation and Entrepreneurship: The Theory of Corporate Taxation and the Swedish Policy Discussion*; jointly with Tino Sanandaji; SNS, 2004),

Ett ramverk för innovationspolitiken (*An Innovation Policy Framework*, jointly with Pontus Braunerhjelm and Klas Eklund; Samhällsförlaget, 2012) and *Företagandets förutsättningar—en ESO-rapport om den svenska ägarbeskattningen* (*Entrepreneurship and the Taxation of Business Ownership*; jointly with Tino Sanandaji; Fritzes, 2014).

Magnus Henrekson has participated in several governmental studies. Among other things, he has written expert reports for the Lindbeck Commission (1993), the Globalisation Council (2008) and the Committee on Corporate Taxation (2014), in which he also served as an acting expert (2011–2014). Since the spring of 2015, he serves as an acting expert on the Entrepreneurship Committee.

In addition to his academic qualifications, he also has experience in international banking (1981–83) and extensive experience as an advisor, board member and lecturer in many different contexts, both in the business sector and in the public sector.

Mikael Stenkula holds a PhD from the School of Economics and Management at Lund University. He received his PhD in 2004 with his dissertation *Essays on Network Effects and Money*. After having worked as a lecturer at Lund University for a year, where he taught microeconomics, he joined the Research Institute of Industrial Economics (IFN) in the fall of 2005. His main area of research is entrepreneurship economics.

After a short stint at the Ratio Institute, Stenkula returned to IFN in 2008. Over the past few years, he has been head of IFN's taxation history project, which has systematically and comprehensively described and analyzed the Swedish tax system from 1862 to the present day. This study is unique in scope—no equally comprehensive investigation of a national tax system has been conducted for any other country. Five senior scholars have been involved for five years, and the results of the investigation were published in 2015 by the American publisher Palgrave Macmillan under the title *Swedish Taxation: Developments since 1862*.

In addition to the meticulous year-to-year documentation of all relevant details of the tax code, the project aims to examine how changes in the tax system affect the economy by guiding people's choices, particularly how the tax system affects entrepreneurial activity and firm behavior.

© THE AUTHORS AND STUDENTLITTERATUR

Mikael Stenkula also teaches at the Stockholm School of Economics and he is affiliated to the School of Business at Örebro University.

Mikael Stenkula is the secretary of the award committee for the *Global Award for Entrepreneurship Research*, the foremost global award for research on entrepreneurship. As its secretary, he is responsible for maintaining its award website www.e-award.org and for coordinating the committee's work. The award is jointly owned by the Swedish Entrepreneurship Forum and the IFN. In 2015, it was awarded for the twentieth time. Among the award winners are many of the scholars who made this book possible, such as Zoltan Acs, David Audretsch, William Baumol, David Birch, Israel Kirzner, Josh Lerner, Paul Reynolds, Scott Shane and David Storey.

© THE AUTHORS AND STUDENTLITTERATUR

INDEX

© THE AUTHORS AND STUDENTLITTERATUR

© THE AUTHORS AND STUDENTLITTERATUR

© THE AUTHORS AND STUDENTLITTERATUR